A Spark of Total Darkness

Decolonising Jewish Thought

by Rabbi Adam Zagoria-Moffet

A Spark of Total Darkness

DECOLONISING JEWISH THOUGHT

by **Rabbi Adam Zagoria-Moffet**

Published by Izzun Books in St Albans,
United Kingdom, 2025.

izzunbooks.com
All enquiries to izzunbooks@gmail.com

Typeset in Cormorant, an original font family inspired by the work of Claude Garamond and designed by Christian Thalmann of Catharsis Fonts

ISBN: 978-1-7390896-7-2

For Azriel,
and for Zimra

עָזִּי וְזִמְרָת יָהּ
וַיְהִי לִי לִישׁוּעָה.

A Spark of Total Darkness

Decolonising Jewish Thought

Introduction

A Spark of Total Darkness

You, darkness, of whom I am born–

I love you more than the flame
that limits the world
to the circle it illumines
excluding all the rest.

The dark embraces everything:
shapes and shadows, creatures and me,
people, and powers–just as they are.

It lets me imagine
a great presence stirring beside me.

I believe in the night.

Rilke, Das Stunden-Buch, I. 10[1]

The title of this book, *A Spark of Total Darkness,* comes from a phrase frequently found in the Zohar: *botsina de-qardinuta.* This enigmatic metaphor is nearly impossible to pin-down to a single meaning. As usual, the Zohar revels in the interlocking paradoxes of polysemic language. However, Professor Daniel Matt, in his masterful translation (The Pritzker Zohar, Stanford University Press) helps us immensely:

> **Spark of impenetrable darkness *(botsina de-qardinuta)*,** "A lamp of impenetrability." Though *botsina* usually means "lamp," here "spark" is likely. [...] *Qardinuta* recalls a phrase in Talmud Bavli Pesaḥim 7a: *ḥittei qurdanaita*, "wheat from Kurdistan," which, according to Rashi, is very hard. [...] See Zohar Ḥadash 2a,

> where *qardenuta de-sihara* means "eclipse of the moon," corresponding to the Hebrew *qadrut ha-yareah̩*, "darkening of the moon." Shim'on Lavi retains the reading *botsina de-qardinuta* but renders it *sheviv ha-qadrut*, "the spark of darkness."[2]

This quick survey of the many possible translations aids us in trying to understand the concept: a lamp which shines forth darkness, a radiating eclipse, a black light, a glimmer of gloom. Poetry may suit it better than theology – but the idea is surprisingly ubiquitous across religious literature, particularly among mystics. Pseudo-Dionysius called it 'a ray of divine darkness'[3] and Gregory of Nyssa, 'the luminous darkness'.[4] Often, to approach the biggest and most interesting questions in life, we have to be willing to accept answers which are themselves paradoxes.

This book is an attempt to try and narrate my understanding of those ideas which are a 'spark of darkness', which, by definition, cannot be explained easily, and to share what I have found with other spiritual seekers who may be illumined by them, as I have. Each chapter is devoted to one of these ideas. I have tried to be concise and organised in presenting them, and I have equally tried to avoid abundant citations.

Most of all, I have tried, as best as possible, to avoid technical jargon and Kabbalah inside-speak (despite my great affection for both). In this, I hope to follow in the footsteps of a much grander project, and one that changed my life many years ago, Rabbi Adin Steinsaltz's exceptional work, *The Thirteen Petalled Rose*.

The subtitle of this book is a persistent theme throughout: the decolonisation of Jewish thought. By that I mean that nearly every chapter contests the conventional reading of Jewish ideas. This is, in a sense, a revisionist theology. The aim of applying such a critical lens is not to innovate, but instead to renovate – to return to a Jewish mode of thinking free, as much as possible, of certain Western influences. While Christian hegemony is particularly highlighted in this book, Christianity is not the only intellectual system to dominate Jewish modes of thinking, as Islam and Zoroastrianism have had their own impact on Jewish ideas. However, in the modern West, many Jews, including highly educated and 'religious' ones, look at their own traditions through predominantly Christian eyes, without being aware of how prevalent this interpenetration is.

From God to Creation, Prophecy to Politics, throughout this book I have aimed to challenge myths and misconceptions that many of us, Jews (and rabbis) included, have about Judaism. This project is complex and inherently incomplete – I claim no exclusive authority to have done this work of decolonising Jewish thought fully or correctly. I hope only to show a method by which we can look at Jewish thought through Jewish eyes, and question our assumptions about what 'Judaism' is.

First among such assumptions is the pernicious idea that Judaism is a religion. This idea supports all that comes after, and so Chapter 1 is dedicated to questioning the idea that Judaism is a religion at all. Then, in Chapter 2, we contest the conventional conception of God, pointing to Judaism's radical bifurcated view of the divine as both everything and nothing. In Chapter 3, we challenge the conventional narration of creation as an event in the past tense, suggesting instead that we think of creation as an ongoing process shaping the perpetual present.

Chapters 4 and 5 deal with the political and interpersonal dimensions of Judaism – first by considering the notion of authority and power, and then by looking at the legacy of the Sages who founded and formed Judaism and the models they left us to perpetuate it. Chapter 6 deals with morality, attempting to dissuade and deter us from using Christian language around 'sin' and 'sinners'. Chapter 7 explores the mode of prophecy – what it was, is, and could be as a method of spiritual practice, and Chapter 8 revisits the path of Halakhah, now centering on *mitsvot*, and in particular, why we should bother to do them at all.

Chapters 9-11 takes us on a journey beyond this world, dealing with the classic questions of metaphysics: what are souls and do we have them (Chapter 9), why do bad things happen to good people (Chapter 10) and what happens after we die (Chapter 11). Lastly, Chapter 12 revisits the abstract, encouraging us to think beyond the Christian calendar and reclaim the Hebrew calendar and its concomitant conceptions of time and history. We conclude in Chapter 13 with a reflection on symbols, returning to the *botsina de-qardinuta* and attempting to restate the goal of this overall work: encouraging Jews to pursue an authentic engagement with God and tradition free of all the misperceptions placed upon it by others.

The ideas explored in *A Spark of Total Darkness* are not mine – not really. Almost every chapter is itself a dialogue with the thinkers and teachers who have had the greatest impact on me, and on my incredible friends, colleagues, *ḥavrutot*, and students that I have been blessed to have.

In particular, I owe tremendous debts to British philosopher John Gray, whose work on Christianity and Atheism features prominently in Chapter 1 and as a result in the overall thesis of the book. This was supported by *Dominion* by Tom Holland, a fabulous intellectual history of Christianity, and the framing laid out in *Anti-Judaism* by David Nirenberg. I owe a great deal to Ḥakham José Faur, whose innovative renovation of the classical Andalusian approach to Jewish thought is still woefully understudied, and whose masterful *magnum opus* is the interlocutor for Chapter 4. Chapter 5 would not have been possible without the thought-leadership of Rabbis Daniel Nevins, Joel Roth, Louis Jacobs, and many others, as well as the education in Halakhah and halakhic change I received thanks to the Jewish Theological Seminary.

The influence of the Nazir (Rabbi David haKohén) on my understanding of the prophetic tradition was fundamental to Chapter 7, and my study of Rabbi Yehudah Ashlag frames Chapters 8 and 9. For the latter I'm particularly grateful to Professor Eitan Fishbane, who supervised my MA thesis on Rabbi Ashlag's political thought, *The Communist Kabbalist*. Rabbi Harold Kushner's hugely influential little book *Why Bad Things Happen to Good People* helped me to refine my thinking about suffering in Chapter 10, and the work done by Rabbi Aryeh Kaplan to share the Kabbalistic literature of cosmic cycles and *shemittot* was essential for Chapter 12. A few thinkers are present throughout all chapters – chief among them is one of my great role models, Rabbi Elia Benamozegh.

I have had the tremendous privilege of being a congregational rabbi for seven years – all of which has been in the service of what is unarguably the best synagogue on earth. My gratitude to the fabulous people who make up St Albans Masorti Synagogue is endless, and the opportunities I've had to learn and grow (and teach) have shaped so much of my thinking.

In particular I owe great thanks to the fantastic students who have regularly attended my *Jewniversity* course for the last few years, as well as all those who have been listening via the podcast (available wherever you get your podcasts!). I originally set out to write this book after finding that in so many of my *shi'urim* the same basic message was coming across: that Judaism is rarely what we think, and that so often it is more complex, more confounding, and completely compelling, to a much greater degree than most have come to expect.[5]

My colleagues in the Masorti movement here in the UK are the best anyone can hope for – special thanks are due to Rabbi Natasha Mann for always being willing to brainstorm anything, at any hour; to Rabbi Roni Tabick for being my guide to both mythology and to Anglo-Jewry, to Rabbi Oliver Joseph for literally walking the way with me, and to Rabbi Jeremy Gordon for being the best sort of mentor – accessible whenever needed and always impeccably honest. I owe so much to Rabbi Mark Greenspan, whose kindness and curiosity are so effortlessly on display, both on the *bimah* and off, as well as to Earl Schwartz, a *lamed-vavnik* if there ever was one, and without whom my rabbinic journey would have ended at Ginkgo Coffeehouse on Snelling Avenue.

I owe the biggest thanks to my partner, Mikayla. It was Mikayla who insisted I become a rabbi, who encouraged me to explore my bizarre and bountiful interests, and who has always been my first and best *ḥavruta* in all things. She has heard me rant about many of the subjects in this book more times and with more vigour than any reasonable person should have been subjected to. I'm especially grateful for that, as well as her wisdom and wit.

I have been looking for answers to the 'Big Questions' my entire life. I have sought them within Judaism and without it, but ultimately have come the closest to understanding answers that work for me within the variegated tapestry of Jewish thought. I hope that my presentation of them here similarly helps you, the reader of this book, to feel the spark of impenetrable darkness, the adamantine depths which shine forth from the lamp with no light, and to begin to answer the questions which can only be sought in darkness itself.

If this book leaves you with more questions than answers, then in many ways its aims will have been accomplished. I have found that anyone who claims to have all the answers simply isn't asking the right questions – and I have endeavoured to not make such claims. Questions are themselves the goal, as Rabbi Avraham Galante once wrote in his own commentary on the Zohar, cited by Danny Matt in the Pritzker Zohar: *a question is already half of the answer – for without the question, there wouldn't be an answer at all.* Similarly, the darkness is already half the light, for without the darkness, there wouldn't be any light at all.

Rabbi Adam Zagoria-Moffet
St. Albans, United Kingdom
Rosh Ḥodesh Tevet 5784 / 1 January 2025

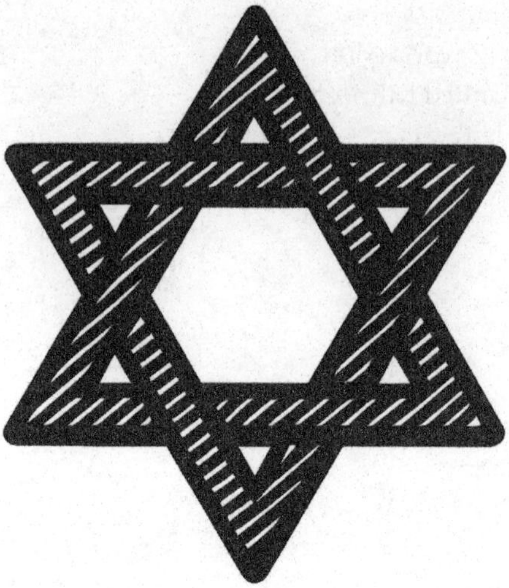

Chapter One

Relinquishing ‘Religion’ // *Judaism*

So profound has been the impact of Christianity on the development of Western civilisation that it has come to be hidden from view.

Tom Holland, Dominion

To explore, as this book intends to, what Judaism is, we must first consider what it is *not*. Disentangling the core of Jewish thought, text, and theology from the many layers laid upon it is not a simple task. For most of Jewish history has taken place in exile – a fact which alerts us to the great and difficult task we must undertake: to decolonise Judaism itself. Due to the long years of intellectual influence (much of it coercive, aggressive, or abusive) on Jewish thought, it can be hard to read Jewish texts with Jewish eyes. Even if we are fully immersed in Jewish learning, we are still products of our societies. To look at Judaism anew with an authentic appreciation requires us to work to remove the husk of foreign interpretation that, too often, surrounds Judaism.

Dechristianising the Mind

As you're reading this in English, you're very likely a resident of the Christian West. Even if you hardly ever think of your society in such a way, you cannot escape this fact. Yes, Christianity, like most organised religion today, is on the wane. Our societies are more secular than ever, but the relative secularisation of a Christian society does not, in the least bit, make it less Christian.

Many of the key ideas of the modern liberal democratic West are simply Christian notions dressed up in the guise of secular philosophy. Even those which seem to be most opposed to the conventions of Christendom are often unlikely doppelgangers of precisely the ideas they claim to oppose. John Gray, a contemporary philosopher, has written powerfully about the lasting impact of Christian thought on the 'secular' West. "When Christianity was rejected," he argues, "its eschatological hopes did not disappear. They were repressed, only to return as projects of universal emancipation."[6] This transmutation of Christian salvation into the political ideologies of the 20th century is one small example of the persistence of religious ideas, even in a society which is ostensibly secular.

Strangely, it is here we must begin in order to understand why almost all of us are wrong about what Judaism is (and isn't). To illustrate the ways in which Christian thought unwittingly shapes how we understand Judaism we need only a few examples: the obsession with progress, anthropocentric humanism and the belief in creation *ex nihilo* (from nothing). These are each inherently Christian – the first a translation of Christian salvation doctrines, the second a consequence of Christological theology, and the third a simple misreading of the shared text of Genesis.

Doing Great, Getting Better

Consider the idea, which we all take for granted as obvious, that society gradually and steadily improves over time. Technically called 'meliorism' – more conventionally we simply refer to this notion as 'progress'. It is an absolute expectation of the modern West that we will pay homage to the dictates of progress, shirking all else in a futile quest to advance its theoretically inevitable march. Politicians, theologians, and everyone in between evoke the belief in capital-p Progress to justify practically anything (and everything), but 'Progress' is just the salvific redemption of Christian thought rewritten into secular terminology.

"If anything defines 'the West,'" John Gray argues, "it is the pursuit of salvation in history. It is historical teleology – the belief that history has a built-in purpose or goal – rather than traditions of democracy or tolerance, that sets western civilization apart from all others."[7] To pursue Progress is to be willing to sacrifice in honour of this agnostic animistic force – salvation in history. Tens of millions of lives were offered up on that altar within the last century, and yet, questioning our absolute belief in progress remains a heretical gesture. Red Army massacres during the Russian Civil War and the imprisonment and beating of Italian intellectuals under *fascismo* during the same years were both the products of a prioritisation of progress above all else, despite their ostensible political differences.

The work of Stephen Pinker (*Better Angels of Our Nature*) attempts to demonstrate – through an abundance of statistics and an unhealthy reliance on charts – that everything is universally better now than it ever was before, thereby applying the dogma of progress's saving power onto the interpretation of history. Pinker's aspiration for an ever-improving march of historical progress is admirable of course – but is itself deeply religious, imbued with the assumptions of Christian theology. Once again, we can rely on John Gray here: "the radical Enlightenment belief that there can be a sudden break in history, after which the flaws of human society will be forever abolished, is a by-product of Christianity."[8]

If the ideas of the Enlightenment, ideas we take for granted as obvious and good, are simply secularised Christian theology – then how can we pull Judaism free from such a hold? After all, most of us, rightly, would not want to disavow *all* the ideas of the Enlightenment. Liberty, human rights and free societies shouldn't come at the cost of needing to embrace salvation, messianism and apocalypticism. One approach is to try and restore Judaism to the centre of this tradition through the abusive use of a hyphen, inventing the 'Judeo-Christian Tradition.' There is no such thing.

As David Nirenberg has shown in his book *Anti-Judaism*, the entire intellectual construction of the Christian West is designed to oppose Judaism. Evidence for this abounds in the mass graves of the pogroms in Europe and the detailed records of the Inquisition. The only beneficiary to the absurd claim of a 'Judeo-Christian Tradition' are Christians seeking to shirk their responsibility for two millennia of antisemitism and lend authenticity to their theological agenda.

If we were to succumb to such intellectual laziness and use phrases like 'Judeo-Christian Tradition', then we may be inclined to imagine that the critiques of Christian thought in this chapter could apply equally to Judaism. To the extent that many Jews have themselves adopted these Christian ideas (salvation, messianism, apocalypticism, creation *ex nihilo*, and many more), this can be a useful critique. The problem, though, is that traditional Judaism doesn't *actually* share in these beliefs, putting the lie to the fiction of Judeo-Christian anything and freeing us from needing to justify ideas that we cannot sustain. To take just one example, that of apocalypticism, Gray reminds us that, "ancient Judaism contained nothing resembling the idea that the world was about to come to an end. Christianity injected the belief that human history is a teleological process."[9] This difference, in how Judaism views time, is a subject we will return to at the end of this book (See Chapter 12).

Whether planning the apocalypse or advocating for progress, we can see the subtle dominion of Christian ideas on Judaism. That isn't to say that Jews must oppose progress. There are benefits and drawbacks to the belief that life is ever-improving – and it is a perfectly sound theology to uphold – but it is a distinctly Christian one. While there is no doubt that many metrics of human quality of life have improved, and dramatically, the conclusions Pinker and others draw go beyond the data.

If we step back and look at history with a broader view, or, more importantly, look at the concept of the 'good' through a more inclusive lens – the picture is different. Human lifespans are longer and infant mortality is lower, but economic inequality is trapped in a cycle of booms and busts and the cost of our human flourishing may prove a third mass extinction event, likely already underway.

We don't need to believe that everything is always getting better. Judaism, free of Christian coercion, is free to acknowledge the reality of history and the complexity of our contemporary world. With 'Progress' as with many other ideas – such as the semi-religious secular doctrine of humanism. Humanism itself is a product of seeing progress as a proven creed, but humanism is another iteration of Christian ideas framed in secular language.

Not Quite Touching - Human and Divine

In the most literal sense, Christianity is enclothed with humanism because in Christianity, God is a human being. The worship of ourselves has never been elevated more than when sanctioned as sacred by the Christian West. In this, the legacy of Christianity has been to build upon the theological structures of ancient polytheism, which made gods out of human beings – only slightly larger and more powerful than ourselves, but with the same anxieties, arguments, and anger management issues. So long as the Divine is in any way a human self-reflection – whether we are speaking of Zeus *or* Jesus – we are entrapped in seeing ourselves and our world only through our own eyes.

In this, Christianity betrayed its Jewish background and returned to a polytheistic impulse which Judaism had rebelled against – for as Gray correctly identifies, it was Judaism that "gave birth to the idea of an invisible reality" with its "ban on images of the deity." Gray continues:

> At this point a type of introspection became

> possible that had not existed before. If God is invisible the inner world might be unknown to us just like that unseen God. It was Christianity that introduced the notion that God resembles humans – even, in the myth of incarnation, becoming one of them. God was then no longer an invisible presence but a divine personage, which could be known with as much certainty as we know ourselves. The possibility that much of our inner world might be hidden from us was lost.[10]

The great insight of the Torah is the rejection of any kinship between God and humanity, and the sacred preservation of that 'inner world which might be unknown to us.' An unseen and alien God was the innovation of our ancient ancestors who first journeyed into monotheism. God does not look like us (or anything). God does not think like us. God does not know like us. God is, simply put, *not* like us in any way whatsoever. While a simplistic reading of Genesis's claim that we are 'made in God's image' (1.27) may lead us into error, the Sages have always understood this in a non-literal way.[11] The unbridgeable gap between the human and the divine is the necessary ingredient for rejecting the self-centred elevation of humanity to the primary concern of religious life. When, as Judaism insists we must, we sever the link between human and divine, our focus becomes the divine interest, not our own.

To define Judaism as not-Christianity may seem facile, but the so-called *via negativa* helps establish what Judaism is not, helping us to separate out the wheat from the chaff: Judaism as it is versus Judaism as it is conceived of by the dominant culture(s) in which we live. Judaism is God-obsessed, while being completely abstract and often agnostic about exactly what God *is*. What is absolutely certain is that God is not us. Isaiah [55.8-9], as so often the case, makes this clear in beautiful poetic language:

> *Because My thoughts are not your thoughts,*
> *and your ways are not my ways – says God.*
> *Rather, as high as the sky above the earth,*
> *so are my ways distant from yours,*
> *and my thoughts are far from your thoughts.*

A brief summary of how Judaism sees God: God is equally present (or not) in all things (Chapter 2). While humanity is given the divine gift of creative power (through language, see Chapter 7), and are tasked with being God's partners in the ongoing creation of the universe (Chapter 3), humans can claim no more divinity than any other living thing. God is *nishmat kol ḥai* (the breath within all that lives). God is *elohim ḥayyim*, two grammatically-collective nouns that we should read as essentially having an equals sign between them: God = life.

In this, we don't mean the sort of soft-shell diluted diatribes of the ill-intentioned 'spiritual but not religious' crowd[12]. We mean that the closest we can come to God is as the cumulative force that *animates*. The difference between death and life is that life is God and death is not. There is one god for all and all gods are one.

Pure humanism is therefore incompatible with a correct understanding of divinity. Arguably, the inability of humanism to see the Divine as present in death and decay makes a sort of idol out of the individual human life. Instead of our primary concern being ourselves, our primary concern should be all life. Our primary concern should be God. Ḥakham José Faur puts it well when he says:

> The theocentric perspective separates creation from nature and the Book from a book. From this perspective truth unfolds within the

> limitless chasm separating God and humanity. Because the Creator can never be fully known, revelation and the truly mystical are limitless and never ending.[13]

This theocentrism could also be called biocentrism. If God and Life can be interchangeable (*elohim ḥayyim*), then we can put God at the forefront of our minds by giving our attention to all living things. A biocentric outlook (rather than a humanist one) could not envision the divine in a human body, nor would it suggest that everything is constantly improving all the time, in all ways, for all living things. The linear assumption of humanism, that human progress serves as the ultimate and inevitable goal of history, cannot hold the reality of biocentrism, in which a species may excel or become extinct and in which the life-line of any organism undulates wildly rather than growing constantly towards an anthropocentric aim. A biocentric theology would appreciate the complex cycles of life. Life cannot simply continue to grow forever, nor is progress inevitable. The forces of decay and disorder always contest with Life's bloom and bud. God's ordering of all things is the essential ingredient in them becoming alive, because it is God/Life which makes living things grow and flourish and challenges the endemic energy of entropy.

Something from Nothing

The final example, which will be fully illustrated by the discussion in Chapter 3, is how we understand Creation. Christianity has been incredibly successful in convincing Jews that their own sacred text starts with the words 'In the beginning.' It does not. There is no 'in the beginning' in the beginning. Creation is a process that begins with plenty of pre-existent matter, and which is conducted through separation, division, and distinction. God creates through drawing difference – upper water from lower water, light from dark, world from waste, and life from death.

The *tohu vavohu* of the creation story, the 'welter and waste' (as Robert Alter translates it), represents the tendency towards disorder (entropy) and it is personified in the chaotic forces of the sea and darkness. Both the ocean and the night are things in which order dissolves into disorder – in which distinction and separation are impossible. If creation occurs through making separations, then chaos reigns in collapsing them. The Mishnah teaches that we can only say the Shema in the morning once we are certain that dawn has broken. How can you tell? As usual there's a debate:

> When does one recite *Shema* in the morning? From when a person can distinguish between sky-blue [*tekhelet*] and white. Rabbi Eliezer says: 'From when one can distinguish between sky-blue and leek-green.'[14]

Distinguishing two colours allows us to testify to the light. The day is created through the distinction that light affords. To create, God must divide what is already present, and it is boundaries of division and separation that permit life to grow. Creation is therefore not a distinct event, not something that 'happened' at the beginning of time – but a process of defeating disorder and defining distinctions. Jewish sources have always accepted this ambiguity of creation, and even imagined that God experienced the rather human frustration of failure in the process.

The Midrash suggests that God attempted to make the universe many times before getting it right.[15] The recipe for one perfectly-cooked universe is complex. God's challenge, the Midrash teaches, was trying to measure out the two essential universal ingredients: compassion and justice. Too much compassion and the world collapses beneath injustice. Too much justice and the world relapses into ruthlessness. These stories belie an important truth:

creation, properly understood, is not the conception most of us have. The vision of creation present in Christianity has God magic the world into being, all at once, from nothing. There is no error, no effort and no gradual ongoing development. The benefit of believing in a Creation which is inherently imperfect and perpetually present is tremendous.

Juda-ism

Progress (salvation), Humanism (Christology), and Creation (from nothing) – these are but three ideas which Jews assume are part of their 'religion' only because they have been implanted by the intellectual imperialism of the dominant culture. Even from just these few examples we can appreciate how critical it is to question the assumptions we hold about religion, to be willing to revise even the concept of religion. These are but three relatively minor ways in which Judaism, when considered in its own context and free of the prejudices of our contemporary society, reaches a very different conclusion to that of Christianity.

Tom Holland, in his history of Christendom, *Dominion* says:

> To live in a Western country is to live in a society still utterly saturated by Christian concepts and assumptions. This is no less true for Jews or Muslims than it is for Catholics or Protestants. Two thousand years on from the birth of Christ, it does not require a belief that he rose from the dead to be stamped by the formidable – indeed the inescapable – influence of Christianity.[16]

The influence is formidable – so much so that we cannot help but find that our minds have been colonised by Christian concepts. We imagine God to be like Zeus, Greek-myth mediated through

Christian concepts (a handsome old bloke with a beard, a flowing robe, and some epic clouds). We imagine history to be a constant march of redemptive progress designed to reap maximal benefit for humanity (salvation). We imagine creation to be an event that occurred once, and in a vacuum, in 'the' beginning. These imaginings are illusions, alien to the correct Jewish reading (*mikhtav*) of the text (*ketav*) of the Torah. To undo these errors, we only have to admit one simple fact: Judaism is not a religion.

A religion is a set of beliefs that the followers of that 'faith' subscribe to. So long as you agree to certain ideological principles (for example, that Muhammad is the seal of the prophets and no one will come after, or that Jesus is the son of God and the only lord and saviour), then you are a follower of that religion. Judaism is of an entirely different category. The word, 'Judaism' is descriptive – 'Judaism' as an -ism is simply a reference to the insights and practices of the Jewish people and their mobile national library, the Tanakh (Hebrew Bible). While there are many laws and rules that govern the individual and collective life of the Jewish people (*mitsvot*), as far as mandated beliefs go, there are only two.

The Two Things A Jew Must Believe

There's a fabulous debate among the Sages regarding how many of the Ten Commandments (*aseret hadiberot*)[17] the Israelites actually heard at Sinai. The consensus seems to be that they bailed long before they could hear more than a part of God's auditory self-revelation. Some believe they heard the entirety of the *aseret hadiberot*, others suggest they heard only the first two commandments, and some propose they heard nothing but the first letter, an *alef* (meaning the entirety of the national revelation was the silent sound following a sharp intake of breath).

The most convincing position is that the Israelites heard only the first two statements[18] – in part because the tense of the words and the tone of the message changes dramatically between the first two and the rest. Yet, the first two also stand apart not just because of their grammar, but also, at least according to Maimonides, due to the fact that they are *obvious* - they don't *need* to be revealed:

> The difference, according to Maimonides, between the first two commandments, which were heard by the whole people, and those that followed, which Moses alone received, is that anyone can fully grasp the first two commandments, which express God's existence and unity, by means of an entirely rational proof.[19]

The first two statements are: (1) "I am Adonai, your God, who brought you up from Egypt," and (2) "You shall have no other Gods beside me." These are the only two that are worded in the first-person, in which God seems to be speaking directly to the people, and they are the only two that hint at any sense of a mandated belief. They are clear and, if we believe Maimonides, self-evident. Therefore there are only two beliefs that a Jew *must* hold: 1) we know God through history, and through the Exodus in particular, and 2) God is singular, unique, and alone. You could label these very simply as: 1) identity and 2) singularity. These, and only these, are the things that a Jew must believe.

One way to remember these two mandatory beliefs is to engage in the typically-rabbinic practice of alternative reading (*ketiv/keri*), specifically by slightly re-vocalising the Shema. If you change only one vowel (from a *sheva* under the *shin* to a *kamats*), then the central statement of Jewish belief would read: *"Israel heard: Adonai is our God, Adonai is One."* Instead of a command *("Hear, O Israel!")* the verb becomes a descriptive perfect aspect with Israel as the subject (*"Israel heard"*). This gentle re-reading of the Shema can serve as a reminder to us of the only two required beliefs for a Jew

– the only two theological statements which were heard directly from the Divine at Sinai: 1) Adonai is our God (identity), and 2) Adonai is One (singularity).

Judaism is not a religion. Or, more accurately, Judaism is not *only* a religion. There are beliefs which make up a part of the complex of Jewishness but they are few in number (literally two, as we have seen) and fairly non-prescriptive. Most of the key questions that 'religions' attempt to answer (the afterlife, the nature of the soul, the beginning and end of the world, and so forth) are open ones in Judaism.

In this book, we will explore some of them and offer partial pictures of the polysemous answer(s) that are provided. However, because these broader theological ideas are not *mitsvot*, not commanded as part of the *berit* (covenant) and therefore not mandated beliefs, they are matters of philosophy. As a result, there is a huge leeway of possible beliefs that one can hold about these questions and still be well within the acceptable framework of Jewish community. Unlike the dogmatic structure of religions, which legislates against thoughts, the only beliefs that push someone into the realm of *minut* (heresy) are those which contradict the two mandatory principles – the identity of God and/or the singularity of God.

Judaism for Jews

Embracing the realisation that Judaism is not a religion liberates us from needing to make it fit into predetermined Christian categories. It permits us to re-read our texts with new-old eyes. It frees us to reconsider God, creation, authority, morality, prophecy, and theology. This is not some puerile quest for purity – there is no such thing. We cannot pretend that Judaism has not been influenced by Christianity (or Islam, or Zoroastrianism, or others) in profound ways. We cannot purge these influences – nor would we want to do so.

To attempt to strip Judaism back to its core, free of any outside influence, is an icarionic task – it is inherently self-destructive. However, we can both accept the complex and often syncretic history of Jewish belief while also applying to it an examination of its ideals, an exacting test of its textual truth. We may not be able to completely remove non-Jewish influence, but neither must we tacitly accept it and allow it to shape the way in which we read our own texts and traditions.

When we allow ourselves to indulge in the unfashionable exercise of intellectual decolonisation, we can appreciate how much of Judaism is misunderstood and misinterpreted. So much of the rejection and disgust many Jews feel towards Judaism is not towards Judaism *per se* but towards the problematic overwritings of Jewish texts that circulate in Jewish communities thanks to Christian influence.

The fact that so many Jews believe that their tradition advocates Original Sin in the Garden of Eden story[20], that Judaism believes in a Devil or that Judaism adopts the same sexual ethics which Christianity later retroactively applied to the Torah – is a tragedy. It is these concepts which drive Jews to reject Judaism, but there are likely many Jews who may find that the Judaism they rejected is itself a façade, an illusory foreign apparatus of intellectual occupation. When we resist that and question its dictates, we may find a Judaism free of dogma, empowered and empowering.

Why Jews are All Atheists

Martin Buber once said that, "the atheist staring from his attic window is often nearer to God than the believer caught up in his own false image of God."[21] Buber would have been well aware that a large number of traditional Jews were attracted to the language of atheism and agnosticism. So many Jews are active and committed members of the Jewish people, attend synagogue regularly, and still call themselves atheist, because the God they are rejecting is the same one that Judaism rejects. To be an atheist is to reject Christianity and its God-concept, not to reject the notion of Divinity. To not believe in the god whom atheists don't believe in is simply to reject our own self-image made divine, the human archetype having undergone apotheosis.

True pursuit of God often puts one on a path of doubt and scepticism which, to the Christian mind, approximates atheism. Yet, in the vein of Maimonides and his radical endorsement of apophatic theology, this extreme scepticism is actually seen, in Jewish eyes, as a religious quest in its own right. The degree to which Maimonides rejects any concept we can make of God, any name we can use, any appellation we may apply as 'illusion'[22] is so extensive that to take the project of the *Moreh Nevukhim* (Guide for the Perplexed) seriously is to approach a certain superficial similarity to atheism in the pursuit of apophasis.[23]

Apophasis is more difficult than simply negating (God is not good, God is not blue, etc). Faur attempts to give us an idea:

> Apophatic knowledge is not merely the rejection of a positive attribute or the correction of a mistaken opinion. It involves a dynamic process: apophasis is defined by the very process of negating a positive attribute. This type of negation is not accomplished by removing a contradiction or amending a mistake and accepting the "right" view on the basis of faith. It must be demonstrated by a *burhan* (plural *burahin*) 'proof established on the principle of contradiction'. There are two stages. Initially, there is only negation

> without a positive proof (*burhan*). At this level there is no apophatic knowledge, and doubt will linger in the mind of the believer. The second stage requires a positive proof (*burhan*), demonstrating why such a positive attribute cannot apply to God. Only then apophatic knowledge is realized.[24]

To know God we not only have to say what God isn't, we have to prove it. What a strange position to be in! It would seem our primary religious duty may be to completely extract Judaism from the trappings of 'religion'. Unfortunately, while there is much in common (a shared rejection of Christian dogma), in this regard we cannot look to atheists as fellow-travellers. In fact, the vast majority of today's atheist advocates (the so-called 'New Atheists') are themselves simply perpetuating Christian doctrine dressed up in contemporary philosophy. Despite claiming to distance themselves in every meaningful way from Christian thought, they end up replacing 'salvation' with 'progress', 'God' with 'nature', and 'religion' with 'science'.

John Gray suggests that, "Contemporary atheism is a Christian heresy that differs from earlier heresies chiefly in its intellectual crudity."[25] The 'New Atheists' of Richard Dawkins and his ilk have done nothing other than change the window dressing on the underlying core assumptions of Christianity. They have enshrined as their primary belief one that is inevitably indebted to Christian thinking (humanism) and they have doubled down on the meliorationist position - reading history as a linear story of gradual redemption leading to a future, technology-driven messianic age in which progress will be perfected.

John Gray mounts a stirring critique of these 'new Atheists' in his book *Seven Types of Atheism*. He doesn't do so to defend religion, but rather to criticise Dawkins, Daniel Dennett and Sam Harris (among others) for being *insufficiently* atheist. Over the course of the brief book, Gray searches for an authentic atheist tradition. He ends up looking towards mystical sources and Jewish ones – and in particular appeals to idiosyncratic Jewish philosopher Lev Sheshtov as a possible example.

To present Sheshtov's writings on religion out of context, they could easily be mistaken for standard Jewish theological speculation. Here's one quote from his work *Athens and Jerusalem* which sounds downright spiritual: "What a sigh of relief men will breathe when they suddenly discover that the living God, the true God, in no way resembles the one whom reason has shown them until now."[26]

God is unknown and unknowable? It's hardly radical stuff, especially considering the legacy of negative theology in Jewish thought in Maimonides and others, whose radical doubt reduces us to being only able to speak of God by shutting our mouth first. Sheshtov was hardly 'religious' in the Christian sense and there's little evidence that his Jewish identity informed his thinking, but what he had to say about God and 'religion' would fit quite easily into nearly any Jewish thinking:

> Within the 'limits of reason' one can create a science, a sublime ethic, and even a religion; but to find God one must tear oneself away from the seductions of reason with all its physical and moral constraints, and go to another source of truth.[27]

If you're going to offer a real alternative to Christian theology in the modern West, it cannot come from simply secularising Christian ideas and repackaging them as 'atheism'. There is a counterpoint to Rome/Athens, and it is Jerusalem. There is an alternative approach to spirituality, morality and belief which offers a considerably different take on most key questions we face. It exists and it flourishes underneath a layer of Western Christian/Secular overwriting.

If we have the courage to peel off that outer layer that has been artificially imposed, we will find a resource-rich tradition (*masoret*) which has preserved an altogether different way of thinking. How then, do we do the work of recovering the authentic intellectual tradition of Judaism and redeeming it from the false binary of Atheism versus Christianity? Throughout the chapters of this book, we will aim to do exactly that – abandoning some of the ideas that we have taken for granted, relinquishing the hold placed upon us by 'religious' institutions, teachers, or expectations, and revising the very conception of what religion is.

Chapter Two

Nothing and/or Everything // *God*

"...what God must actually be—a power vibrating in our every atom, built into the explosions of distant stars, and circling the dust of worlds you and I will never be able to contemplate. We are part of some vast, mysterious, eternal Whole set in motion by a force so awesome that it is ultimately unknowable. Do you feel me? We can't always see the direction or meaning of it all, but to even glimpse this tiny corner of the Whole—what an incredible opportunity. What a grave responsibility."
Stephen Markley, The Deluge

Whatever Judaism is or is not (*not a religion*), it is irrevocably centred on the question of Divinity. We have established that the only two mandatory beliefs in Judaism are the identity of God and God's singularity. Typically both are conveyed by the shorthand term 'monotheism' – but what does that really mean? Is there only *one* way to believe in one God?

The Three 'T's

In *The History of Magic*, Chris Gosden argues for a typological definition of humanity's attempts to make sense of reality. According to him, all human societies have been and are still variations on the triple helix of science, religion and magic. All three of these interpretations of reality aim to address, as Gosden describes it, three T's: Transcendence, Transformation and Transaction.

Bronze Age ancient Near East society was heavily structured around a magical interpretation of religion which placed undue emphasis on transaction. The relationship with the world of spirits, demons and the dead was one of exchange. Because the notion of divinity was diffuse (in the animistic sense) and diverse (in the polytheistic one), transcendence was not the primary focus of Egyptian or Babylonian religion.

The innovation that occurred during the Late Bronze Age collapse[28], among the people who would come to be called Israel, was a reorientation and rebalancing of the three T's, placing transcendence in a newly central role in religious life. The Torah preserves much of what preceded it, in this regard, but it also recontextualizes it. For example, the *Kehunah* (priesthood) has no shortage of transactional spiritual objectives (notably the system of sacrifice as well as ritual purity), and transformation is preserved (now rewritten on a national scale as the story of a people rather than through individuals such as shamans), but both are overshadowed and undergirded by the new role of transcendence in the primary innovation of Israelite religion: monotheism.

Is Israel really the first community to adopt a monotheistic worldview? Considerable evidence points to a connection with the renegade pharaoh Akhenaten and his attempt to reform ancient Egyptian religion[29] - although any certainty is evasive due to the active erasure of Akhenaten and his capital Amarna from the historical record. Akhenaten promoted the reduction of the panoply of gods in the Egyptian pantheon to a single divine force: called only the Aten, and depicted abstractly as the sun and its rays reaching out, each ending in an outstretched hand.

It is hard to imagine that this great religious revolution could have happened among the elite of Egypt during the same time a Hebrew Egyptian prince was discovering the unity of divinity in the desert – and there *not* be some connection. While speculation has abounded as to what the link may have been between Akhenaten and the emergence of Israelite monotheism, there is every possibility that the repression of Atenism by Akhenaten's son and successor, Tutankhamun, and the persecution of the

Atenist priesthood sowed the seeds for Moses's later rebellion against the gods of Egypt and the authority of the Pharaoh.

While the possible Atenist inspiration for Israelite thinking remains only speculation - we can be certain that as Israel gradually attempted to put into practice the monotheistic dictates of the Torah (particularly Deuteronomy) it was resisted from within and without - with widespread public derision for the reforming religious impulse within Israel and bafflement and disgust from its neighbours. Although a simplistic reading of the Israelite experience would suggest everyone was equally convinced, the numerous tirades by the *Nevi'im* (literally 'spokespeople' but conventionally translated as 'prophets') against those who resisted Israel's religious revolution is testimony enough for us to understand that monotheism was never as simple or as easy as it may first seem. In the Late Bronze Age (1300-1100 BCE), the idea that all divinities were one unity was so radical it, like most good ideas, took many attempts to gain widespread adoption. The Israelites were early adopters and innovators of the concept, but they also imbibed the new ideology in fits and starts, with as many setbacks as advances.

Why was monotheism so radically rejected by the people first exposed to it? Principally, as the story of Exodus demonstrates, it is because monotheism is incompatible with a worldview that sees absolute authority in any human person, institution, or state. The political import of the Torah and its ideas about governance, states, and leadership will be considered more in depth in Chapter 4, but it is worth mentioning in brief this key element before turning to the question of what monotheism actually means.

A consequence of acknowledging that ultimate authority is singular is the implicit rejection of all *other* authority. To say that there is only one God is to make that God equally accessible (or inaccessible) to everyone. 'One' and 'all' are exchangeable adjectives. If there is one God, then that is the God of all. Conversely, all gods must be one and the same God. Both sides of this are needed: all gods are one God who is the one God of all. That was the radical revolution in thought engendered by the people of ancient Israel and their constitution, the Torah.

True monotheism is exceedingly rare. That is because it is actually very challenging to accept both parts of the above statement. When we begin to imagine the divine, as we inevitably do, we often fail on one or both counts. Either we suggest that God is *this* one but not that – or, we believe that there is only one God, but that it is in some way limited.

Theolomega

The great paradox of the monotheistic revelation of the Torah is that it is almost inherently impossible to believe. If we imagine a shape like a horseshoe (or like the Greek letter Omega), the truth (that all gods are one who is the god of all) lies in the empty space between the 'legs' of the letter. We cannot quite reach it. As soon as we get close we immediately start to drift away again. That is the unfortunate reality of the truth – it is almost, by definition, unattainable (or at least, impossible to hold onto for any period of time).

How do we grasp God without being able to break out from the black lines of the letter's sweep and take hold of the empty space in the centre? The closest we get is to make a jump from the nearest point, reaching out momentarily, before being pulled back. The Sefer Yetsirah (Gra Version 1:6) calls this 'running and returning'. Derived from Yeḥezkel's (Ezekiel) description of his divine vision - with the 'holy beings running and returning', (1.14) the sense the language creates is one of vibration, vacillation, an active dynamic energy of tension and torque, twisting our minds towards the truth before being overcome by the gravity of reality and losing our hold.[30]

This implies an important idea: to approach the truth we have to largely approximate it – it cannot be held for long in our minds. We may reach it momentarily but just as quickly, it slips away. Like a child darting across the burning sand of a summer beach, we have to constantly go and return, flitting between what we know and what we don't. Only in the movement itself do we find the revelation of the Divine, and only ever for just a moment.

It is nearly impossible to discuss this 'running and returning' in practical terms, but we need to understand what the two points are that get us close enough to make the jump. Those two sharp corners, the 'elbows' of the Omega, where the letter's shape bends towards the truth are our destination. They reflect the duality of theology which most approximates truth, that is, the two distinct methods of monotheism.

In a short-form prose piece, Argentine poet Jorge Luis Borges imagines a spiritual crisis taking place for William Shakespeare. His brief story, titled *Everything and Nothing*, ends in this way:

> The story goes that shortly before or after his death, when he [Shakespeare] found himself in the presence of God, he said: "I who have been so many men in vain want to be one man only, myself." The voice of God answered him out of a whirlwind: "Neither am I what I am. I dreamed the world the way you dreamt your plays, dear Shakespeare. You are one of the shapes of my dreams: like me, you are everything and nothing."[31]

Simply put, there are two versions of monotheism: God is either nothing (no-thing) or everything (every-thing). Perhaps in recognition that both these points are equally close to the transcendent but unattainable truth, and in keeping with the imagined self-revelation to Shakespare in Borges's piece, God is *both* everything *and* nothing.

Both ideas are equally acceptable as approximations of the truth. While to the casual observer these appear to be completely opposite theologies, their apparent opposition collapses in the truth that they both point towards. The assumption that the truest version of something is attained by taking the 'two aspects that seem most in opposition and synthesising them' is central to most mystical philosophies. It is perhaps best articulated by the modern mystic, Carl Jung, who made the alchemical formulation of the concept as *coincidentia oppositorum* (the coincidence of opposites) a key part of his psychological worldview.[32]

In the realm of Jewish theology, this phenomenon (of holding the productive tension of apparently opposite concepts) is richly sourced. The notion of a *maḥlokhet leshem shamayim* (an argument for heaven's sake), or the oft-cited maxim of Rabbi Abba that *eilu ve-eilu divré elohim ḥayyim* (both these and those are the words of God who is Life)[33] each testify to the assumption that truth is attained by going towards paradox and a dialogue of opposites rather than avoiding diametrically opposed concepts in favour of dogma. So we must endeavour to not see 'God is everything' and 'God is nothing' as only opposite statements, grammatically or theologically. Instead, we have to work to see them in dialogue and to reach for the place they both point towards.

Where a theology of nothingness and a theology of everythingness coincide is in a sphere of belief most likely called by academics 'theistic naturalism'. In the technical parlance of theology this means a belief that God is expressed primarily through the natural world, but not restricted to it. Others may call this 'panentheism' (the world is within God but God surpasses it). What's critical is that we must find a way to establish a theological footing in which we can hold both statements true: God is nothing and everything.

Nothing and/or Everything

Typically the 'God is nothing' argument relies on negation and on seeing God as essentially and inviolably other. It suggests that the closest we can come to speaking of God is silence – that any words are inherently incorrect. This God has no names, no qualities. This leads us towards seeing the Torah not as God's self-revelation per se, but rather, as Rabbi Louis Jacobs called it, 'a human record of revelation.' Maimonides's *Guide for the Perplexed* built upon earlier philosophic work to attempt a cohesive negative theology in such a vein, in which God could not be described or directly apprehended. The challenges of a purely 'God is nothing' approach is that it deprives God of any personhood or personality and diminishes the world of any real enchantment. It leaves us with an idea of God which is an absence, a black hole described by its edge alone but with content which is unknowable, a God who is supremely transcendent, but as a result, incredibly distant.

The apophatic approach of Maimonides and others is subtractive: God is *not* human *nor* animal, God is *not* male *nor* female, God is *not* spiteful *nor* caring, etc. The idea is that the closest way to approximate something which is by default incomprehensible is to eliminate everything it is *not* and whatever remains is the closest possible conjecture of the truth. This draws us ever closer to 'God is no-thing' in the most literal sense, and encourages an awe-struck silence in the face of the indefinable divine.

The other pole of the Omega is the 'God is everything' argument. This suggests an additive approach to theology – rather than saying what God is not, we simply never stop saying what God is. Here our key word is not 'not' but 'and'. God is human and animal and vegetable and mineral. God is good and evil and kind and awful and compassionate and cruel.

Rather than approximate the truth through silent contemplation, the method of prayer and practice is a voluminous one, with more and more words being used. Images are not only celebrated, they're compiled – with a text like the Zohar using numerous complex and contradictory images all at the same time, pushing our perception of the paradox of God's identity through a glut of description. This is the God of myth and Midrash, who can be anything and anyone because they are everything and everyone. The challenge of this approach is that if we ever stop the additive exercise, even for a second, and go: 'this here is God,' then we've fallen into idolatry.

So how do we choose? Both are the closest we can get to the truth but neither is actually the truth. Both offer benefits to religious life, thought, and practice, but both have drawbacks. No doubt most simply chose a side, immediately denouncing the other side, not realising how similar both approaches are. Instead, we have to, as Borges suggests, accept that God is both everything and nothing. This means we get the benefit of both approaches. We can, at times, find God in silent contemplation, rejecting any description or conception as false. At other times we may revel in the lush maximalism of mysticism and myth, with a God who is described in erotic terms and has limbs that can be measured in millions of miles.[34]

It is impossible to hold both these concepts in the mind simultaneously – but by 'running and returning' between the two, we can get as close as allowed to the truth of God's existence. Inevitably, some of us will spend more time on one side or another. Perhaps we feel comfortable with only one or the other, perhaps we need both – it doesn't really matter, so long as we can acknowledge that within the Jewish community, both 'God is no-thing' and 'God is every-thing' are equal attempts to approach the practically unattainable goal of real and true monotheism: all gods are one god who is the one god of all.

Not only are both approaches equally valid in Jewish spaces, there is also considerable parity in their representation within Jewish sources. While it is a gross overgeneralization, the type-species for 'God is no-thing' is the 'negative theology' of Maimonides, in which God is reduced and reduced in an attempt to get a clearer picture through establishing what God is *not*. Similarly, it is the mythologically-rich intellectual landscape of early modern Kabbalah which best represents the opposing approach, that of 'God is every-thing.' There, particularly in the many and florid articulations of Lurianic Kabbalah, God is complex, multiple, and composite. The Tikkuné Zohar, in a passage famously used as an introduction to many *siddurim* (prayer books) puts it this way: "You, God, are one – but not in number."[35]

The apophatic approach of Maimonides and others is subtractive: God is *not* human *nor* animal, God is *not* male *nor* female, God is *not* spiteful *nor* caring, etc. The idea is that the closest way to approximate something which is by default incomprehensible is to eliminate everything it is *not* and whatever remains is the closest possible conjecture of the truth. This draws us ever closer to 'God is no-thing' in the most literal sense, and encourages an awe-struck silence in the face of the indefinable divine. The alternative additive approach, which seeks infinity in the combinatorial complexity of adding everything up, is usually found in Kabbalah, but in many ways its roots are in the Hebrew Bible.[36]. It is this model which offers a theology uniquely well-suited to the modern mind, and which we will explore below.

God, Living and Everlasting

While there is much to say that credits the 'God is nothing' argument, the other end of the Omega – in which we attempt to reach the truth through combinatorial complexity – holds more promise for our contemporary world. In such a model, the nearest it is possible to approach what God *is* (and it does, forever, remain an approximation) is as the concatenation of all living things at once. We purposefully are not using the terms 'pantheism' or 'panentheism' or worrying over the distinction. Instead, we need to look at the question from the bottom up. From our point of view, how do we begin to conceive of a God who is *nishmat kol ḥai*, the animating spirit of all life?

Purely as a thought experiment, try this. Hold in your mind your own life and consciousness, then gradually add to it and combine with it that of other people – first those you know personally and then gradually strangers – eventually holding gently to the idea of what the combined life of 8 billion people would be. Have it in mind? The concerns, desires, and designs of the entire human population all at once? Great, that's only a start. Next you have to add all the other living things – the remainder of non-human animals (keep in mind 97% of all animals are invertebrates), the entire kingdom of plant life, the complicated webs of fungi (of which mycologists estimate we are only aware of about 5% of species), bacterial organisms in their multitudes, and even the borderline cases such as viruses. If you can imagine all of these things as one tremendous additive identity, then perhaps that is the closest possible approximation of what God *is*.

Many of those who would identify as 'spiritual but not religious' or perhaps even 'atheist' would say that what they take to be the ultimate reality (or God) is life itself. They are not wrong. Or at least, Life Itself (the combination of all living things) is the closest we can get to imagining the additive infinity of the Divine. Hinted at by that frequent Hebrew appellation, *elohim ḥayyim* (God/Life), Life Itself also is a useful way to frame the narrative of Creation as an ongoing attempt to counterbalance entropy, chaos, and death. The scale required to appreciate Life Itself as a Divine stand-in is tremendous, and difficult to hold in one's head. All competition between life happens within the context of the great body of God.

This poses the challenge of identity. If we accept this idea of biological monism, then we have to also accept that the centre of our focus is not humanity but biology writ large. In other words, in light of an additive theology that sees God as the Life in all Worlds (*ḥei olamim*),[37]anthropocentric thinking seems incredibly short-sighted. Our myopic obsession with ourselves prevents us from acknowledging the Divine in all living things. Similarly, as we discussed in Chapter 1, our self-divinization is indeed a sort of idolatry – represented by, but not limited to, much of contemporary mainstream Christian theology.[38]

On a different scale, the problem of identity could be stated in this way: if God is best understood as Life Itself – is God the disease or the cure? The poison or the antidote? When a bacterial infection invades one's body, the immune system recognizes this other life form as an enemy – and rightly so, as competition for limited resources within the body plays a big role in health. It is inconceivable that we might think of the protective white blood cells and the invading bacterium as being one in the same thing. However, in truth they are both living organisms, both attempting to fulfil the two prerogatives of all life: 1) extract maximum energy from the environment in order to 2) reproduce as much as possible.

Whilst it wouldn't be good for human health if we see the immune cells and the bacterial invasion as being essentially co-identical, in truth both have more in common than not. All living things are variations on the same theme, the underlying melody of divine consciousness – and all life, while competing and killing and destroying one another, are facets of the same stone. Can God be such a compound identity and still be preserved as a monotheistic singularity?

A God who is more or less Life Itself is both incredibly accessible and yet simultaneously very difficult to recognise as such. This God is an ever present, ever energetic force which we can find within ourselves and within the beautiful, complex, messy world of biological organisms all around us. Thinking in this way, we must do away with the idea of God as *a* being. Instead God *is* Being. This distinction is more than syntactical; it changes our very conception about how one accesses the Divine.

The River and the Radio

Imagine you find yourself in a forest – a lush woodland completely empty of any other people. Still and quiet, you listen carefully and hear in the distance a burbling stream, perhaps even a freshwater river. You realise that not only are you lost, but you are also very very thirsty. As a result, your whole orientation becomes centred on trying to find your way to that river. What can you do? Perhaps the first step is observation – are there other animals nearby that might show the way to the river? Can you hear from which direction the sound of the water is coming? Once you've made up your mind to seek it out, the only way to find it is for you to move – to pick up your feet and follow the sound of the water.

Perhaps you'll come across a path in the underbrush where others trod before, perhaps instead you'll cut through the woodland in a completely new path. Maybe you'll get distracted on the way there – confuse the sound of the wind for that of the water, give up and sit under a tree for a while. Yet always it is an unassailable fact that the river is there, flowing, constantly – it will not move its course to get closer to you. It does not disappear when you stop being able to hear it. Your ability to find it is only a factor of your own effort and attention. If you succeed in seeking out its cool waters, you can slake your thirst, swim in its depths, and channel its power to grow and sustain life.

Like the river, God is omnipresent in the world, in Life Itself. We imagine ourselves to be far away, but only because we are incredibly bad at listening, observing, and following the sound of the flowing water. Far too many people (predominantly 'religious' ones) act out their spiritual lives as a childish protest. They find a tree they like the look of and make camp – waiting for the river to come to them. All they'll ever have is the sound of the river in the distance, but they'll never get to taste its waters.

If quenching your thirst is really the desire, the only way to do so is to change *your* position – to begin to search out the path or find a new one, and to find the Divine where it already is. There are many pitfalls and distractions, many illusions which can occupy our woodland walker and keep them forever trapped in thirst. But, for the person who can correctly identify the facts of their situation and is willing to move themselves to seek out the living waters, there are no barriers. The river is accessible to all who seek it out, but it will not change its course while you stand still and insist.

Consider another analogy: you are a radio – antenna, speakers, and all. God is a brilliant radio broadcast, accessible on a certain frequency. If you power down the radio, it does not affect the broadcast. If you tune the dial to the wrong frequency and hear only static, it is not because the broadcast you're looking for has ignored you or neglected you. If you want to hear the station you seek, you have to tune the radio appropriately – but regardless of whether you do or not, the radio waves continue to emanate in exactly the same way, on exactly the same frequency, continually unheard and ever present in the electromagnetic field that pervades all of space and time.

There are many who have rejected God because, foolishly, they are waiting for the broadcast to change frequencies to their own, rather than turning the dial to tune themselves into what is already (and always) there. There are many who have lamented the absence of divinity and simultaneously failed to realise that they themselves are its vehicles. We are the receiver and transmitter – the broadcast is picked up by our correctly-tuned antennae, but we also possess speakers, able to share what is received with others, becoming a conduit for divinity.

Like God, the number of listeners to that original transmission doesn't have any effect on the quality or persistence of the broadcast – it is the same whether billions are tuned in or no one is. We can see living things the same way. All organisms are radios – the frequency that animates them, that brings their speakers to life and carries sound from great distances is God – and no matter how many billions of organisms there are all playing the same station, the signal remains forever the same. Like a radio, there is plenty of noise, static, and interference that can confuse the keen listener. Like a radio, there's technical problems with the radio itself that can make it unable to pick up the broadcast. But regardless of whether the radio is tuned and able to carry the signal, the station plays on.

For us to fully manifest our potential we have to find the correct tuning, gently adjusting the knobs of our embodied radio sets. The transmission doesn't change, but we do, and constant adjustment is likely. But reception alone is not sufficient. If we have the volume down we may pick up the signal but may not be able to hear it, and certainly unable to share it. We cannot transmit what we haven't first received, but we also cannot settle for listening only for our own sake. Once attuned to the divine frequency we can also become signal boosters for it, helping others to hear the transmission and teaching them how to find its tuning in themselves.

If we can accept both these principles: that God is best understood as the additive complexity of all living things thought of at once, and that God is omnipresent in those living things as and when they seek out that source of life – then we have a responsibility to transform our thinking about religion from an anthropocentric obsession to a biocentric reality. We have a responsibility to awe, and a duty to work to see God, to seek out and embody the divine. Moreover, the biocentric 'God is everything' approach offers us a chance to face the most present and pressing problem of our time: the eradication and extinction of life.

Everythingness and Ecotheology

Mara Benjamin, a scholar of Jewish ecotheology, correctly diagnoses that: "Jewish modes of speaking about ultimate reality are, of course, variegated and polyvocal, [... but] the vast majority of the exoteric tradition is incompatible with contemporary ecological knowledge."[39] Exploring the 'God is everything', monotheism, as we have done, allows us to address and explore a fully present God without straying into the idolatry of seeing God as only nature and nothing more.

Jewish theology has, until very recently, completely failed to account for an accurate understanding of ecology. The *via negativa* of Maimonides leaves an image of God which is increasingly diminished from the world. In ever removing any adjectives from the Divine we drive God out of the world, making the notion of God as the World-Life harder and harder to relate to. While to many the otherness of God in Maimonides's theology is a selling point,[40] one of its unfortunate outcomes can be a disregard for the world, its ecosystems, and its creatures.

One can be so infused with a vision of God that is unspeakable (for to put it into words is to abandon the nothingness) that anything that *is* becomes a barrier to divine transcendence rather than a vehicle for it. Rather than the world being a route of access to the divine, the world ends up being a burden, preventing a purely abstract intellectualism. If the goal is to help people see the immanence of the divine within the world, the Life animating all things, and thus create a sense of care and responsibility, we need to pursue a different path.

In contrast, in the 'God is everything' approach to monotheism, God is embodied and ennobled in the world around us. There are, of course, dangers to this – we must constantly resist the temptation towards idolatry, towards 'something'.

We must always push on to see God as more and more, never complete, never fully described. When it comes to theology, certainty is almost always a bad sign. Despite its pitfalls, the additive approach offers a much better chance of articulating a theology which can actually aid us in our efforts to preserve the world around us.

Key to these efforts is an endorsement of the mythical and an appreciation for the spiritual methodology of quest. The journey of faith is one Jews have eschewed for far too long. God will not come to us – we must move, explore, err, correct, collate and compare our knowledge of the path to the river, the correct frequency of the radio. The language and method of *quest* is more needed than ever, but as with many quests, the thing we seek is often to be found where we started. Rainer Maria Rilke, whose devotional poetry in his *Das Stundenbuch* (Book of Hours) gives voice to the challenges of such a quest, writes:

> You are the future,
> the red sky before sunrise
> over the fields of time.
>
> You are the rooster's crow
> when night is done,
> you are the dew and the
> morning bells
> maiden, stranger, mother, death.
>
> You create yourself in ever-changing shapes
> that rise from the stuff of our days –
> unsung, unmourned, undescribed,
> like a forest we never knew.
>
> You are the deep innerness of all things,
> the last word that can never be spoken.

To each of us you reveal yourself differently:
to the ship as coastline,
to the shore, as a ship.

Book of Hours II.21

Against Idolatry

If God is Life and Life is sacred, then making *human* life the sole focus of religion is idolatry. Making any one thing into God is idolatry. God is either nothing or everything, but cannot ever be, in any sense, *some*thing. As soon as we say that God is the sun but not the moon, male but not female, human but not animal, heavenly but not earthly, we are restricting God to somethingness, and thereby committing the great crime of idolatry. This is an active danger for the 'God is everything' approach to Jewish theology. If, while adding together all life, we stop, finding ourselves satisfied – then we have failed. To truly avoid idolatry we have to put great effort into making *all* life the divine concern, not just our lives.

What would a theology look like which is properly biocentric? How do we begin to tune our collective radios to the signal and to recognise the sound of the river's patter in the distance? The ideas above can help us to begin this shift, but it is a weighty and difficult task. Accepting that God is all life challenges many of the notions conventionally found to be fundamental to religion.

While it may be true that in the scheme of our theological omega (theolomega) both 'God is no-thing' and 'God is every-thing' are paths on the way to truth, the majority of the horseshoe shape that marks out the distance between them is idolatry. Idolatry is the belief that 'God is some-thing'. If God is this but not that – if God is limited and boundaried, consigned into the coercive bounds of 'something' – that is what we call idolatry.

Several things should be clear: 1) monotheism is a lot more complicated than we often make it sound, 2) there are two ways of approximating the radical truth of monotheism, both of which are incomplete and at times, incoherent, 3) those two theologies (God is nothing and God is everything) are not as opposite as they seem, and in fact, the ideal approach is to hold both of them, whether through force of will in synthesising their ideas or through meditative vacillation between the two poles, 4) all of us have the right and the privilege to choose between these two monotheisms, to do so as often and as violently as we like – thereby giving ourselves a richer and more complex spiritual life.

Arguably, more weight is needed on 'God is everything' in contemporary Judaism, partially to counterbalance its historical repression, and partially due to the potential it has to help us remedy the problems our world faces. However, both approaches need to be validated, and everything that falls between them, every version of 'God is this, but not that', every iteration of 'God is something', needs to be rejected. Only then can we see that the two extremes depicted by the Omega above are closer than we think – that everything and nothing are practically touching. In his novel *Slaughterhouse Five*, Kurt Vonnegut draws our attention to another theological diagram which seems to illustrate this well, and which is appropriate to conclude on: "Everything is nothing, but with a twist."[41]

O

∞

Chapter Three

The Perpetual Present // *Creation*

Nothing is sudden. Not an explosion – planned, timed, wired carefully – not the burst door. Just as the earth invisibly prepares its cataclysms, so history is the gradual instant.

Anne Michaels, Fugitive Pieces

Constant Creation

Creation, as it is conventionally understood, is an **event** – it happened, once, a long time ago. Exactly how long ago is irrelevant for the moment. The point is: one can plot Creation (as it is usually thought of) on a timeline. It is discussed as no more than a simple occurrence.

It is a discrete, recognisable point in time. Distant, but definite – that is what most mean when they talk about Creation. However, that is not the only narration of how the world is created, nor is it the one articulated in the text of the Torah or in many of the Jewish traditions that interpret it.

In particular, the Jewish mystical tradition has long flirted with alternatives to this 'conventional' Creation model. In its own typical way, Kabbalah avoids any dogmatic statements of absolute belief – however, a tendency is not difficult to discern. There is a subtle suggestion that 'Creation' is not an event in time, but instead an ongoing, dynamic, process. Moreover, this process of creat*ing* is one which requires the active participation of the creat*ed*.

Read broadly, we can see Creation as an ongoing process, never quite reaching the desired stasis and completion. A process without progress, the expansion of Creation is not one-directional. While the creative process, due to its origins in a cosmic catastrophe, tends towards entropy, disorder and chaos, the active input of God/Life helps to rebalance the input/output and keeps the universe in a dynamic system of *constant creation*.

Nothing Comes from Nothing

The pithy phrase *'nothing comes from nothing'* originates from the ancient Greek philosopher Parmenides and captures the historic objection among many classical philosophers to the 'conventional' (by which we mean, Christian) notion of Creation we discussed above. Parmenides's apparent disregard for the notion of *creatio ex nihilo* (creation from nothing) was shared by Lucretius, as well as by many philosophies rooted in the Vedic tradition (most notably, Jainism). In addition to these, it is also possible to outline a Jewish perspective which rejects the notion of creation from nothing without even needing to look beyond the grammar of the Torah itself.

The grammatical case for a more complex picture of Creation relies very heavily on the very first word of the Torah and the name of the first book: *Bereshit*. The Masoretic Text (MT) unquestionably vocalises this word with an indefinite article as a prefix: **בְּרֵאשִׁית** – however, in the vast majority of translations, from the biblical period itself onwards, and including nearly all English translations prevalent today, the word is rendered as *'In the beginning'* featuring the definite article *'the'*. While to some this may seem to be a purely persnickety question of language, the artificial addition of the definite article meaningfully changes the first sentence of the Torah.

Read correctly, the first line of this sacred text – which informs not just Judaism, but all Abrahamic faiths – should be something *like*: 'When God began to create the heavens and the earth...' or perhaps even 'At the start of God's creating the heavens and the earth...' This itself should lead us to see Creation as something that does not occupy a discrete moment on the timeline. Both '*When God began...*' and '*At the start of God's creating...*' are vague and relativistic suppositions about Creation. Both of which also inherently imply an active and ongoing notion of creation, which occurs against the backdrop of pre-existent reality.

In the commentary of the most famous *parshan* (commentator), Rabbi Shlomo Yitsḥaki (better known as Rashi) on this first verse, he is quite plain in pointing out the problem with the conventional Creation story:

> Scripture [in its opening words] is not teaching the order of creation [as it does afterwards] ... for if this was what it was teaching, it should have written "first (*barishonah*) God created the heavens," for the word *réshit* (start) in Scripture is always grammatically connected to the word that follows it... [and thus] **בראשית ברא** ... is the equivalent of "in the beginning of God's creating."

Rashi is correct in pointing out that the phrase endorses Creation as a process, and he doesn't have to look far for more evidence, as the first chapter of Genesis goes on to label explicitly that *at least* four things were already around when the creating began: some kind of chaotic substance (*tohu vavohu*), darkness (*ḥoshekh*), water (*mayim*), and divine breath/wind (*ru'aḥ elohim*).

So, if the plain meaning of the text is so obvious, how is it that literally *every* contemporary rendering of this verse into English could be wrong and centuries of scholars of multiple religions have eagerly endorsed creation from nothing without even a second thought? The error was introduced early on, and percolates within Western consciousness, gaining strength with time. When the Torah was translated for the first time to Greek, in what is known as the Septuagint (often abbreviated LXX), the translator changed the first word to imply a different narrative of Creation:

ἐν ἀρχῇ ἐποίησεν ὁ θεὸς τὸν οὐρανὸν καὶ τὴν γῆν
"In the beginning, God made the heaven and the earth"

This is the key problem. As literacy with Hebrew largely remains confined to the Jewish community (and even within it, to only a portion), the Greek mistranslation found in the Septuagint has considerably more influence over the Western imagination than the original text. Scholar Ziony Zevit posits that:

> For many Jews since [the Septuagint], even those who read and understand Hebrew well, this doctrine is a truism. When they see and read the Hebrew, they think of the Septuagint translation. When they read a similar translation in English or any other language, they assume that it reflects the Hebrew accurately. It does not.[42]

Thus we can see the need for a re-evaluation of the key text, and a reappraisal of what Creation *is* in the Torah's framework. It may not be, as we likely were told, an event – before which there was nothing – but rather a process that began with primordial matter already in existence and which, as we will see, reflects a form of revelation itself.

We have attempted to demonstrate why creation *ex nihilo* is not a central Jewish belief. Yet, simply showing its flaws isn't enough to suggest what we *should* believe instead about the formation of the world. Decolonising our ideas of creation takes more effort and time than we have space for here – but as a starter, let us review the various approaches to creation found in Jewish thought and their sources in Jewish texts.

Origin Stories

Unsurprisingly, as there are many different interpretations of creation in Jewish sources, any claim to consistency has to be met with incredulity. There's no way that one cohesive idea emerges from such diverse sources. Instead, there are three general trends that can be identified.

1. God created *ex nihilo* – there was nothing before the narrative of Genesis and creation is to be understood as an event that takes place in time.

2. God created out of pre-existent matter – this can be seen in discussions of the Greek idea of *hyle* (a universal matter that can take any form), particularly in the commentary of Nachmanides and others.

3. God created out of emanation – that is, God created out of Godself.[43]

One of the challenges in choosing is that all three of these ideas are formulated in the language and concepts of non-Jewish philosophical systems. Emanation is the doctrine taught by Neoplatonist thought which took hold in early mediaeval Jewish thinkers such as Rabbi Shlomo ibn Gabriol and the nascent kabbalistic movement. Pre-existent *hyle* (a literal Greek word) is cited by Rabbi Moshe ben Naḥman, but his source is ultimately Aristotle who used the word for a raw chunk of wood to refer to all matter prior to its imprint by form. Lastly, the *ex nihilo* doctrine which is so often taken at face value in Jewish communities is itself likely the product of contact with early Christian thinkers in the Tannaitic period, due to the Septuagint warping the meaning of the Hebrew text, as we saw above. If we look away from these philosophical approaches and instead seek out answers to the riddle of creation in Midrashic sources, we don't gain any additional clarity.

The Talmud discusses[44] in depth what items were created at the end of the first Shabbat (that is, after creation supposedly 'concluded'). The list is broad and fascinating and includes a well, a grave, and a donkey. The collections of Midrash (Midrash Rabbah) offer a variety of interpretations on this theme, including the idea[45] that a handful of things were created before Creation (again lampooning the notion of creation from nothing). Elsewhere in the same collection Rabbi Abbahu famously teaches[46] that God created and destroyed worlds over and over until one (ours) occurred that was pleasing, an idea that's backed up[47] as well in the commentary on Exodus. Later midrashic collections, like Midrash Tehillim and Pirké deRabbi Eliezer get even more specific and therefore opaque. Midrash Tehillim suggests[48] that there were 974 generations who lived *before* the creation of the world, and in Pirké deRabbi Eliezer a mythological explanation is offered[49] in which the heavens were created from the light of God's robe (a sort of emanation) and the earth was created from a snowball God made from the ice under the divine throne and cast into the waters, somehow inexplicably making dust.

If we were pursuing the sort of dogmatic theology that predominates in many faiths, then we would have to choose one of the three philosophical options suggested above or build a flimsy theology on the myths and Midrashim of rabbinic literature. Thankfully, that need has never been present in Jewish thinking. All three ideas have coexisted for two millennia and have even, through the medium of some very creative thinkers, been blended and innovated. Chief among those innovators was Rabbi Yitsḥak Luria (also known as the Ari), whose 16th century reworking of mediaeval Kabbalah introduced several ideas which would permanently reshape Jewish thought.

Cosmic Catastrophe: Luria's Myth

It *all* began by breaking. At the cusp of the modern world and in the midst of the sweep of Renaissance thinking, Luria put forward a new mythology of creation – one centred on creativity, and on cataclysm.

Before anything came into being, when the universe was chaos and void, the only thing that existed was a pure, undifferentiated, infinite Light. It was in every place possible, because at that time there was no such thing as *place*. In every direction, to every degree, there was the Infinite Light. In order to begin the process which we call 'creation,' the Light had to recede from a particular spot, creating a 'place,' a vacuum empty of anything, for the only 'thing' was the Light. Held back at the edges of this void, the Light meant to assemble a universe inside the vacuum – but if it simply filled it back in, everything would again be overwhelmed with pure undifferentiated Light.

In order to allow for difference and differentiation, the Light created something to hold the space. It formed vessels of material reality – the containers which were meant to hold the world. Once the containers were in place, the Light trickled back in, very slowly – so as not to overwhelm this new reality. However, even this slow flow of Light was too much, and the vessels shattered like crystal, dispersing into innumerable pieces.

This catastrophic destruction couldn't be reversed, so instead the Light attempted to form a universe inside the void a second time. This time the trickle of Light into the vessels was barely anything – a hairsbreadth compared to the width of the entire universe. Yet, in this smaller quantity, the system was stabilised.

The light poured back into the void, now structured as a world, and in that new world it took on many different forms, creating all material and spiritual reality and infusing itself into everything that lives, from galaxies and nebulae to dust mites and mitochondria.

Thus, the universe, *our* universe – is a second try. The cosmic collapse which characterised the first attempt at it resulted in fragments of the original vessels scattered throughout the universe – embedded in all things, waiting to be discovered, gathered, recombined, and reunited. Luria's narration of creation artfully combines all three ideas we saw above: it 1) allows for a discrete start (the moment the Infinite Light began to retract), 2) describes a single universal substance that takes many forms (the Light itself), and 3) permits the process of emanation (the Light is God and fills the vessels of material reality).

This myth of Creation may sound like a jumble of motifs from a pop-science programme, but Luria's conception of Creation was informed by his readings of Jewish mystical and philosophical sources, as well as his own innovation. Luria called this myth, *shevirat hakélim* (the shattering of the vessels) and it provided a basis for his entire worldview, one in which God is an Infinite Light equally present in all living organisms and one in which we bear the partial responsibility to help find, collect, and repair the shards of that first attempt at creation which are in the world all around us, including within ourselves.

Luria referred to this process of repairing the original cosmic scaffolding as various things. When discussing how it related to personal character development it was *tikkun atzmut* (self-repair), and when relating it to a broader goal it was nothing less than *tikkun olam* (world-repair). By this, character building and creation advancement were interlinked – our efforts to make ourselves better people go hand in hand with our efforts to make the world a better place. This fed into the common notion in Kabbalah, as well as many mystical systems, that there is a correspondence between things of varying scales. In the language of Hermetic philosophy, this is 'as above, so below', but in the mythologising language of Kabbalah, it comes as the notion that a human being is a literal microcosm. This is stated and quoted often by the Midrash, which says clearly: *Adam olam katan, v'olam adam gadol - 'A human is a small world, and the world is a large human'.*[50]

Luria's mythology of creation accepts that Creation was not a moment, but a process. As he spells out the discrete stages, and acknowledges that the final one (repairing the world) is still underway, he does so with the considerable backing of Jewish tradition which has always strayed from the 'conventional' Christian conception of creation. He blends the three possible beliefs we mentioned above into a single mythological description of cosmic catastrophe, including elements of creation from nothing, pre-existent matter reformed into many shapes, *and* God's reveal through emanation.

Reconsidering these models of creation are critical for us to push back against the facile version of Creation many of us were taught: God as a stage magician pulling a rabbit out of a hat. Instead, Judaism offers us a complex, dynamic, and ongoing approach to creation. Luria's description of creation gives us a way to blend all three rabbinic interpretations of Genesis *and* offers us an ethical dimension to the creation story. Ultimately, that is the most important outcome. Our concern isn't with cosmological accuracy but ethical import. Whatever beliefs we may hold about creation are acceptable within Jewish thought, so we may as well choose a *functional* theology which offers ethical motivation and spiritual inspiration.

The great benefit of the Lurianic model of creation is the role that it affords all living things: that of partners. Due to the catastrophic origins of the universe, the world we inhabit is inherently imperfect. There remains within it a component of chaos which is the key to understanding suffering and evil (see Chapter 6). This myth of catastrophe and repair also suggests that there is a role to play for humanity, not as the most important lifeform *per se*, but perhaps as the one with the most capability to assist in repairing the world.

One of the (many) rabbinic readings of the curious phrase that the human being is made 'in the image of God' is the idea that, like God, we possess the power of creation. Like God, we can use language to bring order to disorder, to separate and distinguish, to defame and destroy. As a result, we become God's *literal* partners in furthering the ongoing process of creation.

Partners in Creation

Inevitably, our discussion of the 'correct' understanding of Creation's mechanics is frustrating. The Lurianic myth is widespread in contemporary Jewish sources precisely because it just so happens to be *useful* as a way of understanding creation for the world in which we live.

When dealing with non-mandatory beliefs (such as the nature of Creation here or the Afterlife in Chapter 11) we should aim to find ideas that are *functional*. What we believe about Creation matters because it changes the way we view nature, the universe, our place in it, and our responsibility towards it. In that spirit, we should focus on Jewish sources on Creation which emphasise the particular role that human beings play in the perpetual present, aiding ongoing creation.

Arguably, the greatest contribution Jewish sources can make to our understanding of Creation is to show us that continuing to complete the cosmos is *our* responsibility. This is a belief which functions as a key part of Jewish theology and ethics, and yet is discussed superficially. Below, we try and trace the development of the idea that humanity are partners in the endeavour of creation, precisely to show that it (like most ideas in this book) is not some modern interpretive valence, but rather a core tenet of Jewish tradition.

Some of the earliest sources are those in rabbinic literature. In the Talmud the idea is referenced so casually that we can easily imagine it was *obvious* to those who heard it. In the context of discussing judges and judgement, Shabbat 10a records: *"All who judge a judgement truthfully, it's as if they are a partner with God in the creation of the world."* The consequence of this partnership role is that we have to accept and appreciate the fact that Creation is, by definition, *imperfect*. Whether through Luria's mythological vessel-breaking catastrophe or simply by virtue of observing the world around us, our tradition has no reservations about deeming what has been created as incomplete.

In the Midrash, the Sages teach us:

> All that which was made on the six days of creation requires extra action [to be complete], like mustard that needs to be sweetened, or lupin beans which need sugar, or wheat that needs to be ground – even humanity requires repair.[51]

Nothing is quite finished, including us – and that's okay. To understand these sources we need to disentangle the ideas of creation/completion and find language to articulate the role of the creat*ed* to be co-creators of themselves and the universe. This midrashic concept is affirmed and expanded in the Zohar, a mediaeval anthology of earlier *midrashim*, embellished and extrapolated to new interpretative heights. There, the text suggests the partnership is more akin to a relationship:

> Once the world was created, not a single thing was firmly established until an impulse arose in the Will to create the human being, who would engage in Torah and for whose sake the world would endure. Now, whoever gazes upon Torah and engages in her, as it were, sustains the world. The blessed Holy One gazed into Torah and created the world; a human gazes into Torah and sustains the world.[52]

Here then we have the fullness of both ideas we've seen: first, that the world is built to be incomplete and second, that it is the task of humanity to collaborate on the ongoing work of Creation. If we jump to more modern sources, we can see the same idea being explored by such a variety of sources. The centrality of the principle is confirmed by the diversity of its referents. To take only a few examples: the Malbim, the Kedushat Levi, the Ramḥal, and Rav Ashlag.

The Malbim, a 19th century Torah commentator from Ukraine, has a beautiful explanation of the partnership implied by the Torah and Jewish tradition. His comment on Leviticus 26.12 is worth quoting in full:

> *"And I shall walk about amongst you and be for you as God"* [Lev. 26.12] There are two distinct levels to this: the first is that the essence of God is within [humanity] completely, as their souls are divine, and through sanctity they can respond and collaborate on the work of completing reality. In this way the righteous are imagined to be like sharecroppers (tenant farmers), made into partners with the king in maintaining an orchard. Sure, they don't own it, but they are partners in it because of the

> work they put into it and the repairs they have made – they built its fences and planted its choicest crops. So too the righteous are like sharecroppers of God, for they guard the Great Orchard which is the world, they sustain the world that was created through ten utterances by keeping the Torah and *mitsvot*. They collaborate with the King in all his labours and thus are properly made into partners with the Holy Blessed One in the ongoing work of creation – they live amidst the great garden in order to labour in it and to protect it through Torah and *mitsvot*. God says to them: 'Look, I am just like you', for in their works they move the rows and furrows according to their own custom, guiding the world towards love and tranquillity. This is like what was said: "'Who rules over me?' A righteous person"[53], and many more such statements of our Sages.

The Malbim provides for us a beautiful metaphor of collaboration and partnership – we are like tenant farmers and God our landlord. The work could not be done without our effort – the landlord's act of acquisition doesn't make the land fruitful in itself. Productivity is made possible by the fact that humans possess the 'divine image', that is, which enables us to continue the work of creation.

The Kedushat Levi, an 18th century Ḥasidic teacher, applies these same ideas to a different example, taking as his source the description of the *mishkan* in the desert:

> Construction of the *mishkan* in the desert was an act that paralleled the creation of heaven and earth and corresponded to all known

> aspects of the order in which God created the universe. Seeing that this was so, Betsalél, the chief architect of the project was granted the wisdom to understand how the letters of the alphabet were to be used in carrying out all the details of the task entrusted to him. Nowadays, this ability of Bestalél at the time of his building the *miskhan*, has been granted to the righteous Torah scholars of varying degrees, who are able to reveal insights into the Torah that have not previously been revealed. By doing so, they become partners of God in the creation of the universe.[54]

Note that the Kedushat Levi makes explicit what was only implied in the Malbim's analogy: it is the power of language that affords us the privilege of partnership. This reading of *betselem elohim* (in the divine image) is not unusual, but it is applied here to great effect. Understanding how being made in the divine image affords us the possibility of collaborating on creation is essential.

We cannot make the mistake we raised in Chapter 2 of admitting an anthropocentric theology. While notions of partnership afford a special role to humans, it is not an exclusive role. The Malbim, and many others throughout the Jewish tradition, emphasise that the exalted status of humanity is not a result of some indefinite human specialness, but only due to the divine image within them. We are sacred not because we are fully human, but because we are partially divine.

This is expanded upon further by Rabbi Moses Ḥayyim Luzzatto (18th century) in his work of theology, *Derekh haShem*:

> God decreed and arranged to create some things complete and other things incomplete

> – and then made an additional creature which would possess the possibility of balancing these two types of creation. God gave to this creature the means by which it could repair itself and attain perfection and thereby remove all traces of imperfection. This is why humans are imagined as being in God's likeness — in that they can do what God can, and thus can cleave to God and benefit from God's goodness.[55]

It is not our own power that provides us with the privilege of partnership – it is the divine within, exemplified by language – the tool of creation and the weapon of destruction. By sharing in the divine power of language we also share in the responsibility to *continue* creation, not reverse it. Twentieth century mystic and activist, Rabbi Yehudah Ashlag, in commenting on Jeremiah 30.3 (*And you shall say to Zion, you are my people (ammi))*, said:

> We should read it not as *ammi* (my people) but as *immi* (with me), that is, you are with me as partners. For the righteous are the literal partners of God. God has begun the Creation, but the righteous complete it.[56]

So we come to it: "the righteous are the *literal* partners of God." God has begun Creation (but not 'in the Beginning') and it is up to those who are creat*ed* to complete it – to repair the breaches, to lift up the sparks, to aid the divine mission of the Torah and to spread justice, goodness and knowledge throughout the world.

It *matters* how we think about Creation – because how we think about Creation changes how we think about our lives and our task on Earth. What we imagine the beginning entailed (or didn't) shapes our understanding of the present and the future.

There is something beautiful and burdensome about this task. There can be no sensible approach to Judaism which does not validate the heaviness of what it means to be literal partners with the divine. The first step towards embracing such a role for ourselves is, no doubt, to become aware of it. We cannot fulfil a responsibility that we weren't conscious of. By challenging the conventional understandings of creation we begin such a process. Rabbi Ben Tsiyyon Uziel explained this need beautifully:

> We are bound and bowed to the laws of nature and its causes, to societal conditions and to variable physical states which can affect our choices. All of the time that we go about unconscious [of these factors] we are void of knowledge and wisdom, and lacking in vigilance over all aspects of our actions. But, we do have free choice to overpower all of these causes and factors, the perspectives and aspirations of our society in the game of life. If we seek to know it, we can realise our mission – the mission of humanity, created in [God's] image and graced with knowledge from the source of all wisdom and knowledge. Then, we will always remember our responsibility to both God and humanity.[57]

Remembering our responsibility begins with questioning creation. Creation is not an event that happened 'once upon a time.' Creation is an ongoing process in which we are required to collaborate – because we have within us the divine image, the power of language, and because we have been charged with such a lofty task by the notion of covenant (*berit*).

Attempting to shift our minds away from the Greek and Christian philosophical notions of creation 'from nothing' allows us to embrace creation as a participle, to perceive the power and privilege of being partners with the Divine in the perpetual present, and to pursue peace and justice, pushing the world ever towards completion.

Chapter Four

Hierarchy or Horizontalism // *Authority*

Judaism has, throughout unparalleled trials, preserved its passion for justice and its desire to contribute to the defence of the rights of men of all races and origins, along the lines of the very principle with which it was entrusted two thousand years ago.

René Cassin, Ten Commandments to the Rights of Man

No King but You

One of the primary misconceptions facing modern Jews is the question of Judaism's engagement with politics. Today, innumerable rabbis give sermons and teach *shi'urim* predominantly from the front page of the newspaper rather than the commentaries and legal traditions of the Jewish tradition. In some circles, Jewish ideas have become nothing more than clever coverings for Western political aims – a problem affecting both ends of the political spectrum in the modern west equally. In reality, Judaism has little to say about the politicians or policies of today. However, that doesn't mean that the Torah fails to articulate a political vision for humanity. Notions of authority, sovereignty, violence, and civil resistance are central to the worldview articulated by the Torah.

If pressed, we would have to say that the Torah falls within the political axes (approximately) around theocratic anarchism. That is, the societal system of the Torah is deeply anti-authoritarian while also upholding the centrality (and equality) of the law, with God as the sole arbiter and ruler. Perhaps we are 'legalistic libertarians' in addition to 'theocratic anarchists'. The challenge of language aside, it doesn't take much research to see that our tradition affirms one thing above all else: the absolute rejection of any human pretence to sovereignty.

The phrase '*Én melekh ele attah,*' meaning, 'there's no sovereign but you' is best known from the prayer *Nishmat Kol Ḥai*. These words are not only a frequent refrain in our liturgy, they're also the foundation of the Torah's political principles. There's probably no one who has articulated this dimension of Jewish thought more clearly than Rabbi José Faur. Faur's classical (Andalusian) Sefaradi training and a skilled grasp of Arabic have aided him in the project of defining Jewish tradition across his many books and writings, and set the stage for a sophisticated understanding of Judaism, open to reevaluating the commonly-held myths about Jewish law and life.

In Faur's case, the myth he most sought to bust was that Judaism is another one of the classical civilisations of the West. He contested the idea that Judaism differs only in region and language from ancient Greece and Rome, and that as a result we can see the so-called 'Judeo-Christian' ethos throughout Western history. To Faur, Judaism was the complete opposite of Greek thought. The distinction was not superficial but fundamental. Faur claimed that Judaism was diametrically opposed to ancient Greek thought, but also to that of Arabic, German and practically all other Western intellectual landscapes, for one simple reason: the alphabet.

Faur classifies all societies as either analphabetic (relying on poetry, orality, and authority) or alphabetic (relying on text, context, and interpretation). Judaism, he argues, is the originator and sustainer of alphabetic religion and alphabetic society. In all those societies which existed before the innovation of alphabetic script, there was no choice but to follow the rules set arbitrarily by the humans who wielded power – whether kings or priests or prophets. When social consciousness was determined by the power of the poet, who would memorise long epic tales told orally, there was no capacity for analysis, privileging the poet with a persuasive power.

By transitioning into a consonantal alphabet, the ancient Hebrews *liberated* themselves from arbitrary human authority. Specifically, by putting down in *writing* the laws of the people, a radical democratisation of knowledge and power was engendered. Now, the Torah, acting as a constitution, can be consulted by anyone, its words read and re-read in different ways by different readers. Any claims to absolute authority by anyone other than Hashem are impossible so long as society is governed by a written constitution. God's sovereignty is sustained by the anarchic opposition to human authority.

Alphabetic Anti-authoritarianism

"A fundamental characteristic of consonantal writing is that meaning is not immanent in the text," says Faur. "Consequently, a term may be correctly interpreted in various ways. When pertaining to the Cosmic Book, consonantal density is utmost: the grouping and possible arrangement of the letters, countless."[58] The very fact that half the information needed to transform writing into speech is *missing* allows (or requires) an anti-authoriarian society.[59] By centering the life of the people on Law, the Torah rescues them from the whims of kings and from the rhetorical prowess of gifted orators. In a significant contrast to ancient Greek society, the Torah has no interest in orators or oratory. Rather,

> Given that the Hebrew alphabet rules out vowels, *speech* is outside script representation. Slogans are excluded, once and for all, and with them the whole gamut of theatrics, intrinsic to speechmaking: Moses stuttered, for he was 'heavy of mouth and heavy of speech' (Ex. 4.10) The Hebrew alphabet excludes the language of the analphabetic crowd, 'enthralled' by the 'charm' of the myth-making poet. At that level

> of consciousness, the 'truth' is 'obvious' – as with slogans and graffiti – and will not tolerate analysis. [...] At the poet's song, cultivated intelligence and scientific thought vanishes, as per magic. Once possessed by the poetic truth, the analphabetic crowd will march to the beat of the poet's drum, silently, obediently.[60]

In contrast to the 'analphabetic crowd' which Faur sees in most other societies, the Jewish people are liberated from imperialism, domination and ideology by virtue of their vowel-less text. While it may seem to be tangential to political concerns, there are 'political consequences to analphabetic discourse.' Faur explains that in analphabetic societies, since, "agreement is attained by manipulating the dramatic features of speech, political decisions could only be reached after a long, intense debate." The innovation of the alphabet then is linked to writing: "by excluding the dramatic aspects of speech, writing dissipates the voice of the people."[61] Thus the people regain their power and their voice precisely through text and textual interpretation.[62]

Faur refers to the needed components of a textual revolution as the *ketab* (text) and *mikhtab* (interpretive framework). He calls these a "*sine qua non* for the proper functioning of the Law, both linguistically and intellectually." With such a textual tradition in place, an alphabetic society is formed, one where, "... the governing institutions of the nation, including the judiciary and the political, have only limited sovereignty. Their authority is grounded on, and therefore conditioned by, the Law."[63]

Faur goes so far as to frame all notions of sovereignty 'in pagan political thought' as "a function of might."

> By virtue of his hierarchic superiority, the sovereign issues orders which his subjects

> must obey. Or he founds a State, and then proceeds to frame a series of laws and legal principles whose objectives would be to further strengthen the political institutions of the State.[64]

Meanwhile, "for the Jews, the Law contracted at Sinai-Moab is the great equaliser system because it stands above all governing institutions; political, ecclesiastical and judicial. The ultimate depository of the Law is the people – not the governing authority."[65] Therefore it is intolerable under the Law of the Torah to entertain absolute monarchy.

Even when monarchy is permitted by the Torah it is done so only as a concession, and its permission comes with tremendous restrictions on the king's ability to consolidate power. The King of Israel is heavily restricted to prevent the accrual of wealth and influence, and is himself subject to the Law. Deuteronomy even insists that the king must keep a copy of the Law with him at all times and read it regularly – a reminder that his authority is subsumed under the greater and more significant polity of divine sovereignty.[66]

Therefore, we can see a radically different approach to political authority in Judaism, one that puts it in an entirely distinct category from other classical or modern civilisations. As Faur explains:

> Sovereignty is not the effect of might. The Hebrew Scripture puts forward the principle that God's sovereignty is grounded on the fact that God is the creator of everything. [...] Moreover, the Law was not imposed but was freely negotiated. Thus the overwhelming principle: Law is not a consequence of

> dominion, but of an agreement contracted by two consenting parties. [...] God does not want to govern according to whim and want but exclusively according to the Law. Indeed, the whole dialogue between God and man in the Torah presupposes that God is not *above* the Law or the accepted standards of justice. Fundamental to Judaism is the belief that God Godself observes the Torah."[67]

When we say, *én melekh ele attah* (there's no king but You), we mean it. Any human claim to absolute authority is a violation of the Torah. This is perhaps the most important and most radical idea put forward by the ancient Israelites: that monotheism mandated a rejection of absolute monarchy – that human sovereignty and divine authority were mutually exclusive. "For Israel, the source of all forms of authority is the Law contracted at Sinai," Faur explains. "This means, above all, that all forms of sovereignty are limited, and that political authority is not the fact of might but of the consent of the governed."[68] This liberatory political ethic is what defines Judaism's approach to sovereignty and authority – and it also is likely one of the main drivers behind antisemitism.

Against Authority: Antisemitism

There can be little doubt that the worst excesses of antisemitism find their origin in Christian thought (blood libel claims, accusations of deicide, and the numerous other essentialist justifications for violence against Jews in the West). Yet, it is not Christianity[69] *per se* which made antisemitism a mainstay of human society, but rather Christian claims to absolute sovereignty. Antisemitism is driven by the fact that Jewish thought is fundamentally threatening to all those who claim power for themselves and attempt to use it to coerce others.

The protections which the Torah's law affords to us, those which free us from the arbitrary authority of human pretenders and predators, are precisely those which are most at odds with civil and religious authorities. Analphabetic societies rely on violence to enforce their mythological claims of authority. In the analphabetic West:

> A government which ceases to control violence lacks legitimacy: might *is* right. At the theological level, too, polytheistic systems postulate a perennial conflict between independent cosmic forces. Order is the result of one or more forces *overpowering* other forces. 'Cosmogony' celebrates the birth and battles waged by forces dominating the world. 'Victory' announces the formal installation of the triumphant party and its subsequent monopoly of violence. Without monopoly of violence all hierarchical structures collapse. Israel does not recognise the legitimacy of a law standing upon violence."[70]

Thus even the myths of chaotic divine battle, central to many non-Jewish creation narratives contribute to the political suppression of freedom. By celebrating coercion and violence, and sourcing their legitimacy in epic poetry and convincing oratory, human tyrants consolidate power in imitation of their anthropomorphic deities.

When in Ancient Greece one would read about great King Zeus overthrowing his father Cronus and the other titans in a world-shaking war (the Titanomachy), the message is not opaque – Zeus is in charge because he has the power to enforce his will through violence and to determine the law based on his whim. Meanwhile, the Jewish story doesn't involve a war between the gods.Where

Hashem does battle another it is against Pharaoh, a human being claiming powers that aren't his.

To the Israelites, few things are closer to blasphemy than the idea that human beings possess absolute power. Pharaoh is compared by Ezekiel to "a great crocodile crouched in the Nile claiming 'this is mine and I made it.'" (29.3) In the words of Faur:

> The Jewish form of governance enrages tyrants and their worshippers. [Their] hatred of the Torah goes beyond madness and the purely pathological. To the high and mighty, to obliterate Jews and what they stand for in every which way is a solemn duty bordering on the spiritual and the sublime.[71]

Thus antisemitism can be seen as a way to suppress the radical political message of the Torah. In fact, antisemitism may be little more than hatred of Jews based on the Jewish claim to reject all human authority. Tyrants threatened by a system which cannot be controlled by them, attack the legal framework of Jewish thought. Dictators seeking to claim complete power target the people who retain complete independence. Such authoritarians, such antisemites don't just seek to disavow Judaism but to destroy it.

"Although commonly seen as a 'religious' phenomenon, hatred against Israel is political in its motivation," says Faur. He then asks a telling rhetorical question: "How can a *Rex* or a Pontifical ruler be expected to exercise absolute sovereignty over his subjects, when a high-profile radical minority refuses to subject itself to the absolute sovereignty of anyone?!" Therefore he comes to the conclusion that, "antisemitism is the preferred strategy of political and religious systems claiming unlimited sovereignty."[72] The truth in this logic is compelling. How else can we explain the fact that antisemitism is equally cherished as a political tool by *both* the extreme left and the extreme right? What is it that binds Nazism and Stalinism together? It is a claim to absolute authority. Any totalitarian system – regardless of its ideological lineage – will necessarily see Judaism as its enemy.

Thus the nature of antisemitism – it is not an ethnic or religious prejudice, but primarily a political one. "There is no record of a people, other than the Jews, who have been the continuous object of persecution and vilification from antiquity to the present."[73] That persecution has come from both Christians and Muslims, both European and non-European societies, across several millennia and regardless of the religiousness or assimilation of the Jews whom it targeted. How could it be that antisemitism can flourish in so many environments, cultures, locations and times? It is, as Faur asserts, because, "the sin of the Jews is political. The principles upon which the Governance of Israel rests are anathema to pagan political ideology."[74]

It is the horizontal nature of authority which is essential to the Torah's Law which is such a threat to human tyrants bent on dominion and domination across all times and places. It is not a religious dispute (in part because Judaism is not a religion), and the threat is not from immigration or cultural distinction or theological persuasion[75] – the threat Jews pose to the authoritarian claimants of the world is more foundational and more political.

> Antisemitism is not a clash between spiritual systems, but of certain political views intrinsic to European ethos and society. Specifically, that the Law and liberty put forward by the Torah and embraced by the Jews constituted a challenge to hierarchic government and administration. This rendered Israel a unique nation *because* of its legal and political apparatus.[76]

The idea that the root of hatred towards Jews is actually political in nature has a great deal of merit. Antisemitism, after all, has often been *justified* as a political idea. To the Nazis, Jews were in league with the communists and therefore attempting to undermine German victory and German pride from within. To the Bolsheviks, Jews were suspiciously non-proletarian–too intellectual, too analytical, and therefore too likely to be branded under the imaginary stain of being 'kulaks'. To Christian monarchs and church authorities, Jews rejected the authority of Jesus and his emissary the Pope. Therefore, the language used is political language – Jews are traitors, guilty of sedition and sabotage.

The political nature of this hatred is therefore not very well hidden. Judaism stands for the undermining of every tyrant's claim, a rejection of any absolute human authority, and a reliance on the tradition of alphabetic decoding of the text in order to avoid dogmatic and literalist readings of it. To a society which affirms human authority and justifies it through selective literalism with the biblical text, the presence of Jews is inherently threatening.

Torah or Tyranny

To return to the central argument that Faur makes in his *The Horizontal Society*, we must appreciate not only the way in which the Torah threatens analphabetic human authority, but also how it lays out a system in which we are held to a higher authority: through the mechanism of *berit*, covenant.

The word 'covenant' has very formal connotations in contemporary English usage – other appropriate options would be 'deal', 'agreement', 'contract' and similar synonyms. The reason these alternatives may be better suited is because 'covenant' makes it feel very much like an arrangement imposed to solidify a power dynamic rather than the creative collaboration of two equal partners. Radically, the Torah insists that the covenant which centres our entire faith is consensual, bilateral, and inviolable. Faur calls the making of a "bilateral covenant between God and an entire people" an "event with no parallel in history."[77] He suggests that:

> If there ever were a people that contracted a judicial and political system freely and without coercion, it was Israel at Sinai-Moab. The Torah is the fundamental Law of Israel, containing the precepts (*mitsvot*) defining the rules of action and the institutions which have been sanctioned by the entire people in a solemn covenant before God.[78]

'Freely and without coercion' is the critical bit. While there is a minor midrashic tradition that God threatened the Israelites with destruction if they refused the covenant[79], the plain reading of the Torah itself affirms the Israelites willing and repeated consent to the terms of the covenant. One of the barriers we face in understanding this fully is the very language of '*matan Torah*' (literally, 'giving of the Torah') to describe the encounter at Sinai.

Matan Torah makes it sound as though God showed up with a fully formed covenant and gave it to us, unilaterally and without a process of negotiation. In reality, the Torah describes the gradual accretion of the covenant's terms, from universal comfort offered to Noah after the flood, to the first personal and national assurances offered to Abraham, to the moment of Sinai, all the way until the Israelites encamped at Moab, waiting to enter the Land of Israel.

The misunderstanding of the Torah's multivocality and its misappropriation by analphabetic culture has led to many errors. Perhaps, none is more pernicious than the dangerous discourse around the concept of *torah min hashamayim*.

The Torah itself never claims to be 'from the heavens,' nor to be written by God. It is only in fairly recent Jewish history that Christian textual traditions insisted on a backwards-compatibility, attempting to make the Hebrew Bible over in the latter-day image of the New Testament. The Torah, understood on its own terms is divine, sacred, and a record of God's self-revelation to Moses and the Israelites – but it is not a platonically perfect form, descended from the heavens to dwell among us. Rabbi Louis Jacobs, whose principled stand for the traditional view of the Torah resulted in him labelled a heretic and cast out of the 'orthodox' world, articulated the real understanding of revelation powerfully:

> Revelation is not the communication of infallible information, as the fundamentalists claim, nor is it the outpouring of 'inspired' sages and poets, as the modernists conceive it. Revelation is the self-disclosure of God in God's dealings with the world. *Scripture is thus not itself revelation, but a humanly-mediated record of revelation.* It is a story composed of many strands and fragments, each arising in its own time, place and circumstances, yet it is essentially one, for it is throughout the story of the encounter of God and humanity in the history of Israel.[80]

This completely sensible paragraph inspired a decades-long rift in the British Jewish community, entirely because a new generation of 'orthodox' thinkers, approaching Judaism as Christian doctrine, refused to see the aberration that their biblically literalist views were against the grain of Jewish intellectual history. What Jacobs articulates here, that Torah is 'not itself revelation, but a humanly-mediated record of revelation' is completely consistent with Rabbi Faur's explanation of alphabetic society.

Of course the Torah is not a record of speech (divine or otherwise). If it were then it would be no different from Homer. If it were a record of speech it could not be, as it is, polyvocal and abundanr with diverse and often contradictory meanings.[81] To suggest that Torah is *min hashamayim* is to restrict it to a single, analphabetic form, one based on the power of rhetoric and fixed into an authoritarian hierarchical structure. Perhaps it is no accident that the people who were most threatened by Rabbi Jacob's insistence on the traditional view were the same ones who attempted to foist a Christian authoritarian hierarchy onto Jewish life.[82]

Dealing with the Divine

The choice is this: Torah, or tyranny. One cannot have both. It is precisely because that final version of the *berit* is ratified by the people with their full consent and bilateral understanding, that it becomes inviolable and eternal. As Rabbi Faur explains:

> Since God is themselves bound to the *berit*, the *berit* is eternal. Neither God nor the people can abrogate it or introduce any additions to it. A deity that can dissolve a covenant, reinterpret it, or change one contracting party for another, is one more tyrant in the long history of tyranny – not the God who contracted the *berit* with Israel at Sinai-Moab. Members of other monotheistic religions *have* to believe. Jews *choose* to be Jews. More precisely, they and God *choose* to believe in each other. The Torah is the document attesting to the *berit* or the choosing of God-Israel.[83]

This fact – that both parties to the contract are equally obligated under its terms – is itself a radical political statement. As Jews, we are unused and unwilling to submit to human authority because we have already obligated ourselves in a contractual relationship with a superior authority. Yet, just because the *berit* is made with God doesn't mean that God has coercive control over its conditions or its enforcement. Even God "cannot determine the interpretation of the Torah. A fundamental condition for rabbinic discourse is the exclusion of divine intervention (either in the form of supernatural oracles or miracles). To establish 'meaning', authorial perspective must be excluded."[84]

Thus the 'author' of the *berit* is irrelevant to its application. This point is made powerfully by the famous story of the Oven of Akhnai – worth quoting in full. What begins as a debate about the kashrut of a particular type of oven spirals out into a fundamental legend of Rabbinic Judaism, floridly illustrating the fact that God, while the Torah's author (in a sense), is not its primary interpreter:

> The Sages taught: On that day, when they discussed the matter [of the oven of *akhnai*], Rabbi Eliezer provided every possible answer in the world to support his opinion, but the other sages did not accept his explanations from him.
>
> After failing to convince the majority logically, Rabbi Eliezer said to them: If the *halakhah* is in accordance with my opinion, this carob tree will prove it. The carob tree was uprooted from its place one hundred cubits, and some say four hundred cubits. The majority said to him: One does not cite halakhic proof from the carob tree!
>
> Rabbi Eliezer then said to them: If the *halakhah* is in accordance with my opinion, this stream will prove it. The water in the stream turned backward and began flowing in the opposite

direction. They said to him: One does not cite halakhic proof from a stream!

Rabbi Eliezer then said to them: If the *halakhah* is in accordance with my opinion, the walls of this academy will prove it. The walls of the academy leaned inward and began to fall. Rabbi Yehoshu'a scolded the walls and said to them: If Torah scholars are contending with each other in matters of *halakhah*, what is the nature of your involvement in this dispute? The walls did not fall because of the deference due Rabbi Yehoshu'a, but they did not straighten because of the deference due Rabbi Eliezer, and they still remain leaning.

Rabbi Eliezer then said to them: If the *halakhah* is in accordance with my opinion, Heaven will prove it. A Divine Voice emerged from Heaven and said: "Why are you differing with Rabbi Eliezer? The *halakhah* is in accordance with his opinion in every place that he expresses an opinion!"

Rabbi Yehoshu'a stood on his feet and said: "It is written: 'It is not in heaven'" (Deut. 30:12). What is the relevance of the phrase "It is not in heaven" in this context? Rabbi Yirmeya says: Since the Torah was already given at Mount Sinai, we do not listen to a Divine Voice, as You already wrote at Mount Sinai, in the Torah: "Follow the majority opinion" (Ex. 23:2). Since the majority of the Sages disagreed with Rabbi Eliezer's opinion, the *halakhah* is *not* ruled in accordance with his opinion.

> Years after this, Rabbi Natan encountered Elijah, God's spokesman, and said to him: What did the Holy Blessed One do at that time when Rabbi Yehoshu'a issued his declaration rejecting the Divine Voice? Elijah said to him: The Holy Blessed One smiled and said: "My children have triumphed over Me! My children have triumphed over Me."[85]

This story is foundational to rabbinic Judaism for a reason – it establishes the principle, unquestioningly, that it is up to *us* what the Torah means. Even when the Author themselves intervenes to advocate for Rabbi Eliezer, it is still not enough to validate his interpretation. In that regard, the Torah functions like a constitution. In fact, Faur advocates for the view that, "the Torah is the first Constitution establishing an independent judiciary system with full judicial authority"[86] in human history. How, then, is that judiciary meant to work?

We have been bereft of the judiciary established by the Torah (the Sanhedrin and the legal system that once surrounded it) for many years. As a result, there has not been 'official' interpretations of the *berit* since the Temple's destruction – and yet, as we'll explore more in the next chapter – that has not stopped rabbinic Judaism from continuing to innovate and explicate the Torah. The judiciary's role moved out of the hands of the Sanhedrin and into those of the people as a whole. Rabbi Faur tries to clarify this judicial task, in keeping with the principle of a bilateral, consensual, and inviolable *berit*:

> The interpretive mission of the judiciary is to *institute* the legal meaning of the text. Their function is to implement the law, not to resolve textual ambiguities, past or future, or impose their interpretations on the *meaning*

> of the text. Therefore, as long as the law is implemented in accordance with the norms ascribed to it by the judiciary, the text may be interpreted differently.[87]

Here is the key tension of so much of Jewish life: we need to create a certain degree of consensus around *practice*, around the norms of applying *halakhah* to life – and yet, we can (and should) preserve the right of any one to interpret the text anew. Essential to this distinction is the acceptance of a different notion of 'truth', one often at odds with the European West.

Truth and Trustworthiness

Exclusive claims to truth often fall short in Jewish thinking – in part because so little is actually mandated as belief, and in part because the alphabetic nature of the text permits and permissions polysemous readings of it. Even when the judiciary (in the form of the Sanhedrin of old or in the contemporary institutions of rabbinic leadership in our world) functions properly, it is not in charge of dictating 'truth'. As Rabbi Faur puts it:

> In Israel[88], the judiciary does not embody the spirit of some sort of *europaischen Menschetums*[89] in charge of administering the 'truth'. Their authority to adjudicate and promulgate new rules on the basis of exegesis is limited to areas that fall within the jurisdiction of the court, what is commonly known as public law, not to matters of faith and dogma.[90]

The idea that we are not actually bothered about administering 'truth' is critical. Notably, it doesn't mean that we reject the concept of 'truth' but rather that truth by definition is self-obvious. It doesn't need to be revealed, only affirmed. This is reflected even in language. The Hebrew word for truth, *emet*, is itself a contraction of the longer and more archaic term *emenet*, which literally means 'trusted'. Thus *amen* and *emet* actually share the same root – when we affirm our agreement with something we are verifying it. Jewish belief doesn't ask of us any leaps of 'faith' – the *emunah* (trust) which we affirm (*amen*) in verifying the truth (*emet*) is a purely descriptive endeavour.

We are asked to look at the world and to affirm what is true: that there is one God to all and all gods are one, that to place anything in a definitional relationship with God, to say God is 'something' is idolatry, to offer to humans the power that rightly belongs to the Divine is blasphemy. Judaism is not a religion, nor is it a political philosophy – it is a methodology of *reading* the cosmic book which is the world in which we live and affirming all that is true and good within it.

Rather than rely on some sort of hierarchical authority to dictate belief, we as Jews are armed with the two mandatory beliefs of the *shema* and the alphabetic matrix of the Torah's text. In a correct weighing of the idea of *matan Torah*, Rabbi Faur says that, "since the Torah was given to the Jewish people, it follows that they, too, have the right to interpret it and determine its meaning, judicially by the courts, and morally and doctrinally, through their schools and sages."[91] That right can never be renounced nor abrogated – not by God, our partner in contractual commitment, nor by ourselves through difference and diversity, nor by any human authority attempting to usurp the divine by claiming absolute sovereignty.

Chapter Five

Putting the 'Fun' in Fundamentalism // *Sages*

The important point for us is that acknowledging Torah as eternal does not mean acknowledging our understanding of Torah as eternal. Our understanding of Torah can change, and when that happens, we will begin to permit actions our ancestors thought that Torah forbade, or we will begin to forbid what they thought Torah permitted. And we will be right in doing so; for we can do no more (and no less) than follow the best interpretation of Torah that we have.

Professor Zvi Zohar, Tradition and Legal Change

Putting the 'Fun' back in 'Fundamentalism'

The Jewish tradition is the founder and foundation of all the Abrahamic faiths – an impressive claim to fame for a tiny group of people who have never even gotten close to a worldwide population of 20 million. Despite the incredibly small size of the Jewish people, Judaism has had an indelible impact on humanity.

Many people in the world who are not Jewish and have never met someone Jewish have first names derived from characters from the Torah and know many of the stories of the Torah. That is, to put it lightly, incredibly bizarre. By population, Judaism is not even in the top ten world religions, but by *influence* there are none that surpass it.

Yet, among the family of Abrahamic faiths, Judaism is unique for quite a few reasons. One of them is this: in Judaism, being a fundamentalist would make one *more* lenient and liberal about most issues. That's correct – to be a true 'fundamentalist' (in the sense of returning to Judaism's founding methodology) would be *fun*. Looking back at Jewish history, and the ways in which Jewish law is established through the system of Halakhah, we can appreciate how flexible the fundamentals of Jewish life can be, and what the issues are with much of modern Jewish life.

Unusually, Judaism has only grown more ossified over time – what once possessed flexibility, worldliness, and an open-minded appreciation of the diverse offerings of surrounding cultures has transformed into a twisted and tortured vestige of its former self. Furthermore, Jews and non-Jews alike perpetuate the problematic perception that reactionary and modernist forms of Judaism are the authentic ones, somehow seen as consistent with the early history of Jewish community.

To unpack these claims we need to understand a bit of Jewish history – in particular, who the Sages were and what they were trying to accomplish.

Who Founded Judaism?

One way to explore this is to ask what seems to be a very simple question: 'Who is the founder of Judaism?' The answer is not straightforward. Is it Abraham? If so, little of his life and time resembles what Judaism comes to be and it is difficult to imagine Abraham putting on *tefillin* or holding a Pesaḥ *seder* (though the Midrash likes to try!). Is it Jacob? After all, he is our literal namesake (Yisra'él) and the particular ancestor of the twelve tribes that made up the ancient Israelite polities. Is it Moses? He has perhaps the strongest claim, seeing as he originated the final articulation of the covenantal relationship between the Israelites and God via Sinai. Perhaps it is Ezra, without whom it is likely that Judaism would have disappeared?

This is the correct question to ask, but the answer is harder to find than it first seems. One contender for the title of 'founder of Judaism' is Rabbi Yoḥanan ben Zakkai (c. 10 BCE - 90 CE). Ben Zakkai is, in effect, the forgotten founder of Judaism, the proverbial type-species of the rabbinic movement. He was an academician, an advocate and an ambassador. He led the group we now know as the *perushim* (Separatists/Pharisees) who, after the destruction of the *bét hamikdash* (Temple), became the primary representatives of Judaism and shaped what Judaism was to become. There is a direct line between Ben Zakkai and the development of Rabbinic Judaism, in a sense, making him our forgotten founder.

Most of Jewish practice and belief during the Biblical period would be unrecognisable to us today. Judaism as we know it has little to do with animal sacrifice, ritual purity or priestly status. How did such a transformation take place? Ben Zakkai is critical to this story, but it started long before his realignment of Jewish life in the 1st century CE.

The Hasmonean Revolt (160s BCE), which we still celebrate on the festival of Hanukkah, ultimately failed. Designed to restore Jewish sovereignty and defeat assimilation, the Hasmoneans became the very thing they opposed. Within two generations of the valorous Maccabees, this nationalist project had devolved into foreign occupation and assimilation (again). This prompted a small movement of scholars who wished to *separate* from the Temple and its practices. These people are ultimately known as *perushim* (separatists)[92] thanks to the labelling done by historian Flavius Josephus (c. 37-100 CE). By the time that Josephus named them, the *perushim* were already several hundred years old.

While the *perushim* still participated in the annual pilgrimage festivals and the obligatory sacrifices at the Temple, they gradually came to see the Temple as a barrier to spiritual life rather than the centre of it. This is due in large part to a perception that under the Hasmoneans and their allies the Temple had been corrupted and the authority once held by the *kohen gadol* (High Priest) was diminished, if not destroyed. In place of the Temple and in an attempt to complement its flawed offerings, the *perushim* started a parallel structure of spiritual life – focussed on study and action, morality and ethics, and an egalitarian approach to accessing the divine, drawing focus and importance away from the priesthood, the Temple, and Jerusalem.

The *perushim* set up two institutions which gradually transformed Israelite society: the *bét hamidrash* (academy) and the *bét hakenesset* (synagogue). They didn't completely reject the *bét hamikdash*, but by making it only a single star within a larger constellation of spiritual authority, they rebalanced how people saw and interacted with the Temple. In the academies they created a curriculum for learning Torah and developed rules for its interpretation – an example of which we saw in the previous chapter and the famous story of the Oven of Akhnai. In their academies, the *perushim* debated the *torah sheba'al peh* (the oral Torah) which was the cultural heritage of all Jews, conceiving of it as a complement and supplement to the *torah shebikhtav* (the written Torah). They placed great value on meritocracy rather than heredity (in contradistinction to the monarchy and the priesthood).

They wrote works of legal theory, ethics, theology, story, myth, and magic. These were all simply *torah sheba'al peh* – the cumulative collection of the habits, practices and customs of the nation of Israel. In protest at the fusing of the role of King and that of High Priest by the corrupt Hasmoneans, the *perushim* made sure every academy had two co-leaders who worked as a dialogic pair (*ḥavruta*) and modelled the particular principle of the *perushim*, that great value was to be found in a *maḥloket leshem shamayim* (an argument for heaven's sake).

The heads of the academies and the lower ranking teachers gradually started going by the title of *rav*[93], and hence the *perushim* are better known to us as the Rabbis, or Sages. The Rabbis are therefore the collection of several hundred individuals who led and developed the academies, schools, courts, and synagogues of Judea between roughly 200 BCE and 200 CE. Right in the middle of that period falls our potentially forgotten founder, Rabbi Yoḥanan ben Zakkai.

In 66 CE, after several decades of routine revolt and more than a few minor civil wars and tax rebellions, all the various Jewish militias, gangs, and resistance organisations agreed to mount a full scale national revolt against Roman occupation of Judea, known as the Great Revolt, or the First Roman-Jewish War. The Romans had taken advantage of a weakening geopolitical situation and finally finished off the Hasmoneans about a century prior to the outbreak of the Great Revolt. Many different factions, who themselves differed on the key aims of the revolt, attempted to collaborate in a war of national liberation.

Surprisingly, they were initially moderately successful – so much so that the Romans needed to mobilise reinforcements from around the Mediterranean to help put down the revolt. With several legions operating, first in Galilee and then in Judea, and with the various Jewish armies spending as much time fighting one another as they did the Romans, victory for the occupying power was inevitable.

As the war worked towards a conclusion in the year 69 CE, the most extreme group in the coalition, a savage gang of young men who called themselves the *kana'im* (Zealots) promised to fight until the very end. They took refuge in the Temple compound in Jerusalem, along with thousands of civilians and enough food, water, and medicine to last up to a year under siege.

The Romans did as the Zealots expected and laid siege to Jerusalem, breaching its walls and massacring its civilians. Due to the Temple's positions and reinforcements, they faced a harder obstacle in taking the Temple Mount, and so laid siege to it as well. The Zealots, increasingly advocating for self-sacrifice and glorifying martyrdom, believed that the civilians who had taken shelter in the Temple were insufficiently motivated to resist the Romans and so, in a logic-defying gesture of self-sabotage, burned all the food that had been stored up to enable people to survive the siege.

By the summer of the year 70, it became clear that there was no way out. That is where Rabbi Yoḥanan ben Zakkai enters our story. Most of the leaders of the *perushim* and the heads of the academies were locked in the Temple compound under siege. Some were sympathetic to the Zealots, some to the Romans, and some simply uninterested in the political battle to restore national sovereignty to Judea. It was Ben Zakkai who, according to our tradition, had his students drug him and smuggle him out of the siege in a coffin, as only the dead were allowed to be brought out to be buried. When the poison wore off and he jumped up out of his half-dug grave, he asked immediately to speak with the Roman commander in charge.

Bizarrely, they indulged him – and a conversation is recorded between Ben Zakkai and Vespasian[94]. Ben Zakkai asked Vespasian to let him and a handful of other academy heads leave the siege. He sought to go to Yavneh, an out-of-the-way village far from Jerusalem, and promised to focus only on preserving the rabbinic tradition, not on further military resistance to Rome. Even more bizarrely, Vespasian agreed.

It was at Yavneh in the years that followed the Destruction where Judaism as we know it was formed. Thanks to Ben Zakkai and his students, the rabbinic tradition that they inherited and which traced itself back to the earliest strata of the *perushim* was preserved, and he worked tirelessly to rebuild the academy and synagogue structure, as well as to train new students. There was no intention to create something new, but through his compromise,

Ben Zakkai ensured the preservation of Jewish life until today. All of the various sects and movements of that first century (the *ḥasidim*/Essenes, *tsedukim*/Saducees, *kana'im*/Zealots, and others) disappeared – lost in the flames that consumed the Temple or in the war's aftermath and the subsequent dispersion. The only flavour of Judaism which survived the existential bottleneck of 70 CE is that which Ben Zakkai smuggled out with him and restored at Yavneh.

The Rabbinic Project

The Rabbis were not conservationists – the traditions which Ben Zakkai rescued from the edge of extinction didn't become ossified into a preserved specimen. The Rabbis recognised that if Judaism was going to continue to survive, it could *never* become fixed and inflexible. If it did, it ran the risk of being wiped out all over again. As a result, they built upon their predecessors to create a spiritual system which is anti-authoritarian, egalitarian and multivocal, and which perpetuates the self-criticism needed for healthy and sustained growth.

The first written text of the Rabbinic tradition, the first book-version of the *torah sheba'al peh* was the Mishnah. The Mishnah is a surprisingly radical text, its innovative nature often obscured by the way in which it is studied (or not) today. To see the rabbinic project in action we have to return to the Mishnah – not just its teachings (although sometimes those as well), but its methodology.

To create the Mishnah, Rabbi Yehudah haNasi (135-217 CE), a patrician member of the *perushim* and friend to Roman emperors, went to everyone he knew and asked them their practice and their opinion about the various *mitsvot* (duties commanded by the Torah). In doing so, HaNasi preserved the multivocality of the rabbinic movement - many *mishnayot* contain both a claim and its opposite. Most have citations which can go back several generations, showing the intellectual lineage of an idea or interpretation. The Mishnah also modelled the principles of interpretation (attributed to Rabbi Yishma'él) and the precept of argumentation for heaven's sake.

None of this sounds as radical as it is. Imagine constructing a legal code, designed to answer discrete questions of daily life, and then including two rulings, one of which opposes another. This multivocality can come about through preserving the opinions of several distinct rabbis or through preserving a minority opinion even when a majority concur. It is also visible in the many and various rulings where different schools of thought are recorded and included, such as those where Bét Hillel and Bét Shammai disagree.[95]

This method of law-making, recording multiple binding opinions simultaneously, is the secret to Halakhah. It is also difficult. To retain such a methodology requires a taste for complexity that authoritarians cannot tolerate. Even within Judaism, there is a tendency to vacillate – to validate the Mishnah's method and then to disregard it in equal measure. The tension between Talmud (which functions like the Mishnah) and the later project of Codes[96] is a continual tug-of-war. Arguably, in modern times, it is the impulse to codify (and thus oversimplify) which has won out.

So, to be a 'fundamentalist' in Judaism would mean returning to the *methodology* of the Mishnah, not necessarily the rulings of the Mishnah. It is the methodology of multivocality, debate and good-faith improvement on the text through established procedure which characterises the rabbinic movement – but it is precisely this Mishnaic methodology which has been in decline among modern Jews.

Is the Mishnah Masorti?

To understand how and why contemporary Jewish life has betrayed the spirit of Rabbi Yoḥanan ben Zakkai and the intention of the Mishnah, we have to once again dive into history, although this time not quite so far.

What most people today call 'Orthodoxy' is a modern invention. It is a term which represents an incoherent approach to Jewish sources, entirely inconsistent with the ways that our ancestors interpreted the Torah through the evolving body of rabbinic literature. How did we get here? What went so wrong that we now have a large and growing segment of the Jewish world who are holding fast to a deeply problematic and entirely novel Judaism? The answer, as with so much about our modern world, begins with the French Revolution.

Prior to 1791, Jews had no civil rights in Europe. Jewish communities lived as explicitly second-class citizens, doomed to the whims of their Christian neighbours and masters. With rare exceptions, Jews were not permitted to live where they wanted, work in whatever profession they preferred, marry whom they wished, or hold most of the key roles in civil society. Jews were literally and metaphorically on the margins of society.

With the radical political promise of the French Revolution and especially the Jacobins, civil rights were extended to Jews for the first time in European history only in 1791 (interestingly, not in 1789 with the *Declaration of the Rights of Man* – it took two more years for the Jacobins to come around to the idea that Jews were people too). The sudden possibility of participation in civil society caused an extreme reaction in many Jewish communities, particularly in young people for whom the change was considerably more significant.

Now, with the promise of complete equality, Jews could marry, work, move, and live however they wanted. Such freedom was dizzying – and as Napoleon's conquests spread the French legal system across the continent, Jews were liberated from the ghetto (at least physically) in dozens of countries. In the thirty years between 1790 and 1820, a considerable portion of the world's Jewish population went from being marginal barely-tolerated foreigners to being accepted (at least in legal terms) in their societies. Jews joined the army, ran for office, began training for a variety of professions, and built organisations and networks to protect their newfound freedom.

Inevitably, such a rapid change had drastic effects on the religious life of European Jewry. The first big crack came in the 1840s in Germany where the Reform movement was established. Built around the principle of active and enthusiastic assimilation, Reform Judaism in this period was committed to a complete disavowal of all traditional Jewish customs, beliefs and practices.

In the eyes of Reform leaders, a French Jew was simply another *citoyen*, a Frenchman who happened to be 'of the Jewish persuasion'. Reform communities began removing all references to the particularism of the Jewish people in their services, began saying their prayers in the vernacular language rather than Hebrew, began building their synagogues to look and feel like churches (including clergy robes, organs, and stained glass windows), and worked to make any trace of Jewish distinction disappear. Traditional practices such as *kippot* and *tallitot*, *kashrut* (dietary laws) and *shabbat* observance were all dismissed as irrelevant relics.

While this was extreme (and often purposefully so), the counter-reaction was equally extreme. Rabbis concerned about the approach of Reform Judaism began to organise, trying to figure out how to articulate a response. Centred around the Ḥatam

Sofer (Moses Sofer, 1762-1839) an anti-Reform Jewish movement grew up first in Hungary. There, completely bizarre and extreme statements were taken as central premises, including the famous condemnation that 'anything new is prohibited by the Torah.' These anti-Reform activists, rather than attempt to assert the value of traditional Judaism, completely overcorrected in an attempt to freeze Judaism in time.

Rabbi Joel Roth, in discussing the evolution of *halakhah*, often used the analogy that the development of Judaism was like a chess game. The Torah sets out the rules for the game – which squares are black and which white, what pieces there are, how those pieces can move, etc. The Rabbis took those rules and began actually developing the game – its strategies and tactics, they recorded their games and studied them, but they *kept playing*. Moves were made on the board, completely within the rules set by the Torah, but with the underlying assumption that the point was to *play* the game, to keep changing, adapting and evolving within the confines of the Torah's laws.

When Reform Judaism began following the upheavals of the French Revolution, it was as though they came along and tipped the entire chess game over. Unwilling and uninterested to preserve the rules any longer, they abandoned the game – moving pieces wherever they pleased with little concern for procedure or precedent. However, if Reform Judaism tipped the game onto the floor, the nascent Orthodox movement did something only a little less radical: they turned the game into a museum piece.

As though putting a glass dome over the entirety of the chessboard, in Orthodox Judaism, spirituality and law became about history. We can talk *about* the game that already took place, but we no longer play. We can look at the positions on the board at the moment it was frozen, but we can't do anything *new*. Both of these approaches compromise the actual game of chess – because neither is *playing* any longer. One walks away from the board and the other turns it into statuary.

Immediately during this period, there were people who questioned these two extremes and advocated for a return, not to the laws as they were in the past (originalism), but to the methodologies as they were in previous generations (fundamentalism, in our sense). In different places in the Ashkenazi Jewish world these people all began to protest the extremes of Reform and Orthodoxy and seek a return to an approach consistent with the Mishnah, with the Rabbis, and with the two millennia of Jewish legal reasoning which preceded the French Revolution.

The Masorti Methodology

In the United States, Masorti Judaism emerged as a response to the excesses of Reform. Following the famous Treyf Banquet of 1885, a group of Reform leaders broke away and began calling themselves 'Conservative', in an attempt to signal their belief that the Reform movement had overcorrected. In Central Europe, many gathered at the academy of Rabbi Zekharya Frankel, who was attempting to chart a traditionalist middle path which he called 'positive-historical Judaism'. Later, in the United Kingdom, Rabbi Louis Jacobs was forced from the established United Synagogue. Jacobs, who was expected to eventually become Chief Rabbi, was condemned for his suggestion that Jews should be able to discuss the nature of revelation, that perhaps the simplistic idea of *torah min hashamayim* advocated by the Orthodox was stymieing the creative adaptation that made Judaism so special.

All of these movements had the same aim, even though they began differently: to reclaim the traditional (*masorti*) approach to Judaism exemplified by the Rabbis – one of moderation, development, and dynamism. The Masorti approach is one completely consistent with Jewish history and one that, like Rabbi

Yoḥanan ben Zakkai, preserved what was best about what came before us while working to ensure it would continue to develop and change, with robust mechanisms for self-correction and critique alongside a tradition of conservatism and conservation.

Masorti Judaism isn't an ideology – it is just Judaism as it always was and was meant to be. Rather than establish a new 'denomination,' the aim of thinkers like Rabbi Jacobs was to return Judaism to its liberal, creative, dynamic roots[97], to purge the modernist extremes from contemporary thought and practice and preserve the diversity and complexity of tradition.

While the three movements mentioned above all had to deal with the contingencies of European and Anglo-American society, the story was very different in most of the Sefaradi world – a point that proves the claim that a moderate Masorti Judaism is far more consistent with our past. Because the ideas of the European 'enlightenment' and the subsequent political extremism of the French Revolution didn't reach as fully or as deeply into most of the Sefaradi world, we can see there what might have happened in the absence of religious reactionism.

There is an incredible and deeply under-studied tradition of Sefaradi *halakhah*, theology, and philosophy which occurs simultaneously to the modern upheaval in much of the Ashkenazi Jewish community (18th-20th centuries). Since there was no radical break with the past, there was instead a natural evolution. In that classical Sefaradi world, the metaphorical chess game carried on, new mid-game moves innovated by Sefaradi sages and missed entirely by European Jews too busy guarding the board from play or tossing it overboard.

Sages like Rabbi Yosef Messas, Rabbi Abduallah Somekh, Rabbi Yosef Ḥaim, Rabbi Ḥaim David haLevy,[98] Rabbi Ben Zion Uziel, Rabbi Eliyyahu Benamozegh, Rabbi Solomon David Sassoon,

Rabbi Solomon Gaon, Rabbi David de Sola Pool, and many many more have preserved a *masorti* Judaism without the need for labels or for the structures of a movement. That is because their approach, and that of the classical Sefaradi scholars, is the one most consistent with Jewish history, insulated from the vicissitudes of 19th century Europe, and maintaining a commitment to tradition while valuing change and development.[99]

Future-Proofing the Past

If the future of Judaism depends, as the past has, on our ability to protect and preserve the tradition while allowing it to naturally develop and change – how can we get back to such an approach? The key is in method. There is nothing inherently different in terms of sources between an Orthodox and a *masorti* approach to any given halakhic question. They do not differ on which sources should be read, or what texts and theologies are worthy of debate. The difference is one of methodology. How do we resolve the emergent challenges of life today? How can Judaism be continually updated in line with its own multivocal, self-critical nature to be persistently relevant for the perpetual present? One answer may be in the Mishnah itself.

What does Judaism think about *x*? Nothing. There is not a single thing for which 'Judaism' has a cohesive unquestioning answer[100]. Rather than pretend such exists or innovate from outside Judaism, we need to go back to the chess board, take off the glass dome, and keep playing the game – making moves, capturing pieces, and catching up with the world around us. That *doesn't* mean changing the rules of the game or worse, starting all over! The halakhic process and its system of precedent is well established, highly organised and beautifully creative, if we embrace it. Judaism doesn't have a single view on most questions because it has *many* views. This diversity is our strength, and our salvation.

Today we need the Mishnah more than ever before – for its liberal and creative rulings, but even more so for its embrace of a multivocal method. If we were to present the variety of valid opinions on the key questions of our day (gender egalitarianism, Israel, LGBT+ identities, *kashrut* in an industrialised food economy, *shabbat* in a world of service workers and digital nomads, etc) we may regain some of the benefits offered by such an approach and reacquaint ourselves with the power of our tradition to be wonderfully, madly, multiplicious.

Both Reform and Orthodoxy present paths which appear easier. Either it is 'Don't worry about *halakhah*, do what you want' or 'Do what we say - this is the only way'. Both limit the creativity of the rabbinic project. From Ben Zakkai until today, the strength of our tradition is in its complex, contradictory answers to the questions of life. Easy answers are initially appealing but ultimately have to sacrifice either the creativity or the flexibility of traditional Halakhah.

The only path forward is the path back – back to the foundation of Judaism in the *perushim* and the rabbinic movement, back to an open and dynamic Jewish law which allows for self-critique and self-correction, and back to a mindset which is open to the world and yet rooted unquestionably in our people and tradition.

Judaism is a sacred inheritance, preserved against all odds for thousands of years, deeply shaping the world in which we live. Today it is at risk of losing its essential vitality out of an abundance of caution and a desire for easy uncomplicated answers. To recover and redeem what is best we have to affirm the creativity and flexibility of Halakhah, as the epigram to this chapter suggested, "we can do no more (and no less) than follow the best interpretation of Torah that we have."

Chapter Six

The 'S' Word // *Morality*

I lost my way, I forgot to call your name. The raw heart beat against the world, and the tears were for my lost victory. But you are here. You have always been here. The world is all forgetting, and the heart is a rage of directions, but your name unifies the heart, and the world is lifted into its place. Blessed is the one who waits in the traveller's heart for his turning.

Leonard Cohen, Book of Mercy, 50

If it were possible to do so, we should make a great effort to purge all of the English-language *siddurim* and *ḥumashim* of the most offensive and inaccurate word contained within them — the 's' word: sin. The concept of sin with which we as Jews have been saddled was irrevocably shaped by Christian theology. It is a grim vision of blood spilt and eternal damnation, and therefore it is nonsensical for Jews to use the 's' word in attempting to describe a vision of morality emanating from the Torah.

It is often taken for granted that the point of a religion is to instill morality in its adherents. However, since we have demonstrated that Judaism is not truly a religion, we need to investigate what exactly Jewish morality looks like, and why. In Jewish sources, morality is most often expressed through the mode of *halakhah*, which we'll deal with in more depth in Chapter 8. We must outline the ideas explored here first, and in particular, work to define our terms.

Words that must be banned from this discussion in order to even begin to approach a decolonised view of morality include, but are not limited to: saint, sinner, sin, original sin, mortal sin, deadly sin, total depravity, confession, total inability, heresy, eternal punishment, hell, and salvation. All of these concepts have such considerable connotations in Christian thought. These ideas can be useful inasmuch as they serve as the foil for Jewish ideas, helping us to distinguish between the approach to key theological questions between Jewish and Christian thought. They can also frame some very interesting conversations of comparative religion – but they remain unsuitable for describing Jewish thought in meaningful ways.

On and Off the Derekh

In Jewish thought the correct way to live is called *halakhah.* A noun derived from the verb 'to go, to walk', *halakhah* is simply the path one is meant to walk — the Way. The closest semantic analogue to *halakhah* is not 'law' although it is often rendered as 'Jewish law', but instead the Chinese concept of 道 (Tao, Dao) which has a range of meanings, including 'way', 'path', 'road', 'doctrine' or 'principle'. So, let us think of *halakhah* not as 'Jewish law' but as the correct Way of life.

For Judaism, *halakhah* is defined through the *mitsvot* of the Torah and their interpretation through Jewish tradition across the generations. The question facing us presently is this: what happens when one violates one of those *mitsvot* or fails to fulfil one? Inevitably this will happen, as the traditional enumeration of the *mitsvot* tallies up to a daunting 613. Since no one can reasonably accomplish all of them, all the time, in one life, the system must account for passive neglect as well as active violation.

The key word to understand is *avérah.* An *avérah* is a transgression, not a sin. Literally from the root which implies crossing over a boundary, an *avérah* is a purposeful or mistaken abandonment of the Way. This could take the form of being too strict (deviating from the path towards one side), or, more likely, be a result of being too lenient in following the Way (deviating to the other side).

This concept of morality is absolutely essential to understand, precisely because it is so profoundly different from the more familiar language of 'sin'.

There are many intellectual benefits to this image – a path is proscribed by two boundaries, not one. If we imagine attempting to follow a trail in the wilderness, we would call it an error to walk off the path on one side or another, with no meaningful distinction between them. Balance, therefore, sits at the heart of this matter. The Way is defined by its extremes and the boundaries that mark the edge of the correct path. This also means that the 'correct' way to live one's life is not an on/off toggle switch. There is not one 'right' way to live – the Way is a range, and often a surprisingly wide one.

Thus when we imagine morality, the analogy we should have in mind is this: a wide path which stretches out before us and behind us, one which has been marked out by previous generations and by the *mitsvot* set by the Torah and the Sages. The Way is wide but not boundless; there are limits to what is acceptable, and those boundaries are both paired and parallel. Going too far in either direction constitutes an *avérah*. Meanwhile, on the Way itself, there is room for many to walk – correct behaviour is not a specific action, but a *set* of actions, a range of behaviour boundaried on both ends.

This not only provides a basis for the observance of the *mitsvot* but also morality – in Judaism the two are inseparable. To walk the Way is to aim to stay upon it. It is possible to transgress in two directions and success thus requires constant calibration to ensure one is in the middle. This is often reflected in contemporary language, for instance when we talk about someone who has abandoned religious life as being 'off the *derekh*'. The concept is not a modern one though, and is in fact central to the whole construction of morality taught by the Sages. Maimonides, in his codified guide to *halakhah*, the *Mishneh Torah*, writes:

> Two extremes sit opposed to one another in each and every aspect of life – neither of which is the right Way, and neither of which is appropriate for people to walk upon, and certainly not to condition themselves to. If one finds that they have strayed off the path to one side or becomes accustomed to such an extreme, or has already habituated themselves to it and is regularly doing so – they must return themselves to the good Way, the path which is correct.
>
> The correct path is that of balanced attributes for every human character trait. This aspect is equidistant from both the extremes and equalises them within it, tending neither towards one side or another. Thus our Sages instructed that a person should inspect their deeds constantly and measure them, redirecting themselves to the middle path in which the body is whole. How? One should not be quick to anger but neither should they be like a corpse that feels nothing. Instead, search out the balance: only allow anger for something significant for which it is appropriate to be angry, keeping it in reserve so it doesn't continually emerge. Similarly, one should not eat more than that which is healthy for the body, but nor should they eat less [...], and one should labour at their work in order to obtain only that which they need for a satisfied life, [...] One shouldn't be overly stingy, nor should they throw away their money – rather, give it

> to just causes and loan it to those who need it more. One shouldn't be overexcited and foolish, nor should they be sad and despairing – rather, they should be calmly content all their days and do so with a smile. This is the Way for all traits. This is the Way of the Sages. Every person whose character is balanced is called, therefore, a Sage.[101]

The idea that the correct approach to life is about staying on a particular path, and that wandering off of it to either side can be constituted as a transgression, is one of the core aspects of Judaism which have been abandoned in favour of the Christian notion of 'sin'.

But What about Yom Kippur?

Every Yom Kippur, we sit through an entire day's worth of prayers and, for those who engage with only the English translation, are subjected to a constant assault of Christian language. In reality, there is very little of Yom Kippur which needs to be understood as talking about 'sin', 'forgiveness' or 'confession'. While rabbis may continually point out that that's not really what the word means, the fact that it is constantly used makes it impossible to escape. Other language used supports this same problem as well, as exemplified by the vocabulary of the *yamim nora'im* (Days of Awe):

> ***Teshuvah*** is translated as 'repentance' but it actually means a return, or an answer to a question. We are not 'repenting', we are turning around, answering a call, recalibrating our behaviour.
>
> ***Ḥét*** is translated as 'sin' but it actually means something very specific: when an archer shoots

an arrow and misses the target. While obviously used metaphorically, *ḥét* remains the very particular sensation of aiming for something and overshooting. A *ḥét* is a mistake, not a sin.

Kapparah is translated as 'atonement' but it actually means something that covers over, which smooths out, which 'pacifies'[102] or hides. What we seek is absolution, a forgetting of our crimes.

Asham is translated as 'guilt' but it actually was an offence that could be calculated and compensated for, a specific crime that had a penalty, not the emotional state of guilt.

Avérah is translated as 'sin' as well, but it is actually a crossing of boundaries — it is about something straying from appropriate amount.

Vidui is translated as 'confession', but it derives from the word for hand and it implies a gesture of pointing and making known. It is about acknowledging the mistakes one has made, pointing them out. Confession implies guilt, while acknowledging one's own actions is a judgement-neutral exercise.

Conventionally, we might, about Yom Kippur, say a sentence like: '**You confess your sins and then seek forgiveness, atonement, and repent so that you may be absolved of your iniquity**'. Sound familiar?

Well, perhaps a slightly more accurate version would be: '**You acknowledge the ways in which you may have strayed outside of appropriate boundaries and then recalibrate your behaviour to**

fit within the correct range of duty and obligation'. Doesn't that seem like a healthier and happier approach to making mistakes and making them right?

Everyone makes mistakes. Everyone attempts something with the best intention and fails, accidentally or on purpose. Repairing those breaches is essential, but it doesn't require guilt or self-flagellation. This is one of the key distinctions between Jewish and Christian thought, and one of the most essential changes one must make to begin to decolonise Jewish thinking. To succeed though, we must not just get away from the concept of 'sin', we also have to abandon any idea of 'sinners' as well.

No Sinners, No Saints

Judaism does not hold that any person is inherently good or bad. There are no sinners and there are no saints. There is no such thing as inevitable and helpless damnation to 'original sin' (we'll get to that!) nor is there any idea of infallible perfect humans who are incapable of making mistakes. As our prayer books do say, repeatedly, 'us and our ancestors have all made mistakes'. Jewish morality is not defined by the *actor*, but by the *action*. Specific actions can be good or bad – evaluated on how well they adhere to the Way outlined above. An action that draws people away from the correct path is bad; one that helps people to walk the Way is good.

Obviously, there are some people who do more good actions and some who do more bad ones – most of us, of course, do a bit of both. That's the simple reality of morality, we cannot evaluate people, only deeds. Rabbi Adin Steinsaltz lays this out beautifully in *The Thirteen Petalled Rose*:

> As a general rule, there are no attributes of the soul that are good or bad. One cannot

> determine that a given quality is always and with every person the same. In certain societies and cultures, love, pity, and compassion may be considered good; and yet there may also be occasions outside these cultures and even within them, when these qualities could be considered bad, leading one astray into sadness or sin. Similarly, pride, selfishness, and even hate are not always bad attributes. As the Sages have said, there is no attribute that lacks its injurious aspect, its negation and failure, just as there is no attribute – even if connected with doubt and heresy – that has not, under some circumstances, its holy aspect. From this point of view, the good and bad qualities are not set opposite one another, with love always on the side of the good and the other qualities always on the side of the bad. Rather all the attributes, all the emotions, and all the potentialities of the heart and personality are set on the same level and considered good or bad, not according to some judgement of their intrinsic worth, but according to the way they are used.[103]

This is a simple idea, but one that is quite hard for us to digest, living as we do in a world of sinners and saints, angels and demons, heaven and hell. Importantly, we not claiming that there is no such thing as good or bad (moral relativism). Instead, Rabbi Steinsaltz, in keeping with the overwhelming majority of Jewish sources, is simply affirming that the *context* of actions matters, not just their content. To establish whether an action is good or bad we would have to know the full context, its impacts and backgrounds, all the secondary and tertiary effects, etc. In short, it is impossible for us to truly evaluate in full detail how good or bad an action is. That is why we rely on God, who possesses the whole picture, and knows the action and the intention, the content and the context.

This also explains why Judaism is agnostic (at best) about the questions of reward and punishment. The Sages routinely acknowledge that life does not appear fair. The righteous suffer and the wicked profit, and reward seems a cruel promise. However, we must always remember that our perspective on it is limited.[104] We must simply try our best to do good things and not do bad things, and not be too paralysed by the anxiety of never fully being able to appreciate the complex interplay and interdependence of all actions. This even extends to the question of degree in morality, ie., *how many* good actions must one take to be considered among the 'righteous'? Wonderfully, the pursuit is not of perfection.

The Moral Majority

According to Jewish sources, a person only needs to be 51% good.

While that's a slightly tongue-in-cheek way of expressing it, the idea is very much a core part of the way our Sages approached questions of morality. Since we know that everyone makes mistakes and that the provision of free will allows individuals to choose their actions and intentions (although not always their outcomes), it would be foolish to expect that anyone could be *entirely* good. Even the person who does as many good things as they can will still do *some* bad things – some intentionally and some accidentally. Perfection is impossible – a liberating notion that allows us to focus on being as good as possible, or at least, mostly good.

Let's look at the sources. The Tosefta, a collection of rabbinic teachings from the second century, says:

> One who does a single *mitsvah*, it causes good for them, it lengthens their days and their years and they inherit the soil. Anyone who does one *avérah*, it causes bad for them, it plucks off their days and they do not inherit the land. About this one it is said, "*One mistake can destroy much good*" (Kohelet 9:18). With a single crime, this one destroyed for themselves many good things.

Later in the same passage, the anonymous author of the Tosefta writes an amazing line:

> A person should always see themselves as half-innocent and half-guilty, and the world too as half-innocent and half-guilty. If they do a single *mitsvah*, happy are they for they have pushed the world world to the side of innocence. If they do a single *avérah*, cursed are they because they have pushed the world to the side of guilt.

A few hundred years later, in the Talmud on Kiddushin (40b), we find:

> Rabbi Shimon ben El'azar says in the name of Rabbi Me'ir: Since an individual is judged according to the majority of their actions and the world is judged according to the majority of the actions performed in it, one who does one *mitsvah* is happy that they have tipped their scales and the scales of the world to the side of innocence; but if they do one single *avérah*, woe to them! They tip their own scale and the scale of the world to the side of guilt. About this one it is said, "*One mistake can destroy much good*".

> With a single transgression, this one destroyed for themselves and the world many good things.

A few things to notice about this text: 1) it is being spoken by rabbis of great authority. Rabbi Shimon is citing it in the name of Rabbi Me'ir, a provenance which makes it powerful and significant. 2) The text *assumes* that we all know this idea already. It doesn't begin with a normal new-idea formula, it begins with an assumption: 'since we know that an individual is judged according to the majority'. 3) The equivalence between an individual and the entire world is reiterated over and over. The same rule (judgement according to simple majority) is applicable at every level of being – whether we consider one person, one city, one country, or the entire world as a whole.

Lastly, a few hundred years on from that, we find the following in the Zohar:

> On Yom Kippur, these two sides stand: Life and Death. Some are inscribed on the side of life, some on the side of death. Sometimes, the world rests in the middle. If a single virtuous person exists in the world who tips the balance, they are all inscribed for life; but if a single wicked person tips the balance of the world, they are all inscribed for death'[105]

Simply put, it is a given for our Sages that both individuals and societies are judged according to a simple majority. 51% good is good. 51% bad is bad. We are told to imagine ourselves at any moment with balanced scales, and with each and every action we do potentially being the one to tip it, in one direction or another. This is scary – it means that we can do tremendous damage to ourselves and the world as a whole with any given action. Nothing is so small that we can ignore it. But on the flip-side, it is also tremendously empowering. We can do one, small, tiny, good thing – and that can transform ourselves and the world for good.

The Impossibility of Perfection

In recent years, some have begun to consider perfectionism to be almost like a disease – something which is spreading, contagious, approaching epidemic proportions. While the research definitely demonstrates a growth of perfectionist thinking,[106] the root of this social ill is in the Western worldview which believes that humans are defined by the extremes of their own moral behaviours: saints or sinners, rather than people who do good and bad things.

To talk of perfectionism as a disease sounds overly dramatic, perhaps – but the symptoms and prognosis are not good. As a society, and as individuals, we are increasingly feeling that we are not *good enough*. Yet the teaching of our tradition, the notion that what we aim for is a simple majority of goodness, is a powerful rebuke to this. We will never be purely righteous. We will never live a single day without making mistakes. What matters is not whether we made mistakes, but the overall picture, the calculation, the weighing of those mistakes in the holistic picture of our lives.

Think about your own life: surely you have done things you regret. Perhaps even cruel and wicked things. But are they a majority? Once more, we have to push back against the latent Christian ideas which infuse our culture. You are *not* a 'sinner'. No such concept exists. You are someone who takes actions – some good, some bad – and in looking at yourself and the scales balanced before you, you need to weigh the simple majority of good deeds and bad deeds. Does the scale tip towards good? I'd guess it does. And if you find it doesn't, you need to add some more actions to the good side, rather than attempt to empty the bad one. Keep adding until the weight shifts, until you can say that you have done *more good than bad things*.

Even the process of *teshuvah* reflects this. We are meant to see the work of the *yamim nora'im* as focussed on making things right, not on changing our fundamental nature.

We are not the problem, our actions are. Similarly, the solution doesn't come from trying to alter ourselves, to become new people – it is much simpler: we need to change our *behaviour*. Teshuvah is reparation and repair, not rebirth. As Rabbi Moses ibn Ezra reminds us: 'there is no mistake so big that one cannot repair it, and none so small that one needn't.'[107]

Without the idea that judgement follows a simple majority, we are prone to think things are worse than they are. Just as we judge ourselves too harshly by assuming we're 100% bad (or too generously by foolishly thinking we're 100% good), we assume extremes about the world which are not a given. There is no better call to action than this: "the world is judged according to the majority of the actions performed in it."

If that's the case, then when we see something wicked happen, we need to do something good. We need to match wickedness with goodness, one for one, to preserve the balance. Then, once we feel like things are in equilibrium, we simply need to do *enough* good things to keep the scales tipped towards goodness. This is not hard. This is not unattainable. It is simple and straightforward and gives us a chance to use our fears about the world's future to transform it, simply by adding a few more actions, by doing a few more good deeds.

Reflecting this, Rav Kook once wrote of Jewish morality:

> The truly righteous do not complain about darkness, but increase light. They don't complain about evil, but increase justice. They don't complain about heresy, but increase

> faith. They don't complain about ignorance, but increase wisdom.[108]

In this way, a Jewish approach to morality is actually *motivating*, a sharp contrast to a worldview which assumes you are a sinner doomed to damnation. For the extreme examples, like that of the Calvinist theology of predestination, one can not even free themselves by being good – goodness is impossible. In contrast to this, in Jewish thought goodness is accessible and possible and, critically, mathematical: 51%.

Garden of Eden Redux

We cannot leave behind the question of morality without dealing with the root of the misunderstanding we face. The source for the idea of 'original sin' as well as a mythological reading of human 'rebellion' against God is the Torah – sort of. The Torah itself does not endorse the idea of original sin, nor sin in general, nor this universal and eternal opposition between humans and God which is foundational to many Christian traditions.

This is perhaps the hardest idea to purge from our minds. The Garden of Eden story is not a tale of rebellion, punishment, sin and suffering. It is a cautionary tale, yes – but one that is meant to warn us about the dangers of straying from the Way, crossing-over the boundaries of what has been marked for us and falling into error. Our greatest guide to the Garden of Eden story as it is meant to be is the scholar Ziony Zevit, whose 2013 book, *What Really Happened in the Garden of Eden?* helps tremendously to aid us in reading the first few chapters of Genesis through a decolonised Jewish lens.

Rather than attempt to sum up his many and cogent arguments, I want to share his own rewriting of the Garden of Eden story, abridged and paraphrased to be understandable to a modern reader, but with the underlying assumptions of the Torah itself, not its Christian commentators:

> God planned a garden for himself in a place called Eden, a name meaning "Bountiful," located in the most distant northern corner of the world as it was known to ancient Israel. Far off the beaten track in what is now eastern Turkey, the Garden contained many fruit-bearing trees, among which two were special: the Tree of Knowing Good and Bad and the Tree of Life. Grains such as wheat and barley and other edible field plants grew around the Garden.
>
> God made Adam as part of his original plan to have a resident gardener. Formed by God from a clod of wetted soil and vivified by his breath, the human differed from all the inanimate objects that filled God's garden. As an individual, he was a special focus of God's attention. [...]
>
> Time passed. The serpent, one of the creatures formed by God for Adam when he was trying to find a helper for him, engaged Hawwa in a conversation in the vicinity of the Tree of Knowing. With clever rhetoric and linguistic sophistication, the serpent mentioned the intellectual benefits that Hawwa would gain if she were to eat fruit from the tree that God had instructed Adam not to eat from. To clinch his argument, the serpent indicated that despite what God had said about dying to Adam, she would not die if she consumed

this fruit. Driven by a desire for the knowledge of good and bad and convinced by the serpent that she would suffer no ill, Hawwa ate. Then she wordlessly gave the fruit to nearby Adam, who, following her example, ate also.

Both Hawwa and Adam gained knowledge, as the serpent had said. Now understanding that it was inappropriate for them to be stark naked, even though they were alone, they devised girdles of fig leaves to conceal their genitals and buttocks from each other's view. Later, when they heard the sound of God moving around in the garden, they concealed themselves because they knew that it was inappropriate to be seen by a third person wearing only their makeshift girdles, a sort of underwear. More appropriate raiment was required before they could be seen in public by a third party.

God understood from their self- concealment and from Adam's words, "I feared because I was naked," that they had eaten from the tree. When queried, Adam admitted eating the fruit but implicated God by pointing out that he had given him the woman, the very Hawwa who had handed Adam the fruit. She had misappropriated the fruit; he had not. The woman in turn implicated the serpent, who had informed her in a roundabout way that she would not be in violation of the instruction directed to Adam were she to take and eat fruit from the tree, nor would Adam be in violation of it were they to eat together. Each pointed

> finger constituted more than an attempt to deflect blame; it also constituted an implicit defense against charges of culpability based (1) on the language of God's original instructions to Adam and (2) on the specific circumstances of what had actually occurred at the Tree of Knowing.
>
> Distraught at having his plans upset, yet accepting the convoluted arguments of the couple, God addressed sentences to the serpent, Hawwa, and Adam. These did not result in any physical change or harm but did compel each to perceive some element of her or his life differently and somewhat negatively. Though chastised, they were not punished. They had not done nothing deserving of punishment.[109]

Zevit constructed this retelling of the Garden of Eden story from the text of the Torah itself combined with the interpretations and Midrashim taught by the Sages, rather than basing it on popular understanding common in Western culture. Over the course of his book, he explores each aspect of the story and corrects the many misconceptions we have when reading it. The most important thing that he emphasises to us, repeatedly, is that the Garden of Eden 'was not a story about sin.' Zevit says:

> ...No word for sin, rebellion, disobedience, or the like occurs in it – although it does deal with the circumvention of a divine instruction. It was not a story about death or redemption. It was a story about the origins of humanity and human nature, about proper comportment, dignity, the acquisition of knowledge, and, ultimately, ethical self-awareness.[110]

Thus, if we truly want to appreciate what Judaism has to teach us about morality and moral behaviour, we have to start with clarity about what it *does not* concern itself with. Sin, sinners, saints and Satan are all *out*. Instead, we have a sensible approach to morality which focuses on action, encourages moderation, and attempts to empower the individual to 'imagine themselves standing on a perfectly balanced scale.'

We are all walking on the Way, and the path ahead is not difficult or impossible. It is not beyond the sea nor atop the mountains, it is not even in the heavens.[III] Making moral choices is something any of us can do – providing we can strike the 's' word from our vocabularies entirely.

Chapter Seven

Visions and Voices // *Prophecy*

I testify, by heaven and earth, that whether man or woman, Jew or non-Jew, servant or maid, the Spirit of Sanctity dwells on all of them according to their deeds.

Tanna deVé Eliyyahu Rabbah 9

While not quite as problematic as 'sin', the English word 'prophecy' is nearly as troubling. Ask a hundred people what prophecy means and the vast majority of them will tell you that it is about seeing or knowing the future. However, prophecy is not fortune-telling nor future-scrying, not divination nor clairvoyance. To understand why we get this *so* wrong, we first have to understand how the conventional meaning of prophecy was established, and only then can we explore the authentic Jewish sense of the concept – from the biblical period until today.

Retconning the Torah - Christian Prophecy

Putting aside the Hebrew phenomenon of prophecy for a moment, one must first explain why the vast majority of modern people misunderstand the concept of prophecy. Predictably, this is a vestige of Christian theology surviving even in the secular West. Specifically it is a result of the Christian habit of re-reading older texts and adapting their understanding in order to support the New Testament.

In the worlds of fan fiction, there is a useful term for our purposes: *retconning*. 'Retcon' is an abbreviation of 'retroactive continuity' and is a concept that's most easily applied to comic books[112]. The OED describes it as follows: "In a fictional work or series: a piece of new (and typically revelatory) information which imposes a different interpretation on previously described events, often employed to facilitate a dramatic plot shift or account for an inconsistency; (also) use of this as a narrative device."[113] One place this tendency is very visible is in sequels, especially long-delayed sequels written by another author.

When an author changes or reinterprets the original story to suit the narrative needs of a sequel, they are engaging in retconning. In many senses, this is the best way to understand the relationship between the New Testament and the Torah.

The authors of the New Testament were all extremely familiar with the Torah as they were mostly observant Jews. Large portions of the New Testament purposefully reference concepts, quotes, and language from the Torah in order to authenticate the Gospel narrative and eradicate any claim to sole authority on the part of traditional Jewish communities.

This is perhaps most evident in how the Prophets[114] are used. Every strange turn of phrase used by Isaiah (the greatest victim of Christian retconning) is explained away by something in the New Testament. Then, with absolutely no historical sensitivity, early Christian writers could look at the two in consonance and claim that Isaiah is 'proved' in the New Testament.

If there are literary connections between the Hebrew Bible and the New Testament, it is because they were *put there* by the early Christians, retroactively inserting their own theology and anachronistically applying it to texts which were already 600-800 years old at the time of the first century.

This tendency created the belief that the Nevi'im (Prophets) were speaking about the distant future, a belief which is easily discarded once we understand the purposeful deception of false intertextuality. Instead, if we look at the Nevi'im in their own context, we see that they were speaking about their own time and place, mostly about political and social issues, and occasionally about the very near future (such as when Jeremiah is routinely attempting to warn his contemporaries about the growing Babylonian threat).

So if the writings in the prophetic books aren't esoteric keys to the distant future – what can they teach us? While they certainly have much to offer in terms of content (beautiful poetry, incredible images and moral rebukes), the greatest gift of the Nevi'im is not *what* they have to say, but *how* they say it. The Prophets can teach us about the phenomenon of Prophecy (*nevu'ah*) – and even perhaps how we too can partake in it.

Nevu'ah: Speaking/Spokespeople

As usual, English isn't terribly helpful in understanding a very Hebrew phenomenon. Nevu'ah is usually translated as 'prophecy' but it is something very different. In other semitic cognates, the root Nun-Vet-Alef has a range of meanings, but all are centred on sound. In Arabic, *naba'a* is a low, quiet sound – often used for instance in describing the noise that a dog makes – what we might call 'growling'.

Elsewhere, the root is used in a causative form to mean 'causing someone to hear a sound' — what we might translate as 'informing, announcing, proclaiming'. In the ancient Ethiopic texts, the root is rendered as *nababa* and means simply, to speak.

So who is a Navi/ah[115]? The best translation would capture as many of these meanings as possible — perhaps something like 'speaker' or, in a contemporary English idiom, 'spokesperson'. These 'speakers' became such not because of an ability to speak, but because of an ability to listen. Much like a spokesperson today for a political figure, government, or military body, the task of the prophet was to listen to God's voice and then to paraphrase the message for the sake of others.

This is not an incidental or historical aspect of Judaism; it is so central to the whole concept of divine communication and revelation that Maimonides establishes some of the key ideas about Nevu'ah in the very first section of his monumental *Mishneh Torah*, aptly titled 'Fundamentals of the Torah':

> One of the foundations of our faith is to know that the divine speaks through human beings. Nevu'ah doesn't fall upon just anyone – only one who is very wise, heroic in character, and not subject to the whims of their impulses for material things. Only one who has mastered their mind completely and who has an expansive knowledge is fit for prophecy.
>
> A person who has fulfilled all these aspects and is whole in their body, when they enter into The Orchard[116] they will be drawn after all of these great and distant concepts, and if their mind is fit to understand and grasp them, they will sanctify themselves and continue to throw off all mundane minutiae of common people who walk about in temporary darkness.
>
> The one who achieves such a state will be energised, and will educate themselves how not to have any thoughts that are wasted or idle or ordinary. Instead, their mind will be available constantly for a connection to the higher realms which sit beneath the divine throne, ready to perceive all of those sacred and holy forms, and to look with wisdom upon the Holy Blessed One – from the highest realm of the stars down to the lowly orbit of earth, and know all of them.

> Immediately, the Spirit of Sanctity will then be absorbed by this person – and when the Spirit is intermixed in their being, they will attain the level of the angels who are called 'people', and they will transform into a completely different person, understanding weighty things with their mind which surpass the capabilities of even the wisest humans, as it says of Sha'ul (1 Sam. 10.6): "You shall speak with them and be transformed into a different man."[117]

For Maimonides to go into such detail on a topic so clearly esoteric is unusual. Such meticulous attention is itself a considerable rejoinder to the idea that prophecy is a purely historical notion in Jewish thinking. Clearly, for Rambam, prophecy is as relevant as ever. While it is certainly true that the Sages claimed prophecy ceased when the First Temple was destroyed (586 BCE), this was not universally believed[118], as evidenced by the rich and complex history of Jewish mysticism focussed on attaining a state of Nevu'ah.

Maimonides continues to develop a system of Nevu'ah which is, predictably, culturally specific to his own time and place. Contrary to the common notion that prophecy ceased with the start of the Exile, never in Maimoindes's discussion of the subject does he suggest that somehow prophecy is no longer attainable. Instead, prophecy's relevance and accessibility is a persistent theme in his philosophical writing, particularly the Guide for the Perplexed.[119]

Micah Goodman summarises Maimonides's understanding of Nevu'ah thus: "A prophet has balanced moral qualities, a powerful imagination, and intellectual perfection. The prophet is a blend of saint, artist, and philosopher. A person who brings all of the rich resources of their humanity to full realisation may become a prophet."[120] While the standard is no doubt high, nothing is preventing an individual becoming a prophet except for the hard work required to develop oneself fully.

Kabbalah Nevu'it: An History of Prophecy

In keeping with the sense that Maimonides suggests above, Jewish tradition has often embraced the notion that Nevu'ah is something that can be learned, trained, taught, and practised. In fact, within the eclectic body of literature we call Kabbalah, or Jewish mysticism, there is a distinct thread which is focussed not on theological speculation (*kabbalah iyyunit*) nor magical practice (*kabbalah ma'asit*) but instead on learning to hear the Voice (*kabbalah nevu'it*). These mystics often operated on the fringes of normative Jewish life, and approached mysticism in an individual and idiosyncratic way. Below is a short survey of some of the highlights of this tradition, but it's by no means comprehensive or complete.

- *Sefer Yetsirah* (The Book of Creation): this very first work of Jewish mysticism, likely from the 2nd or 3rd century CE, is the cornerstone of all three streams of Jewish mysticism, but was especially important to those pursuing Nevu'ah. Understood by them as a meditation manual, Sefer Yetsirah describes methods of contemplation and meditation which can be used to induce a trance in which one can 'hear' the Voice. Utilising number mysticism (*gematria*) and visualisation and contemplation exercises, Sefer Yetsirah came to be seen as providing the technical vocabulary and methodology for attaining a state of Nevu'ah.

- *Bat Kol* (Divine Voice): throughout rabbinic literature (Mishnah, Midrash, Talmud), something called a 'Bat Kol' is described. Literally a 'daughter of a voice', the Bat Kol is a sort of low-level experience of Nevu'ah, in which a sound is heard which contributes to rabbinic discussions. Several famous debates center around the experience of hearing a Bat Kol, including the famous fallout over the Oven of Akhnai.

- *Hasidé Mitsrayim* (Egyptian Pietists): an 11th-13th century group of Sufi-influenced Jewish mystics centred around the family of Maimonides. Maimonides' son (Avraham) and grandson (Ovadiya) each left texts in Judeo-Arabic describing their attempt to purify their character and therefore achieve a state appropriate to hear the Voice. With the exception of the scholar Paul Fenton, most of the works from this school remain drastically understudied and undervalued in the intellectual history of Jewish thought.

- *Hasidé Ashkenaz* (German Pietists): an 11th-12th century group of mystics experimenting with meditative and contemplative techniques of letter-combination and trance-induction in their own effort to explore the phenomenon of prophecy. Perhaps the chief example of this school is Elazar Roke'ah of Worms (1176-1238) who lived during the First Crusade and his friend/teacher Rabbi Yehudah ben Samuel of Regensburg (1150-1217).

- Provençal Kabbalah: the organised school of thought which we call Kabbalah really came onto the scene in Provençe at the end of the 12th century. There, prophecy was actively pursued. Also known as the 'father of Kabbalah', the mystic Yitsḥak Saggi Nahor (Isaac the Blind), talks about how his father's academy was graced by the presence of a Voice which explained complicated Talmudic problems and taught new interpretations of the Torah.

- Abraham Abulafia: a 13th century wandering, idiosyncratic mystic who was inspired by Sufi Islam as well as Vedic meditation practices, Abulafia is often held up as the prime example of the tradition of Kabbalah Nevu'it. His voluminous books explore techniques for hearing the Voice as well as the contents of his own experiences in listening and teaching.

- Isaac of Akko: a 14th century idiosyncratic mystic, Isaac travelled around the Jewish world exploring the different versions of Kabbalah present at the time. His own writings, particularly his diaries and dream-journals, describe his encounter with Divine messages, through voices heard, dreams interpreted, and encounters with the mundane world.

- Abulafia's students: a varied and eclectic group of mystics around the Mediterranean were inspired by Abulafia's systems and techniques. A few left their own semi-autobiographical works detailing their experiences and attempts at ecstatic states. Two of the best examples are R' Sa'adiya ben Harar (*Sha'aré Tsedek*) and R' Yehudah Albotini (*Sulam Aliyyah*).

- Draa Valley Mystics: a group of 16th century mystics working on the tradition of Kabbalah Nevu'it moved to the Little Atlas mountains in Southeastern Morocco and set up idiosyncratic communities of scholars, often combining a variety of traditions. Chief examples of these are David haLevi and Avraham Adroitiel.

- *Maggidim*: a 14th, 15th and 16th century genre of *Kabbalah Nevu'it* developed in which certain scholars would describe their experience hearing a divine voice. Often called a *Maggid* (Instructor), those who encountered these spirit guides would often attribute interpretations of Torah as well as personal development to their auditory influence. Examples include Yosef Taitatsak and Yosef Karo.

- *Sha'aré Kedushah*: during the explosion of mysticism which occurred in the mid-16th century in Tsefat, in the community centred around Isaac Luria, Luria's primary student, Ḥayyim Vital, wrote a small book which served as a practical guide to achieving a state of Nevu'ah. As with others, he instructs the student to first prepare their character and be of excellent morality, and then to engage in ascetic spiritual practices in preparation for 'hearing'. We'll return to this exceptional text below.

- Magic Squares: in the late 16th and early 17th century, a tradition was developed of meditating on Magic Squares, a type of mathematical contemplation. This drew heavily on Muslim texts such as those of the Brethren of Purity (*Ikhwan al-Safa*) and had a big influence on Christian mysticism of the time (such as Henry Cornelius Agrippa). The prime example that we have of this is Yosef Tsiyyaḥ, a mystic who primarily taught in Damascus.

- The Nazir: David Cohen (1887-1972), who had a PhD in philosophy, is the best example in the contemporary period of Kabbalah Nevu'it. His magnum opus, *Kol Nevu'ah* (The Voice of Prophecy) was only published in 1970 but reflects his encyclopaedic research throughout his life to try

> and give voice to the prophetic tradition. In the book, he argues that all experience of Nevu'ah has always been auditory and that the idea of acoustic revelation is a unique and essential feature of Jewish mysticism.

The Nazir died only two years after publishing the first part of his *Kol Nevu'ah.* Yet even in those fragmentary pieces that have come to light, there is a cohesive approach to Nevu'ah as a type of logic unique to Judaism – an *auditory analogic* logic.[121] In this he was absolutely correct – all experiences of Nevu'ah occur through the sense of hearing and the metaphorical capacity of the Spokesperson. Audition and analogy are the twin forces that permit the divine Voice to reach human beings, and in this we can see that even a thousand years prior, Maimonides suggested a similar conception of how Nevu'ah is to be experienced:

> There are a number of levels among the prophets. Just as with regard to wisdom, one sage is greater than their colleague, so, too, with regard to prophecy, one prophet is greater than another. They all, [however, share certain commonalities]. They receive prophetic visions only in a visionary dream or during the day after slumber has overtaken them, as [Numbers 12:6] states: *"I make Myself known to him in a vision. I speak to him in a dream."* When any of them prophesy, their limbs tremble, their physical powers become weak, they lose control of their senses, and thus, their minds are free to comprehend what they see, as [Genesis 15:12] states concerning Abraham: *"and a great, dark dread fell over him."* Similarly, Daniel [10:8] states: *"My appearance was horribly changed and I retained no strength."*[122]

"All Nevu'ah comes in the form of metaphor and riddle," Maimonides tells us.[123] This form of communication with humanity is flawed, but not impossible. Nevu'ah is indeed rare, but not extinct. While the brief survey of Kabbalah Nevu'it above may aid us in seeing the persistence of prophecy in Jewish thought, the question remains – how do you *become* a prophet?

How to Be A Prophet

The practicalities of prophecy are slightly more complex than its history. One thing, however, is absolutely certain: it begins with behaviour. Morality is a prerequisite for divine communication. Maimonides stressed that above, and the point was made in even greater detail in Ḥayyim Vital's *Sha'aré Kedushah*. This work, which we mentioned above, is the most direct and descriptive guide to how one can attain what Vital calls the Spirit of Sanctity (*Ru'aḥ haKodesh*). The book contains four parts – the first three of which discuss the *theory* of Nevu'ah, and the last[124] section explore practical techniques and strategies for putting oneself into a state ready to receive prophetic communication.

As established, everything begins with character. Rabbi Vital devotes a significant portion of the first section to what is now called *musar*, or ethical literature. There he stresses the priority of proper behaviour as the first step towards attaining prophetic consciousness:

> Understand this well – for although moral character is essential and fundamental, it is not counted among the 613 *mitsvot*. So we find that one must be even more careful about negative characteristics – even more than fulfilling *mitsvot*! For, when one has mastered good character, fulfilling the *mitsvot* will be easy. In this as well, you can understand

> those surprising words of our Sages regarding character, who say that it is humility and meekness which bring about the spirit of sanctity and cause the Shekhinah to rest on someone. So Eliyyahu said (Kallah Rabbati 5): *Torah cannot be explained except by one who is not impatient, and I myself do not reveal myself to someone who is impatient.* This is like what the Sages also said (Talmud Bavli Sanhedrin 88b): *Who is worthy of the World-That-Is-Coming? Anyone who is meek and humble.* There are many sources like this, and none of them mention observance of *mitsvot* – instead, they focus on good character. Look at these things carefully and you will succeed on your path, no doubt about it.[125]

It genuinely is not possible to overstate what a radical claim Rabbi Vital is making here. Character development is *more* important than observing *mitsvot*. Why? Well, one can be an extremely observant Jew who technically upholds a normative practice of *halakhah* in extraordinary detail – and still be a jerk.

This problem was raised by Ramban (Rabbi Mosheh ben Naḥman) when he discussed the concept of *naval bereshut hatorah* (an awful person who still is within the Torah's bounds)[126]. One can be *technically* observant while completely missing the point of the Torah. Hence Rabbi Vital reverses the whole framework: we have to strive to be good first, and then we will effortlessly be able to observe the *mitsvot*. Both are requirements on the path to prophecy, but surprisingly, it is good moral character which should be prioritised.

The good news is, provided we can master our own baser impulses and combine that with a serious engagement with *halakhah*,

Nevu'ah becomes something almost automatic. Rabbi Vital explains that:

> It is very easy for a person to prophesy – to be one who contains all the worlds and by whose actions all worlds are sustained. So it is obvious to us from all this that, contrary to what we might expect, Nevu'ah is practically obligatory in this world, in order to direct humanity to repair their actions and to draw down divine influence unto all the worlds without error (God forbid). [...] Nevu'ah and the Spirit of Sanctity must necessarily exist in the world, and do so easily. Yet, even still, there are conditions to find people who are fit for it.[127]

Having established that prophecy is fairly straightforward, the question remains: *how*? How does one tune in to the divine Voice? Here Rabbi Vital introduces the idea of *hafshatah* (expansion)[128]:

> Now we can explain the concept of Nevu'ah. For, after a person makes their material body purified, without any pollution [...] and they carry no mistakes which damage one of the essential roots of their soul, then when they prepare themselves to adhere to the supernal root, they are able to cleave to God.
>
> Indeed, even if one is ready for this, they need to still learn to expand their soul entirely and to separate it from any aspect of materiality, only then are they able to adhere to the spiritual source. Look, this concept of Expansion is not found written in any of the books that

> deal with Nevu'ah or the Spirit of Sanctity as a literal Expansion (where the soul leaves the body, literally, like during sleep). If this was the case, then Nevu'ah would be no different than a dream like all dreamers have.
>
> Instead, the resting of the Spirit of Sanctity on a person happens while the soul is within the body and they are awake. The real definition of Expansion is this: that one must banish any thoughts whatsoever, and allow the imaginative capacity within to cease from imagining and thinking and contemplating in the normal, worldly way – almost like the soul *has* actually left.
>
> Through this, one can reverse the power of mental imagination in order to imagine and depict themselves as though they were ascending through all of the upper worlds via their soul's sources in them, from one to another, until one reaches the image of their own form in its highest possible essence and engraves the sight of all the lights in their mind as though they're illustrated. Then they can see them through the power of imagination and depict them in their mind here in this world, even though it is impossible to see such things through science, as is known.[129]

It is clear that this *hafshatah* is a sort of meditation – one in which all of the extraneous elements of the self are purged in order to make room for the Spirit of Sanctity to be 'absorbed' into the body, thereby taking over one's consciousness and connecting the lines of divine communication. It feels as though we are almost talking about a voluntary (and desired) form of possession[130] – except the potential prophet here does not lose their identity. Rather, the experience of Nevu'ah is akin to tuning an antenna.

As we discussed in Chapter 2, the analogy of God as a radio wave broadcast works quite well when attempting to conceive of prophecy. The prophet is the person who makes themselves the most efficient and effective antenna for the Divine – so much so that the Spirit of Sanctity actually allows them to 'reverse' the power of imagination and use the person's abstract facilities to receive a divine transmission rather than the usual static that occupies our minds.

One comfort Rabbi Vital offers us is the reassurance that Nevu'ah is attainable by anyone and that there are many routes to attain it. The secretive and censored fourth section of *Sha'aré Kedushah* doesn't present a systematic model of exercises that must be followed, but rather reads as a sort of anthology or commonplace book, a catalogue of mystical methods with which one can hone their mind and reach towards a state of sanctity. Before he shares his accumulated wisdom of techniques in that final section of the book, he offers a last summation of the process of prophecy:

> Look, the preferred way is: to return in complete *teshuvah* for any kind of breakage, and afterwards to re-complete one's soul by performing positive *mitsvot*, by having correct intention in prayer, by engaging with Torah for its own sake with enthusiasm (like an ox in a yoke until its strength is exhausted), by lessening pleasures like eating and drinking, by getting up at midnight (or a bit before), by distancing oneself from any negative characteristics, by separating oneself from all

> other people (even in regards to small talk), and after that by purifying one's body through *mikveh* constantly, and after that by secluding oneself periodically and dwelling on the awe of God, by placing God's name before one's eyes perpetually, and being careful in one's thoughts to be free from any of the concerns of this world, and thereby adhering in love to God with great passion. Through this, it is possible to merit the Spirit of Sanctity in any of these ways we have spoken of. [131]

A Critique of "Jew-Bus"

A large number of Jews in the last few generations have abandoned Jewish life. Not because they have no interest in spirituality, God, or religious practices – but because their experience of Judaism has completely and utterly failed to offer them anything meaningful in these areas.

For too many, Jewish education was simply Holocaust education and Jewish spirituality was a dry social-justice driven appeal to 'ethical monotheism'. While learning about the Holocaust is essential, and being motivated by Jewish practice to act for good in the word is unquestionably central, neither should obscure or overpower the genuine history of Jewish spirituality.

This has happened partially because Kabbalah is largely unknown and little-understood by most Jews. Modern Jews have also made such a strenuous effort to demonstrate that they are 'rational' and to distance themselves from anything with the least whiff of superstition that in their attempt to purge Judaism of its pre-modern traditions they have also hollowed it out. When Jews do seek out mystical traditions they often find the most superficial versions, little more than cults covered in a veneer of exotic esotericism. A deeper and more meaningful mysticism seems to remain out of reach, driving Jews to seek answers elsewhere.

The phenomenon of Jew-Bus (Jewish Buddhists) is but one example that demonstrates how completely we have failed to impart a genuine spirituality within Jewish communal life. Thousands of engaged, curious, learned Jewish people have committed their time to a foreign tradition (and one that many are guilty of working to appropriate), while neglecting the spiritual resources and lineage within Jewish thought. An appeal to return prophecy to its rightful place in Jewish life is one small way to mitigate this Buddhist bleed-out.

Studying the texts of *Kabbalah Nevu'it* outlined above with a competent teacher and engaging in the practices they promote doesn't require complex theological speculation nor magical rituals, spells or materials. The pursuit of prophecy is surprisingly egalitarian, wonderfully accessible, and contains within its teachings great moral dimensions as well as spiritual exercises.

In BeMidbar (Numbers), when Moses is informed by Joshua that something has gone awry, and the ritual crafted by God to share out the Spirit of Sanctity with seventy delegated elders has accidentally included two random young men, Eldad and Médad, Joshua expects him to freak out. It describes Eldad and Médad, these absolute nobodies, as *yitnabe'u*, prophesying – but contrary to Joshua's expectation, Moses doesn't mind at all. Instead, he seems pleased:

> Moses went out and spoke to the people the words of God, gathering seventy men from the elders of the people, and stood them around the tent. God came down in a cloud and spoke to him, and God extended some of the spirit that was upon Moses and put it upon the

> seventy men, the elders; and it was, when the spirit rested upon them, that they spoke as prophets without stopping.
>
> Now two men remained in the camp: the name of the one was Eldad, the name of the second, Médad, and the spirit rested upon them — they were among those recorded, but they had not gone out to the Tent — and they began speaking as prophets in the camp.
>
> A lad ran and told Moses, he said: Eldad and Médad are speaking as prophets in the camp!
>
> Then Joshua son of Nun, Moses's attendant from his youth, spoke up; he said: My lord Moses, contain them! But Moses said to him: Are you zealous for me? Oh, if only all the people of God were prophets, that God would put the divine spirit upon them![132]

This story is easily lost in the fracas of a chaotic section of Numbers. Yet, its lesson is a profound one. Moses is not threatened by the fact that several people have become 'unauthorised' prophets. He is pleased about it. Nevu'ah remains the most egalitarian and accessible expression of Jewish spirituality, one that can yet be rediscovered and reclaimed, and one that has the potential to offer an authentic and original Jewish approach to mystical praxis.

Moses was right – we should be so lucky as to have everyone achieve a state of Nevu'ah, through moral clarity and spiritual conditioning. May it be so that all the people of God become prophets – spokespersons for the Divine – whether man or woman, Jew or non-Jew, servant or maid, the Spirit of Sanctity dwells on all of them according to their deeds.

Chapter Eight

Refining Reality // *Mitsvot*

No one can lead a happy life if they think only of themselves and turn everything to their own purposes. You should live for the other person if you wish to live for yourself.

Seneca, Letters XLVIII

The *mitsvot* are the primary mode with which Judaism is practiced, the steps along the Way which guides us (as discussed in Chapter 6) and the basis for our relationship with God. Despite this, the most fundamental questions about the *mitsvot* are often left unanswered in Jewish communities: *who* is meant to do the *mitsvot?* And, arguably more importantly – *why* should we bother to do them at all? It is this latter question which is the primary focus for this chapter. Before thoroughly investigating that however, it is essential to define what *mitsvot* are and who is obligated in them.

What are Mitsvot?

When the *mitsvot* are discussed with a definite article, it means the list of rules laid out in the Torah. This language could make it seem as though the Torah is a systematic law book, organised in a way that would make constructing a civil society as simple as possible, but it isn't.

Many of the *mitsvot* are not explicit, or often could be interpreted many different ways. This is the role of the Sages, who are the authorised interpreters of the *mitsvot* and help to clarify *how* each is to be observed. Arguably, the entire project of Judaism is one of understanding the *mitsvot* of the Torah and how to apply them – a project that has become a multigenerational discussion focussed on the nature of the *mitsvot* and their meaning.

Translating *Mitsvot*

In this book, the term *mitsvot* is used as it is, rather than attempt to translate it. This is because the many translations available in English are all unsatisfactory, although to varying degrees. There is the conventional rendering of *mitsvot* as 'commandments', which implies a degree of hierarchy which is not always present. There is the modern, apologetic, version as 'good deeds', which implies an ethical intention to the *mitsvot* which is not consistently included and becomes largely nonsensical. Perhaps other terms might be 'responsibilities', 'rules', 'tasks', or 'duties'. Due to the difficulty of such a semantic range and the importance of the *mitsvot*, it is easier to not attempt translation.

Taxonomy

There are many ways to organise the *mitsvot*, which are typically counted at 613. This number is somewhat arbitrary, as it is possible to count them differently and to come to a variety of other numbers as a result. The origin of the number 613 is not actually in the Torah itself – which doesn't itemise its commands – it comes from the Talmud, in a *sugya* in Makkot where Rabbi Simlai suggests that there is a medical correspondence (at the time, it was believed there were 248 bones and 365 organs in the body).[133] Immediately following Rabbi Simlai's suggested total, Rav Hamnuna Sava puts forward the number 611, this time based on the correspondence between that number and the numerical value of the word 'Torah'.[134] Interestingly, one way to see these as complimentary is to say that there were 611 *mitsvot* given through Moses and two given directly by God – exactly as described in Chapter 1 in establishing the two mandatory beliefs linked to the Shema.

Since the time of that debate in the Talmud, there have been *hundreds* of Hebrew works aiming to elucidate and list all 613 *mitsvot*, many of which have been hugely influential on Jewish history and literature.[135] Despite the near-universal acceptance of the notion of 613 *mitsvot* there have been notable and high-profile dissenters from this doctrine throughout Jewish history, including Rabbi Abraham ibn Ezra[136], Naḥmanides, Gersonides, and the Vilna Ga'on. Even if the number of 613 is purely symbolic, it nonetheless conveys the immensity of our task! There is an awful lot to do.

Dividing the *mitsvot* up into categories has often been a tool of understanding and an aid in their implementation. In general, there are three taxonomic divisions which are typically evoked in Jewish thought.

Positive / Negative

This separates the *mitsvot* into things we *have* to do (positive) and things we are told *not* to do (negative). Like a parent or a teacher attempting to guide a child's behaviour, there is a need both for positive reinforcement and for the avoidance of negative behaviour. Corresponding to Rabbi Simlai's original count, the Sages teach that there are 365 positive *mitsvot* (one for each day of the year) and 248 negative *mitsvot* (one for each bone in the body).

Human-Human / Human-God

This scheme divides the *mitsvot* based on their realm of application – they are either interpersonal (*bén adam leḥavéro*) or divine (*bén adam lemakom*). *Mitsvot* are evaluated therefore based on who they are *for*: are they for another person or for God? Interpersonal *mitsvot* like giving money to the poor, paying one's workers on time, or abiding appropriate sexual relationships are distinct from divine-related *mitsvot* such as putting on *tefillin*, observing Shabbat and Kashrut, or hanging a *mezuzah*. One way to think of it is to ask – if one violates this *mitzvah* is there a victim?

DeOraita / DeRabbanan

This distinction is one based on sources. The Aramaic terms *deOraita* (from the Torah) and *deRabbanan* (from the Sages) distinguish *mitsvot* based on whether they are based on a verse in the Torah or were innovated later by the Sages in keeping with the rules of interpretation. Those *mitsvot* which can be sourced in a particular verse hold the greater weight of being labelled *deOraita*. However, many very common *mitsvot* are actually *deRabbanan* – such as lighting Shabbat candles, observing the holidays of Ḥanukkah and Purim, and wearing a *kippah*. If it can't be sourced in the Torah, then it falls into the slightly less weighty category of *deRabbanan*. *Mitsvot deRabbanan* can often be updated or upended depending on circumstances, but it is far more difficult within the system of Halakhah to alter a *mitzvah* whose source is in the Torah.

Who Does Mitsvot?

One of the accusations often levelled against Jews is that they see themselves as superior. This is ignorance at best and an aspect of antisemitic belief at worst, and is not at all backed up by the vast majority of Jewish tradition. While there are some particularly egregious examples of Jewish texts that give into the temptation to, in the face of persecution, claim a sense of greatness that is undeserved, these are the minority and were often criticised for doing so.[137] Yes, the Jewish tradition has always singled out the Jewish people, and it is absolutely essential that we recognise that the nation of Israel has a special *task*, but they are not biologically or ontologically distinct from any other human beings – and certainly not superior.

The idea of being the 'Chosen People' is best understood through the analogy of a family. The eldest child in a family is often tasked with more responsibility–in particular, to set a good example for their younger siblings. Often the eldest child is held to a higher standard and expected to behave more like an adult than their siblings, even if close in age. Jews are not superior, but they are, in a sense, the 'first born'[138] – tasked with the extra responsibility of promoting the message of monotheism and the knowledge of God.

Being Jewish means one is saddled with extra responsibilities, but the 'reward' is none other than the responsibility itself. There is absolutely no notion of any sort of exclusivity, no salvation, no soporific separate destination for the soul. All people who keep the most simple *mitsvot* are understood to be equally righteous. Specifically, this 'lowest common denominator' is known as the *sheva mitsvot bené no'aḥ*, the Seven Noahide *mitsvot*. Because Noah is the ancestor of all humans, not just Jews, the Noahide laws act as a sort of universal morality. The earliest articulation of these seven *mitsvot* for everyone is in the Tosefta on Avodah Zarah:

> Seven *mitsvot* were given to the sons of No'aḥ:
> To establish courts of law
> To eschew idolatry
> To avoid blasphemy
> To not practice sexual immorality

To not shed blood unnecessarily
To not steal from another
To not tear a limb from a living creature

These are fairly universal – and in our modern world, most of them are observed by most people without much thought[139]. Therefore it has never been difficult for Jewish thinkers to acknowledge and admit that there is nothing about being Jewish which affords any superior status. Rabbi Elia Benamozegh explained this himself beautifully:

> I believe that as each people has from God its own special task – for some it is art, for others laws or commerce, of which it makes itself a master and initiator to other peoples. So Israel has from nature its monotheistic religious genius, and nature as well as history unanimously attest to its powerful universal impact as a teacher of religion. The Jewish concept is this: The universe is the great house of God. God is the parent of all peoples. These peoples are children, each destined for their own vocation. Israel is the firstborn, and in the same way that the firstborn was in the ancient family head of household, priest, teacher, hierophant, and curator of the cult of God – thus and not otherwise is Israel's status in humanity as a whole.[140]

Who are the Jews, then, to the rest of humanity? We are the eldest sibling, the firstborn, and the one who has a particular religious vision to share with others. We are not better, we were just first. In a fascinating echo of Rabbi Benamozegh's articulation of this idea, the 20th century mystic Rabbi Yehudah Ashlag reimagined the role of Israel vis-a-vis the nations through the lens of

Marxist-Leninist theory, in which the Party is the 'vanguard' of the revolution, showing the way for others. To Rav Ashlag, the common refrain that *kol yisra'él arévim zeh lazeh* – all Israel are responsible for one another – is the basis for understanding a wider, more humanitarian mission:

> It is not sufficient [...] that all the people of Israel be guarantors for one another, but instead that the whole world be included in this mutual obligation. Everyone admits that at the start it is enough for one nation to fulfill the Torah, that is, only in order to begin the correction of the world, since it would be impossible to begin with all the nations of the world at once.[141]

The role of Jews the is to activate the 'correction of the world' – just as the eldest child is the first to model the role of adult, so too Israel is the first nation to demonstrate monotheism in practice. Rav Ashlag proceeds to analogise Israel is to Humanity as the Patriarchs are to Israel, writing that:

> The role of the people of Israel toward the whole world resembles the role of our ancestors toward the people of Israel. That is, just as the merit of our ancestors sustained us in our development and refinement until we were worthy of receiving the Torah [...] similarly it is incumbent on the nation of Israel, by being occupied with the Torah and the *mitsvot* for their own sake, to prepare themselves and the people of the whole world, until they advance and undertake this exalted labor of loving others, which is ladder to the ultimate purpose of creation, that is, fusion with God.

Jews, therefore, are burdened with sacred purpose – not to rise above others in haughty indifference, but to show the Way and to be, as Isaiah famously suggests, 'a light unto the nations.'[142]

Conversion and Citizenship

If one need not be Jewish to be 'saved' (a completely foreign concept to Judaism), then why be Jewish at all? How can it be that two groups are evaluated equally – one responsible to follow only seven simple rules, and the other liable for *at least* 613 *mitsvot*? It is because of this extreme imbalance that Judaism has rarely promoted conversion, never actively proselytised, and for most of its history, failed to grow in demographic terms. Jews today make up no more than 15 million people out of a world population which has surpassed 8 billion. There is no evidence that there have ever been more 16.5 million Jews on Earth – which was the population estimate in the years preceding the Holocaust.[143]

In the modern world, in which religion is an open marketplace and Judaism is better understood by non-Jews than ever before, rates of conversion to Judaism have increased dramatically. No one quite knows the numbers (and no one would agree anyway), but all Jewish spaces report increased interest in conversion to Judaism and increased numbers of people completing the arduous process of doing so. Why is it so difficult to convert? Precisely because Judaism is *not* a religion. Conversion is actually not about changing belief (although that is often required), but rather about a sort of spiritual immigration.

The best way to understand conversion to Judaism is to analogise it to a naturalisation process that might take place when one immigrates to a new country. If you move to a new country and wish to seek citizenship you have to 1) prove you know the language and history of that country, 2) prove you have been 'resident' for some period of time, 3) prove you don't harbour any beliefs which contradict the values of that country, 4) undergo a period of study which concludes with a ritual acceptance of you as a new citizen of the country.

Essentially, the same contours define conversion to Judaism. To take someone who we currently believe is only obligated in seven *mitsvot* and change their status to burden them with the obligation to fulfil an extra 600+ is potentially an act of harm. Therefore, a successful conversion candidate needs to demonstrate that they understand the *mitsvot* required of them, how to perform them, how to learn more about them, and show that they have participated in the life of a Jewish community for some period of time (often at least a year). This is an appropriate process, considering the severe increase in one's responsibilities towards both humans and God, derived from both the Torah and our Sages, and covering all aspects of life.

Why Do Mitsvot?

Whether you are born to the Jewish people or undergo a process of naturalisation through conversion, the question still remains: there are a huge number of duties you must undertake – why? Jewish tradition offers (at least) three answers to the question of why we should bother to do *mitsvot* at all – each of which we'll attempt to treat in brief below. In short they are: 1) Because God Said So, 2) Because God Needs Us To, and 3) Because We Need To.

1. Because God Said So

This is perhaps the explanation most familiar to those who attended Ḥéder/Hebrew School where a routine answer to any question may simply have been 'because God said so.' In fact, this is quite a developed understanding of the *mitsvot*. In essence – we signed a contract at Sinai to do the *mitsvot* and so we have to. If we don't, we are deserving of the punishment that may occur because of our breach of contract. God doesn't particularly care how we feel about doing them, we simply have to do them.

The power of this is its innate sense of compulsion; the danger, of course, is that it can stymie questioning and curiosity. This mechanistic explanation of the *mitsvot* is not difficult to source in the Torah, as the default assumption the Torah offers is an exchange of responsibility, a contractual covenant for all time, for instance, Deuteronomy 7:

> Now, because you listened to these commandments, keeping and observing them, God will keep for you the covenant of loyalty that he swore to your ancestors; God will love you, God will bless you, God will make-you-many, God will bless the fruit of your belly and the fruit of your soil, your grain, your new-wine, and your shining-oil, the offspring of your cattle and the fecundity of your sheep, upon the soil that God swore to your ancestors to give you. (12-13)

The exchange is simple and straightforward – we do what God asked, we don't ask questions, and we'll get in return what God promised. The promised reward is largely agricultural, which makes sense considering the anxieties of the time, but we don't perform the *mitsvot* to attain the reward per se. It is simply a contract.

We do our part (*mitsvot*) and God does God's (blessings). The fertility and fecundity of the land is dependent on our moral and ethical behaviour – when we fail, so too do the crops, when we behave, so too does the natural environment we rely on. While to some this may seem aggravatingly simplistic and patronising, it has often had its appeal.

Perhaps the most sophisticated and intellectual voice endorsing this view in recent generations was Yeshayahu Leibowitz, who was famous for being an *enfant terrible* of Israeli intellectuals, and who strongly endorsed the idea that it doesn't *matter* why the *mitsvot* are what they are – we do them regardless. For Leibowitz, the whole system is simply about us doing what God asked. He stretches this to unusual extents, suggesting that prayer is useless unless it is part of what is obligatory:

> Only the prayer which one prays as part of the observance of a *mitsvah* is religiously significant. The spontaneous prayer a person prays of their own accord is, of course, permissible, but, like the performance of any act which has not been prescribed, its religious value is limited. As a religious act it is even faulty, since one who prays to satisfy their needs sets himself up as an end, as though God were a means for promotion of their welfare.[144]

Leibowitz adds an elevated flair to the 'Because God Said So' argument, rejecting any other explanation of *mitsvot* as being anthropocentric. In this sense, he structures his argument in opposition to our third explanation (Because We Need To) – yet what the first and third approaches both share is an idea that the *mitsvot* often have no discernible reason. The search for what are known as *ta'amé hamitsvot* (the reasons for the *mitsvot*) has often been fruitless, with many of the Torah's instructions appearing completely impenetrable by reason.

Many have endorsed this view that the content of the *mitsvot* is irrelevant – that is, the fact that we're commanded to put on *tefillin* or avoid pork is meaningless. It could have been anything and it would have been sacred. In an extreme example, the first Ḥabad Rebbe taught: "Had we been commanded by God to chop wood it would be no less a fulfillment of a divine desire than the most meaningful and enlightening deed."[145] While this is potentially a hyperbolic statement of the point – the idea that the *cause* of the *mitsvot*, their rationale, is unknowable is central. In this, Maimonides also expresses a great deal of sympathy with this first position. He suggests that *mitsvot* have no deeper meaning other than being the duties we have agreed to take on. Looking further can itself sometimes be dangerous:

> No cause will ever be found for the fact that one particular sacrifice consists in a lamb and another in a ram and that the number of the victims should be one particular number. Accordingly, in my opinion, all those who occupy themselves with finding causes for something of these particulars are stricken with a prolonged madness.[146]

2. Because God Needs Us To

The second way to answer this question is encapsulated in the notion that we must do *mitsvot* because they have a real effect on the world around us. This idea, which in academic parlance is typically called theurgy, is purely magical. It is this theurgical notion of *mitsvot* which informs a majority of Kabbalah and as a result, a majority of Jewish communities today. If you have ever been accosted by a Ḥabad emissary on a street corner who is unduly keen for you to put on *tefillin* or shake the *lulav* – they are doing this because they believe that the more *mitsvot* that are performed, the closer the Messianic Era comes.

Like all three ideas we are exploring here, there are positive and negative aspects to such a belief. On one hand, theurgy is tremendously empowering: you, purely through observing *mitsvot*, can literally make the world a better place. This anthropocentric understanding of human agency is central to ideas such as that of *tikkun olam* (world-repair) and it can be a powerful source of inspiration and motivation. However, there is a flipside. Believing that your actions have cosmological importance can lead to a sense of extreme anxiety. If doing *mitsvot* can fix the world, then the natural implication is that *avérot* (transgressions, see Chapter 6) can break the world.

This approach implies that prayer is like an incantation and *mitsvot* are like magical spellcasting – performed correctly, they actually change the material reality in which we live. It also, inevitably, contains a portrayal of God who is dependent in some way on such human action. The notion of the divine system which is taught in many kabbalistic schools is one where our actions on Earth act to rebalance, reorient, or unify the complex mechanics of the cosmos and the identity of God. While surprising to those who have been taught that Judaism and magic are mutually exclusive, the theurgical approach to prayer and *mitsvot* sees the practice of Jewish life as magical mechanics – the right words at the right time can change the whole universe.

If God is broken and needs repairing (as the world does), then our task is immense. Performing *mitsvot* incompletely or inadequately is not just a personal neglect of discipline, it is cosmically criminal. Yet the positives of believing that one has the power to redeem all of existence are many.

While this empowered theurgical approach to *mitsvot* is most explicit in Kabbalah, it long precedes it. In a famous example, the Talmud teaches that, "if only [all of] Israel would keep two [consecutive] Shabbatot, they would be immediately redeemed."[147]

From this fairly simple notion that our observance of *mitsvot* can initiate our own redemption, the concept grows over time into one in which any and every individual bears the responsibility to repair the entire world. As the Ḥasidic teacher Rabbi Naḥman of Bratslav puts it:

> Since each person must say, '*the whole world was only created for me.*' (Talmud Bavli Sanhedrin 37) – hence, insofar as the world was created for me, I must at all times see and look into repairing the world and to fill what is missing in the world and pray for it.[148]

Again, this idea does have deep roots in Jewish thinking, even if most of its exponents are products of the Renaissance and onwards. A beautiful *midrash* in Devarim Rabbah teaches that, "if you study the Torah, you do a kindness, for you help to preserve God's world, since if it were not for the Torah the world would again become without form and void."[149] Here we can see that even the fairly passive action of *talmud torah* (studying Torah) has world-redeeming qualities. This could lead us to believe that all we need to do to make the world a better place is sit and study – which obviously was not the intention of our Sages; equally, it could paralyse us, pinned with worry that any misstep would damage the entire fabric of reality.

This second approach, which believes that God and the universe *require* us to do *mitsvot* in order to be whole and/or redeemed, likely sees the world in the most negative light. It is the most sceptical of material reality – seeing brokenness everywhere and believing the power of repair lies in our hands exclusively. Professor Lawrence Fine, who has written incredibly thorough intellectual histories of Lurianic Kabbalah and its influence on contemporary Judaism, clarifies the negative view of the world consequent to this approach to *mitsvot*:

> The material world as we know it, [...], is deemed repugnant, evil, inhospitable, opposed

> in every way to that which is immaterial, divine light and the soul. The project of human life is to separate the holy from the material world, and thus divest that world of all existence. [...] The vision of redemption is a fundamentally spiritual one in which all things return to *olam ha-tikkun* [literally 'the world of repair']. Thus, the *tikkun* of which Lurianic Kabbalah speaks is not that of this world, but of 'worlds' beyond it. **The responsibility for bringing all this about is a human one, not a divine one.** Divinity is, in effect, a passive beneficiary of the actions of human beings.[150]

Each of the two we've explored so far is triangulated with the third approach – which suggests that we do *mitsvot* not simply because we must, nor because God and the world needs us to, but because we ourselves need to. One way to contextualise these three could be to ask: for whose sake do we do *mitsvot*? For the first approach, we do *mitsvot* for God's sake (for the sake of our covenantal responsibility). For the second, we do *mitsvot* for the world's sake (because we hold the power of repair). For our third and final view, we do *mitsvot* for our *own* sake (because they refine our character).

3. Because We Need To

The last answer to the question is the one that is least discussed but likely most-widely believed – that the *mitsvot* are there for our sakes. By performing *mitsvot* we engage in a process of self-development; the *mitsvot* are uniquely structured to act as a programme of spiritual and personal growth. In this model, God doesn't insist we observe the *mitsvot* just because they're a demonstration of divine power, nor does their observance hold cosmic or magical power. Rather, God has given the *mitsvot* as aids in psychological conditioning, a spiritual discipline designed to inculcate in us values and ideals which permit the growth of the person and the maximum relationship with the divine.

Every year, it is shocking to come to the Haftarah on Yom Kippur morning and read the words of Isaiah, essentially reprimanding us for fasting. The Sages made a fascinating choice in insisting we read this passage, and in doing so they sketched a way to approach *mitsvot* which sees them neither as arbitrary covenantal responsibilities nor as magical invocations – but as a method of character development. The full passage (Isa. 57:14-58:14) is too long to reproduce here, but a few highlights are worth including:

> God said: Build up, build up a highway!
> Clear a road!
> Remove all obstacles
> from the road of My people!
> For thus said God, who dwells high above,
> whose name is sacred:
> I dwell in high, apart –
> yet, I am with the contrite
> and the lowly in spirit, reviving their hearts.
> This is the fast I desire:
> to unlock fetters of wickedness,
> to untie the cords of the yoke,
> to let the oppressed go free,
> to break off every subjugation,
> to share your bread with the hungry,
> to take the poor into your home,
> to clothe the naked when you see them,
> to not ignore your own kin.

To be told, in the midst of fasting, that fasting alone is useless – that God has no interest or purpose in people observing *mitsvot* just to do them – is a refreshing slap in the face every Yom Kippur.

The point, it would seem, is not just to do what we are told, but to be motivated by the system of *mitsvot* to act for good in the world, not as a kind of cosmic magic, but as a quite mundane practice of what we might today call social justice. The very first chapter of Isaiah begins with similar remonstrations – a theme built up and reinforced across the course of the book:

> Your new moon and Shabbat observances
> fill me with loathing –
> they are a burden to me –
> I cannot endure them!
> When you lift up your hands,
> I will turn my eyes away from you.
> Though you pray and pray, I won't listen –
> your hands are stained with crime!
> Wash yourselves clean and put away your evil
> doings from before Me.
> Cease to do evil, learn to do good!
> Devote yourselves to justice:
> aid the wronged,
> uphold the rights of the orphan,
> defend the cause of the widow.[151]

To Isaiah, then, the *mitsvot* are there to help us be better people. In this, he is not alone. The psychological dimension of *mitsvot* is one recognised early and often by our Sages, who neither put much stock in magic nor were willing to accept that the *mitsvot* were random commands without reason.

Hence there are many famous passages in rabbinic literature in which the same question is asked in different variations: does God *really* care if an animal is slaughtered one way or another? This becomes the motif which links many diverse passages together, all of which answer an unequivocal no. A great example comes from Midrash Tanḥuma:

> What does God care whether a person kills an animal in the proper Jewish way and eats it, or whether they strangle the animal and eat it? Will the one benefit God, or the other injure God? Or what does God care whether a person eats kosher or non-kosher animals? So you learn that the *mitsvot* were given only to refine God's creatures, as it says, 'God's word is refined. It is a protection to those who trust in God' (2 Samuel 22:31)[152]

The key here is this language of *refinement*. In Hebrew, the idea of *tséruf* implies a very particular and rather technical process: the refinement of molten metals necessary for gold and silversmithing. To refine the metal, one needs to separate the high quality material from the dross – a process typically done under great heat and great pressure, and which leaves the smith with a better quality product by the end. Hence, the third approach is that the *mitsvot* are the tools of *our* refinement.

This concept, particularly around the idea of character refinement, is articulated powerfully by Rav Yehudah Ashlag, as part of his understanding of *mitsvot*:

> These are the words of our Sages in Beréshit Rabbah (44), when they were asked: 'What does God care if one slaughters an animal at the front of the neck or the back?!' [They answer that] the *mitsvot* have been given *only* so that created beings can enhance themselves through them. This enhancement means the refinement of the physical body, which is the purpose of fulfilling the Torah and *mitsvot* entirely. For, 'man is born as a wild ass' – that is, when one enters the world and is born into

> the bosom of creation they are found to have impurities and imperfections. The reason why is due to the prevalence and degree of self-love which one in this world drowns in, a world in which each person orbits only their own centre with no trace of giving to others at all. This, of course, is what we find to be the opposite extreme from the root of divinity and of God – from one extreme to the other – for the divine root is to give absolutely without any trace whatsoever of taking. So it is that the one who is born finds themselves in a total state of taking for themselves without any hint of giving at all – therefore we can evaluate their state as being the lowest point possible, full of the impurity and imperfection which is prevalent in the human world.[153]

Here, Rav Ashlag frames the notion that the *mitsvot* are for our sake by structuring human nature as being diametrically opposed to divinity – God is all giving, we are all taking. In order to be more like God, we have to condition ourselves to *give* more, to be less self-interested and less self-obsessed. The tools to do that, to challenge our natural selfishness and develop a sense of divine love for others, are the *mitsvot*. In this, Maimonides speaks similarly:

> All the *mitsvot* are to [help us to] overcome our negative inclinations and to correct our traits; and most laws of the Torah are instruction from afar from the Great Adviser [to help us] to correct our character traits and straighten our ways.[154]

The *mitsvot* are a carefully-crafted system of spiritual discipline and individual self-development, designed to encourage us to weed out negative character attributes and cultivate positive ones. Maimonides is not alone in seeing this in such a total way – there are similarly dramatic statements made from a variety of sources across Jewish time and space.

The mediaeval work of *musar* (ethical teaching) known as *Orḥot Tsaddikim* (Ways of the Righteous) begins its introduction with a dramatic statement: "If you do not possess refined character traits, then neither do you possess Torah and *mitsvot*, for the entire Torah depends on the refinement of character."[155]

The entire Torah depends on the refinement of character. This sentiment is echoed, hundreds of years later, by the Vilna Ga'on, where in his work *Even Shelémah*, he teaches that:

> All service of God is dependent upon the improvement of one's character since character traits are like clothing to the *mitsvot* and are the general principles of the Torah. Conversely, all transgression stems from unimproved character traits.[156]

Good and bad actions are not the cause of one's character, they are the products of it. Refined character (purified through *mitsvot*) helps to encourage us to act for good in the world, while neglect of the *mitsvot* (and thus a character which remains naturally selfish and unimproved), leads to *avérah*, transgression – in which we stray from the Way.

These teachings offer a third way to understand *mitsvot*, one that triangulates and syncretises the first two – which sees human action as powerful and also understands the *mitsvot* to be part of a relationship of human-divine covenant. However, this third approach allows us to approach *mitsvot* as a personal and psychological pursuit, avoiding many of the negative implications of the first two understandings and offering a modern, methodical, and moral understanding of precisely *why* we should bother to do *mitsvot* at all.

Chapter Nine

The Sundered Stone // *Souls*

My soul, where are you? Do you hear me? I speak, I call you – are you there? I have returned, I am here again. I have shaken the dust of all the lands from my feet, and I have come to you, I am with you. After long years of long wandering, I have come to you again. Should I tell you everything I have seen, experienced, and drunk in? Or do you not want to hear about all the noise of life and the world? But one thing you must know: the one thing I have learned is that one must live this life.

Carl Jung, The Red Book

One hundred hairs fall out of your head each day, and a hundred new ones begin to grow in. Every few days your stomach lining is entirely replaced, with brand new cells taking the place of ones that were shed. Every few weeks the outer layer of your skin is replaced. Every four months all of your red blood cells are different, with one hundred million new cells developing every minute. Every six months you have brand new fingernails. Every five years or so every hair on your head is different; every ten years every cell of bone is different. Every fifteen years all of your muscle tissue is replaced, and it takes twenty five years for fat cells to be exchanged. Of the few things that remain unchanged throughout a lifespan, the only ones worthy of note are: about half the cells of the heart, the neurons of the brain, and the lens which forms the outer part of your eye.

However, a cluster of neurons, half a heart, and a viscous tissue through which we see the world hardly constitutes a full 'person.' If we are constantly in flux, if our bodies are always changing, developing – then who, ultimately, are 'we'? Who is the 'I' that we reference when we use the first person? Who is the 'self' which we identify with our innermost essence as an individual?

A simplistic theology would say that what makes 'you' *you* is the 'soul.' According to most of its proponents, the soul is an indivisible spiritual entity which defines your self and connects you to the realm of the spiritual. The whole notion on which so much of modern Western Christian society is based – that each person has an 'individual,' indivisible soul – seems to be at odds with all of what we know about our bodies.

Bodies change – constantly. They regenerate, replace, and eventually relinquish their hold on material existence. At some point, entropy and ageing overtake that drive to regenerate cells, and we begin to die, regardless of the extent of social and emotional change that comes with age and maturity. The material body simply begins to fail, as is exceedingly obvious, despite our dedication to death denial in modern culture. Yet we are told that despite the inevitable bodily decay, we can rest assured – the solid 'self' which lies within the soul lives on.

If that's true, then there are somewhere in the range of 107 billion souls out there, as that is the conservative estimate of how many human beings have ever lived. That means that for every person alive today on the earth, there are 15 people who have died during the course of history, each of which continued to exist in the form of a 'soul' after death. That of course, is assuming animals and other forms of life don't have our prized 'souls,' which we would be hard pressed to argue, or prove. If we were to include all living things (or even just all mammals) in our 'soul-count', the numbers become inconceivable.

So how can we understand the idea of a 'soul' without feeling like it conflicts with everything we know about ourselves and our universe, and about our changing and fragile bodies? One option is to embrace the biblical absence of any idea of 'soul', a system in which souls simply do not exist, and in their place is the pure and divine exchange of breath.

The Breath of All That Lives

The biblical notion of the self is free of any dualistic division between body and soul. You likely didn't learn it in Hebrew school, but nowhere, not once, not at all, does the Tanakh talk about an immortal soul. The idea of a soul simply does not exist in the Hebrew Bible. Things are alive, it seems, because they have God's breath in them, and when that breath leaves, they die. Breath, body, and blood are all one and the same in the eyes of the Torah. As soon as the 'breath of life' is returned to God, that is it – game over. Arguably, the whole point of the Garden of Eden story is that eternal life is the exclusive domain of God and that when we left the Garden to head East we lost the chance at immortality.

When the idea first entered Judaism that there is a distinct 'soul' which outlives the body, it was likely a result of the foreign influence of Zoroastrianism in the late biblical period, particularly during the years of the Babylonian Exile (597-515 BCE). Thanks to that contact, and the later influence of Greek philosophy, especially Plato, many Jews started to take the idea of a soul as a given. However, even the few Second-Temple era Jewish books that *do* endorse the idea of an 'immortal soul' (Maccabees, Sirach, Enoch and Jubilees) were all explicitly rejected from the canon of the Tanakh[157].

Barukh Spinoza (1632-1677) is mostly remembered today as the renegade Jewish philosopher whose radical ideas about God, the soul and Creation led him to be placed in *ḥerem* (exile) by the Amsterdam community. Spinoza was criticised so heavily not purely for his ideas of God (as is typically thought), but predominantly, for his views about the lack of a soul. In his *Ethics*, Spinoza argued that there can only be one thing which is eternal, and that is God. While we live, we share in that eternity, but to say that we also become (or are) an eternal being would violate the principle of monotheism. Far from being an atheist — Spinoza was in many ways restoring the indigenous, biblical view of life and death.

Steven Nadler, one of the leading scholars of Spinoza today, has argued that the reason Spinoza was put in *ḥerem* was not because he denied the divine origin of the Torah, nor because of his views on God, but precisely because he contested the belief in personal immortality.[158] This is telling – if the most infamous rebel of Jewish thought was orthodox in his theology, and it was truly his approach to the soul and the self which caused his exile, then we can be certain that the notion of a soul is a primary concern (and a significant threat) for Jewish communities.

It would seem that to early Judaism, what you are, really, is a bunch of dust temporarily animated by the Divine breath. That is what we all are. When that breath is exhausted, the spirit that preserved us as living things reintegrates into the whole. It will be used again to bring life to countless other organisms. The whole world of living things – the biosphere – is God breathing in and out, in and out.

Perhaps no text puts it better than Isaiah 40:

> Grass withers and flowers fade –
> when God's breath is exhaled from them.
> Indeed, people too, are naught but grass.

This sentiment is fundamental to Yom Kippur — and to our own reflection on mortality. After all, it is in the Unetaneh Tokef prayer that Ashkenazim recite over and over that we find the powerful poetry of fragility:

> The origin of humanity is dust;
> their end is dust.
> They earn their bread by exertion and are,

as a result, compared to:
a broken shard, dry grass, a withered flower,
a passing shadow and a vanishing cloud.
They are like a breath that exhales and scatters
the dust, like a dream that flies away.

Judaism does not (*or* did not, originally) sustain a belief in soul-body duality, that is, the concept of a distinct non-physical entity which lives inside your body and represents the essence of *you*, the profound quintessence of your identity. That idea simply isn't sustainable. However – if you find the biblical notion of breath-as-life too daunting, there is a compromise position articulated beautifully by Jewish mysticism: the soul exists, but is not a *thing*. Instead, what we mean when we say 'soul' is actually a category, a collection, a complex and compound entity.

A Literal Piece of God

For Spinoza, as for much of our tradition, eternal life was the exclusive province of the Divine. If we can be said to have an eternal life, it is because we have, and are, a piece of the Divine, temporarily instantiated in material reality. *This* idea of the soul – that it is a literal piece of God – forms part of a broader notion within religion sometimes called 'nondualism'.[159] How does this work? We'll attempt to explore what this might mean below, but great caution is required. Since we are so inured to see the soul as a projection or apparition of our physical and material selves, it is genuinely difficult to challenge our own preconceptions around this and think differently. Comfortingly, this is not a new struggle. One of the main systematisers of Kabbalah, Rabbi Moses Cordovero wrote in his work *Elimah Rabbati*:

> The essence of divinity is found in every single thing – nothing but it exists. Since it causes everything to be, nothing can live by anything

> else. It enlivens them; its existence exists in each existent thing. Do not attribute duality to God. Let God be solely God. If you suppose that Infinity emanates until a certain point, and that from that point on is outside of it, you have dualised. God forbid! Realise, rather, that Infinity exists in each existent thing. Do not say, 'This is stone and not God.' God forbid! Rather, all existence is God, and the stone is a thing pervaded by divinity.[160]

Cordovero's use of the analogy of a stone is apt, as this is a repeated metaphor to understand how we can talk about a 'soul' without it meaning anything other than a piece of God. The metaphor of a stone hewn from a mountain is so prevalent that it is almost taken for granted in mystical Jewish sources. One that explains it beautifully is the Kabbalistic textbook *Talmud Eser haSefirot* by Rabbi Yehudah Ashlag. There, he writes, in a vein very similar to Moses Cordovero:

> Know that there is no existing substance in the universe, whether it is perceptible by our senses or not, whether it is intelligible to us or not, which is not included within God – for everything is drawn out from God, and it is impossible for there to be anything which is not within God.[161]

Once that is established, we can better understand our identity, and the question of our souls. Our 'soul' does not represent a pure version of our selves. It represents a piece of divinity, an actual fragment of God which animates our material body. This explains, in one sense, how we are meant to understand what it means to be made *in the image of God*. Rabbi Abraham Joshua Heschel makes explicit what is so often only hinted at, regarding the laws of *avodah zarah* (idolatry):

> Why are we forbidden to make images of God? It is not because God is beyond all images, so that no image could possibly depict God. If that were the case, images would merely be harmless. God *has* an image, and that is you. You may not *make* the image of God because you *are* the image of God. The only medium in which you can make God's image is the medium of your entire life, and that is precisely what we are commanded to do. Everything you do, everything you say, each moment and the way you use it are all part of the way you build God's image. To take anything less than a full, living human being – like canvas or a piece of marble – and call it the image of God would be to diminish God, to lessen God's image.[162]

If we, as living creatures, are a literal piece of God – two questions immediately spring to mind: 1) how can God be divided into pieces? 2) What is the relationship between the fragment(s) and the whole? Both of these are central to a nondualistic understanding of the soul, and both are addressed partially by returning to the metaphor of the stone, this time in relationship with a mountain from which it was hewn. Again, Rav Ashlag takes care to spell out this analogical relationship as part of his pedagogical project of teaching Kabbalah, and the passage (again from his textbook *Talmud Eser haSefirot*) is worth quoting in full:

> Now we come to understand what the Kabbalists taught about the substance of the soul. This is their wording: that the soul is a literal piece of God, and there is no difference between the All and the soul, except that the

soul is only a piece and not the All. This is like a stone quarried from a mountain – the substance of the mountain and that of the stone are one in the same, there is no distinguishing them, except in this: the stone is only a *piece* of the mountain while the mountain is the All. This is a summary of what they have taught.

It seems that these are surprising and radical ideas, and perhaps difficult to understand: how can we interpret the aspect of division and separation when speaking of Divinity? To return to the analogy of the stone hewn from the mountain (which is simply the stone in Whole) – it is actually *cut* from the mountain through the use of a tool like an axe – but when speaking of Divinity, how could we imagine such a separation?

Before we can come to the explanation, we have to explain the meaning of the concept of 'separation' which applies to spiritual things. Know that different spiritual identities are distinguished from one another only through an alteration in form. For example, if there is a spiritual thing which acquires two forms, then it is not one, but two.

I will explain to you about human souls, for they too are spiritual things. It is well known that the law of spirituality is that the forms are simple – this is why there are at least six hundred thousand root-souls, corresponding to bodies. The souls each illuminate the bodies they are within, but each is different –

distinguished by the subtle changes in form in each and every one.

> In a similar way, our Sages discussed the human face, teaching that there are no two which are exactly the same, or the human mind, where each is completely unique. This is symbolised by the body, to distinguish the forms of the souls, until each soul can be understood on its own – this one good, that one bad and the like, according to the ways the forms are defined. Therefore one can see that just like in a physical object, which is divided and separated and cut through an axe and the ability to separate the two pieces over distance – so too with a spiritual object, it can be divided and split and cut through changes in form between one piece and another – and depending on the degree of change in form, that is how we discuss the 'distance' between two pieces. Remember this well.[163]

There are several key ideas here relevant to our discussion: first, the 'soul' is actually just a piece of God, completely co-identical with the All, and second, to understand how a piece of God could be separated from the Whole and then carried off, we have to understand what causes separation in spiritual things. This second point is technical but important: spiritual things are not separated by physical space. Since they don't take up physical space, they cannot be described in the typical three-dimensional coordinates of space. God is not *here*, nor *there*. Moreover, we can't say that the soul is *here* in our body but God is *elsewhere*. Distance is not a factor of space, but of form. Things which are similar in form are close, and things which differ in form are distant.

This concept of 'equivalence of form' is central to Rav Ashlag's whole system – where the primary pursuit of human life is to condition ourselves to be *like* God, thus making our form like God's form. Rav Ashlag articulates this through the structure of giving/taking, as we've seen before, but many similar examples could be used. Since God is always giving and our default is to take, by changing our form to be more giving, more caring, more loving of others, we literally move our soul – the stone hewn from the Divine mountain – *closer* to God. Complete equivalence of form, in which no 'space' remains between how we act and how God acts is impossible, but we strive towards it, aiming for an experience of *devekut* (literally 'adhesion', in which two spiritual things are in the same 'place' because they share identical forms).

One of the components of this theory then, is that when the soul takes on other forms (for a spiritual object can take on many forms at once), it changes and differs. In this way, Rav Ashlag is able to explain the diversity of living creatures while also affirming that all of them are, in substance and identity, literal pieces of God. The only reason we don't perceive ourselves and others *as* such is because the multifarious forms we take on create spiritual distance, separating us from our divine source. Understanding this complexity allows us to understand another idea which has been central to Jewish mystical thinking about the soul: the concept that it is itself a composite entity, not singular in form, but compound and complex.

The Composite Soul

One way to resolve our dilemma is to acknowledge that the soul is in fact a **composite** entity.

Like our bodies and its billions of cells and our planet and its billions of people – our soul, the Kabbalists suggest, is not a *thing*, but is a literal piece of the Divine, made up of innumerable tiny fragments, pinpricks of divine light. They called these *nitsotsot*, sparks, and understood that the soul which we possess during our life is in fact a unique configuration of these soul-sparks. We have, for our short lifespan here on Earth, a special constellation of divine energy, amassed from broken shards of previous worlds (See Chapter 3) and chips off the divine rock. When we die, the sparks that make up our particular soul separate and reconstitute. Some of them may rejoin together in the next life, some may not.

Thus, Jewish mysticism is able to believe in reincarnation (more accurately: transmigration) without having to explain why we don't remember past lives. We live many lives, but each one is a different configuration of soul-fragments. Each life is itself a composite entity, existing for a short period of time and then reemerging into a greater fabric of divine light. The mystics suggest that these sparks actually do fall into groups, that they are shattered bits of primordial soul-roots. Thus, they explain that the things we are drawn to, the people we are drawn to, often hold such extraordinary sway over us because some bit of our soul is magnetically drawn to a similar bit in someone else. A little bit here, a little bit there – regenerating, replacing, reincarnating.

I think this may be the best way for us as modern people to understand our 'selves.' We do have souls, but they aren't so special or unique to some essential version of 'us.' I am who I am because of the unique configuration of sparks which happens to make up the soul I currently possess.

Thus, when we mourn someone who has died, we mourn their soul as a particular combination. What a special configuration of sparks that person was! Just enough of this, a little bit of that. The composition was excellent. That specific combination may never be seen again, but we can nonetheless take some solace in knowing that the sparks which made up that unique soul will be re-used, perhaps have already been re-used. Maybe you recognize some bit in a relative, in the face of a stranger, or in the soul of the wind rustling through the trees. Wherever we go, we are surrounded by soul-sparks, new and old, familiar and strange, ones we have been and ones we have yet to be.

This conception, of tiny soul-fragments continually reincarnated in different bodies, is known as *gilgul* (cycling) and will be discussed more in Chapter 11 – but it is worth saying here that this is neither a fringe aspect of Jewish tradition nor a modern one. Moreover, precisely because it is the approach to 'souls' which is most aligned to the experience of the natural world, it has the best possibility of being a compelling answer to that ever pressing question of 'who are we' for modern Jews. Rabbi Benamozegh, for example, saw it in absolute consonance with the findings of science and reason:

> Gilgul is in agreement with the opinion of the best and greatest among ancient and modern thinkers; it is the supreme, almost unique, means to explain the apparent injustices that are seen on earth, and is, in short, almost necessarily required by Science.[164]

It is this dimension of our discussion which is perhaps most important: as people who live in a world irretrievably shaped by science, how can we endorse a belief in a soul which is person-specific, immortal, and identifiable? If we find we cannot (and we cannot), then we are not alone – not only are there incredible resources within the Jewish tradition to help us in discovering an authentic and sustainable grasp of what 'soul' means, but there are also wonderful examples of comparative thought in other religious traditions.

For example, the Vedic traditions of 'anatman' (no-self) often are remarkably close to the Jewish view of a composite soul – and central to many of those belief-systems is the idea that the many lives one lives possess 'continuity, without identity.'[165] That is, 'reincarnation' is often not thought of by the traditions which teach it in the way that outsiders to those traditions expect. To be reincarnated doesn't mean that you, as you are now, wake up one day in the body of a squirrel. Instead, it means that the pieces that compose your soul are reused and recycled in order to construct new souls in the future – you can be assured that you will continue, but you cannot count on still being 'you' through the process.

Continuity, Without Identity

One way to imagine this compound soul is to consider a pick 'n' mix vat of marbles. When I was a kid, I loved collecting marbles. The variety of colours, textures, and inset features were astounding, and they were both beautiful to look at and enjoyable to hold, spin, and of course, crash into each other. In a local shop there was a big pick 'n' mix marble station, where for a small fee, one could scoop up a random collection of marbles and place them into a small paper bag. Later, at home, I'd spill out the bag and have a look at all the marbles that made up that particular day's haul. Some would be kept, some organised, some lost in the couch cushions, and those that were duplicates or simply not desired returned to the massive barrel of marbles on the next visit to the store.

Imagine that when a living thing is created, a random selection of soul-fragments (*nitsotsot*) are gathered up and placed into a 'bag'. During the lifetime of that creature – whether it is the two hours of the mayfly or the roughly eighty years of a human being – that particular combination of 'marbles' is the soul of that being. Those fragments, in that configuration, animate the body and offer it both identity and divinity. Upon death, that bag of marbles, the soul full of fragments, is spilled back into the collective vat. When they are next needed for another living thing, some of those pieces may yet again end up together, but not all of them, and not in the same configuration. Perhaps after eighty years spent together in a paper bag, there is an affinity, a complementary resonance which those fragments share with one another – a memory of a life lived in composed consonance.

This idea is stated brilliantly in one of the short stories that make up David Eagleman's wonderful collection *Sum: Forty Tales of the Afterlives*[166]. The story, entitled *Ineffable*, is worth reproducing here in full:

> When soldiers part ways at war's end, the breakup of the platoon triggers the same emotion as the death of a person – it is the final bloodless death of the war. This same mood haunts actors on the drop of the final curtain: after months of working together, something greater than themselves has just died. After a store closes its doors on its final evening or a congress wraps up its final session, the participants amble away, feeling that they were part of something larger than themselves, something they intuit had a life even though they can't quite put a finger on it.
>
> In this way, death is not only for humans but for everything that existed.
>
> And it turns out that anything which enjoys life enjoys an afterlife. Platoons and plays and stores and congresses do not end — they simply move on to a different dimension. They are things that were created and existed for a time, and therefore by the cosmic rules they

continue to exist in a different realm.

Although it is difficult for us to imagine how these beings interact, they enjoy a delicious afterlife together, exchanging stories of their adventures. They laugh about good times and often, just like humans, lament the brevity of life. The people who constituted them are not included in their stories. In truth, they have as little understanding of you as you have of them; they generally have no idea you existed.

It may seem mysterious to you that these organizations can live on without the people who composed them. But the underlying principle is simple: the afterlife is made of spirits. After all, you do not bring your kidney and liver and heart to the afterlife with you – instead, you gain independence from the pieces that make you up.

A consequence of this cosmic scheme may surprise you: when you die, you are grieved by all the atoms of which you were composed. They hung together for years, whether in sheets of skin or communities of spleen. With your death they do not die. Instead, they part ways, moving off in their separate directions, mourning the loss of a special time they shared together, haunted by the feeling that they were once playing parts in something larger than themselves, something that had its own life, something they can hardly put a finger on.

Souls, in Summary

In this chapter we have explored several challenging ideas – challenging because by definition the subject matter is complex, but equally so because of all the preconceptions that are so deeply hardwired into our modern Western culture about what the word 'soul' means. For most of us, when we talk about the soul, we immediately imagine it as part of a dichotomous system: body and soul. Such an idea is more complex than it may first seem, and Jewish thought, particularly Jewish mystical thought, offers a more comforting and compelling understanding of the soul.

The soul is not a *thing*, but a collection of sparks, each a fragment of the divine, a literal piece of God. Life is made possible by virtue of a temporary configuration of those divine fragments combining with material reality to form a body; the marker of the physical presence of life and divinity is breath. In breathing, God is present, and when the fragments of divinity are returned to their source, breath ceases and entropy succeeds. While something is alive, its divine animation holds the forces of decay and entropy at bay – breath acts as a bellows to push away the force of death – but this is, by definition, temporary.

The Jewish mystics have a tendency to refer to God as *nefesh hanefashot*, literally the 'soul of souls', a construction of Hebrew grammar meant to demonstrate extremity, a superlative. God is the soul-est, the source of all life and the substance of our self. Through God we live, and through the complex and compound shards of the divine stone within us, we find both God and our selves.

Chapter Ten

A Responsibility to Raise // *Suffering*

My greatest wish for humanity is not for peace or comfort or joy. It is that we all still die a little inside every time we witness the death of another. For only the pain of empathy will keep us human. There's no version of God that can help us if we ever lose that.

Neal Schusterman, Scythe

The chief question asked of religion is rarely about theology (what God is) or of anthropology (what humanity is); it is not usually about metaphysics (the nature of the soul) or metempsychosis (reincarnation). The question that we must ask most is this: why is the world *so* awful sometimes? This is a question about the nature and texture of what we conventionally call 'evil', although, as we'll see, the failure to properly define such terms is itself part of the problem. It is also the question of suffering, ours and others', and if there is meaning to be made in the experience of misery.

Different religious traditions answer this question differently, and there is usually as much diversity of thought *within* a religion as there is between them. This is equally true of Judaism, even if the moniker of 'religion' is not completely appropriate. Within Judaism there are essentially three options for how to make sense of suffering, all of which are well-represented in Jewish sources. There are also, predictably, some options or opinions which are not present in Jewish thought, and we'll quickly begin with those.

First of all, Judaism recognises that suffering is a real and potent thing. The custom in many religious writings to simply try and reframe the pressing question of unhappiness by denying the existence of suffering is not one that Jewish authors are prone to indulge in. Suffering is real, powerful, and practically universal. However, while we don't deny suffering, we also don't assume it is meaningful, or attribute it to personal agency in the form of a malevolent counter-deity (Satan, the Devil, Ahriman, etc). God, we affirm daily, is equally responsible (or not) for all things, good and bad, pleasurable and miserable. Isaiah doesn't allow us to think otherwise, as his striking clarity is irrefutable:

> I am God, and there is no other.
> Except for me, there is no divinity.
> I surround you, but you do not know Me.
> This way, they can know, from east to west,
> that there is none but me.
> I am God, and there is no other,
> who forms light and creates darkness,
> who makes peace and creates evil.
> I am God – I do all these. [45:5-7]

It is impossible to read a text such as this and then conclude that there is a powerful agential angel responsible for evil. We must leave any idea of devilish anti-divine tempters at the door. While there are several references to *ha-satan* (the adversary) in the Hebrew Bible (notably in the Garden of Eden story as well as Job), that character is nothing like the anti-God so central to the vast majority of Christian traditions (and a good portion of Islam), where Satan/Lucifer/the Devil/Iblis is responsible for much of the suffering that humans endure.

In the absence of a Devil to blame, we are stuck at our starting point, with two assumptions inviolable to Jewish thought: evil is real, and it cannot be written off as the wranglings of a demonic force. Thus we must try and account for two things: the *origin* of evil and the *explanation* of evil. To do so, there are three primary methods, none of which are completely mutually exclusive. Indeed, they often overlap and intertwine in Jewish sources, and individuals are, as always, free to find the approach to this question that suits them best. Like with the question of the afterlife (see the next chapter), our view on evil, as Jews, is largely up to us – provided we neither deny its existence (which would be cruel) nor attribute it to some lesser demon/deity (which is a cop-out).

Three Options

The options presented below are derived from the wonderful book by Rabbi Harold Kushner, *When Bad Things Happen to Good People*. While they do not exactly match the structure of *When Bad Things*, the three configurations of theodicy (an academic term for the question of evil and/or suffering and its discourse) assume the same three claims about God, and acknowledge that the choice we face is of which two to pick. This trilemma (three part dilemma) has long been attributed to ancient Greek philosopher Epicurus, whose name becomes the metonym for heresy in Rabbinic Judaism (*epikoros*), but Epicurus likely didn't say it, and even if he did, sometimes heretics are correct as well.

In short, if one acknowledges evil as a real experience, and if we are unwilling to attribute suffering to some external evil agent (no denial and no devil), then only *two* of the following three adjectives can be true of God: 1) omnipotent (all-powerful), 2) omniscient (all-knowing), and 3) omnibenevolent (all-good). God simply cannot be all powerful, all knowing and all good - all at the same time. The presence of so much suffering in the world contradicts it. One of those three has to go, and the resulting three configurations offer us options for how to understand suffering. To state it in clear terms before we explore more:

The Three Suppositions:

Omnipotent – all powerful
Omniscient – all knowing
Omnibenevolent – all good

The Three Combinations:

> **Option A = 1+2, but not 3 = God is omnipotent and omniscient but not omnibenevolent** (God knows what's going on and *can* fix it but doesn't want to), AKA *God is ill-tempered.*
>
> **Option B = 1+3, but not 2 = God is omnipotent and omnibenevolent, but not omniscient** (God can fix things and would do so, but doesn't know what is going on), AKA *God is ignorant.*
>
> **Option C = 2+3, but not 1 = God is omniscient and omnibenevolent, but not omnipotent** (God knows what's going on and *wants* to fix it, but isn't able to), AKA *God is impotent.*

We are left with having to choose between which imperfect God we like best: ill-tempered, ignorant, or impotent. Jewish sources endorse all of these at various times and in various texts. We'll explore a bit of the first two, but then devote our focus to the third, which holds the most merit for modern minds, and has the best chance of helping to motivate us to action.

The first idea, that God knows what is going on and perhaps *could* fix it but doesn't, has many sources to evidence it in the Torah itself. God often seeks to explicitly punish humanity, bemoans having created humanity, and more than once has to be stopped from an impulsive murder spree by one of the human heroes of the text. At one point [Ex. 32], Moses literally shames God into not murdering the entire population of Israelites, not by appealing to compassion, but by appealing to the reputational damage such a killing spree would incur... among the *Egyptians.*

This vision of God is one who is capricious, cruel, and often at odds with the language of compassion and mercy that is used so often elsewhere. In this notion, we experience suffering because God can't control God's temper, wants to punish us, or deems our misery a key part of our spiritual development. In some Jewish sources this is discussed as *yisurin shel ahavah* (loving sufferings), and the idea that God causes us suffering because it's good for us (or helps to expunge our misdeeds, as Islam often suggests), is not rare.

The second idea, that God has the power to fix everything and would do so if God knew about it, offers us a distant, ignorant God. This is the God of the Hebrew notion of *hester panim* (hidden face), who plays hide-and-seek with the world, who took several centuries to notice the Israelites' suffering in Egypt, and who, in the Garden of Eden, has to genuinely inquire, *ayekha,* where are you? While it may be comforting to believe that God *would* fix all the awful things about life, it doesn't inspire much confidence. The religious pursuit under this model tends to encourage us to take actions to get God's attention. Prayer and fasting become central, as the idea is that, with enough self-inflicted suffering, we can force God to pay attention to all the rest of the suffering.

Neither of these fully account for the *origin* of evil, and both are deeply unsatisfactory. Why work as hard as a Jew must to develop a relationship with a God who is either an ill-tempered torturer or is clueless and concealed? Therefore, our best chance of developing a workable theodicy for the modern world, rooted deeply in Jewish thought is the third option: we have to dispense with the idea that God is omnipotent.

All-Powerful is Overrated

If we can take a step back, we may ask, why is it that we even think of God as *omnipotent* in the first place? Yes, it is clear that the Torah and the Hebrew Bible endorses the idea that God is the only God. There is no other. God formed the universe in which we live and sustains it still, every moment of every day, in the soul-sparks of every living thing. Yet none of that, strictly speaking, means that God is all-powerful. God is very *very* powerful – no doubt more powerful than anything else by quite a significant margin – but 'all-powerful'? To accept the third option presented above isn't actually very challenging, because a look into Jewish sources may demonstrate that God was never omnipotent to begin with.

Certainly God is not all-powerful in the Tanakh. God is routinely frustrated by all the things that are beyond the reach of the divine – most notably, human will. By definition our aggressive insistence on human will and freedom means that God is *not* all-powerful. Rabbi Abraham Joshua Heschel wrote often about the fact that "omnipotence is not a Jewish idea."[167] He attributed the gradual assumption that Judaism, like its Abrahamic cousins, advanced a notion of God as all-powerful, to the influence of Islamic theology on the post-Talmudic generation of Sages.[168] In fact, the innumerable *midrashim* and *aggadot* of Rabbinic Literature which affirm a non-omnipotent God is evidence enough of this.

The real question is: since God is not all-powerful, is that state a result of God's choice or simply a description of God's nature? In other words, is God limited voluntarily or necessarily? Many ingenious ideas have been conceived to help answer this – the most beautiful of which is the notion of *tsimtsum* (contraction) in Lurianic Kabbalah. There, God is envisioned as self-contracting prior to forming the universe(s) in which we now live. In order for there to be anything that was not-God, a voluntary and necessary sacrifice needed to take place, in which God retreated, leaving an empty space, a void in which emanation and creation could then take place.

This goes sideways fast (as we discussed in Chapter 3) and the resulting *shevirat hakélim* (breaking of the vessels) results in a world in which God is limited and catastrophe has struck. The conditions are non ideal, and they leave a considerable amount of room for chaos to operate within. Since the preeminent quality of God is order, chaos, randomness and entropy can be seen to counteract the influence of the divine animating force in the universe. In God's obligatory compromise state, there is simply a certain amount of brokenness that remains. That can be seen as the cause and origin of what we experience as evil. God is not responsible for evil because God is not all-powerful. Instead, God requires our assistance in the continual creation of the world, purging the chaos that remains and restoring the broken pieces of prior worlds back into their ideal configuration.

Isn't it better to choose to believe in a God who yes, is not all powerful, but is a God who we can connect with, who needs our help, who is dependent on us as actors and partners in creation? Isn't it easier to comprehend evil when we see it as a task to undertake, a challenge to respond to, rather than as the result of God's malevolent or benign neglect? As far as functional theology goes, the third option of those presented by Rabbi Kushner's structure is by far the best. God is not able to stop all the ills of the world. God is aware of them, and wants to see the project of creation and the conquering of chaos completed, but, simply, purely, essentially – cannot. Not without us.

Human Evil, Natural Evil

One of the key points of any discussion of theodicy is the categorisation of evil. That is, are all sufferings the same? Are the awful tragedies of war indistinguishable from the disasters inflicted by hurricanes? Can we really see the harm caused by violent crime as being essentially identical to the harm caused by chronic disease? This leads to an important separation of two *types* of evil – which can, at times, lead to a more sophisticated understanding of the nature of evil in consonance with the third position outlined above (that God is not all-powerful and requires our action to complete creation and conquer chaos).

If one accepts that there is such a thing as agency – some degree of free will no matter how small – then human evil (that caused by people's free choice) is easy enough to explain. One of the 'red herrings' of theodicy is that anytime a discussion of suffering is raised, inevitably, someone will reach a point in which they shout out: 'But what about the Holocaust?!' It is a certainty, a guarantee, a timeless law of the universe that all debates around suffering inevitably pass through Auschwitz. Yet, upsettingly, the Holocaust is the type of suffering that's *easiest* to explain. There is no mystery. Nazi Germany was not a force of nature, it was a product of human choice. Perhaps we don't want to accept that for millions of people the Holocaust *was* the result of their free choice, that they wanted it. However hard that truth about our fellow humans may be to swallow, its factuality remains intact.

Indeed, a large part of the confusion surrounding how we talk about suffering is the conflation of human evil with natural evil. A murder is not the same as a monsoon, the harm one person inflicts on another is distinct from the harm caused by a hurricane. To answer Auschwitz is not difficult, but its lessons for us perhaps remain unlearned. Rabbi Heschel, in a powerful speech given in 1967 said:

> The question about Auschwitz to be asked is not "Where was God?" but rather "Where was man?" The God of Abraham has never promised always to hold back Cain's hand from killing his brother. To equate God and history is idolatry. God is present when man's heart is alive. When the heart turns to stone, when

man is absent, God is banished, and history, disengaged, is distress. What should have been humanity's answer to the Nazi atrocities? Repentance, a revival of the conscience, a sense of unceasing, burning shame, a persistent effort to be worthy of the name human, to prevent the justification of a death-of-man theology, to control the urge to cruelty.[169]

So, let us address and then dismiss human evil, for now. Human evil is the easiest to explain: the Torah is clear on the fact that humans are given the choice of how to act, and that often, to their detriment, they choose violence, harm, and destruction. "The God of Abraham," Heschel reminds us, "never promised always to hold back Cain's hand from killing his brother." To expect otherwise is absurd, and frankly, to think too highly of humans. As we discussed in Chapter 6, humans are not 'sinners', but nor are they 'saints.' A large part of the suffering that is experienced in the world is simply a result of individuals' and societies' bad choices.

But what of the suffering that comes about which can claim no human agent? What of disease and flood and famine and natural disaster? To answer these we must turn to those choices above – either God is unaware, uninterested, or unable to completely prevent such suffering. Yet, in addition to justifying or absolving God from this equation, we must also reevaluate our own place in it. According to many Jewish thinkers, a large part of the suffering we experience is perspectival. This doesn't diminish the misery associated with it, but it does help contextualise the bigger picture.

Take the small example of a bacterial infection. If your body is won over by the bacteria's offensive capabilities, if your organs begin to fail because the bacteria flourishes within them, if the resources of your cells are reappropriated for the sake of this invasive parasite – to whom is it bad, and to whom is it good? Obviously to us, it is suffering. Yet to the bacterium, it is a wild success, a glorious celebration of life and growth. Should we concern ourselves with the perspectives of bacteria? Probably not. Nor need we willingly surrender to the life-goals of other organisms that come at the expense of our own flourishing – but we also cannot forget that the suffering implied by such an encounter is not itself universal.

The strategy of Maimonides in particular, in his *Guide for the Perplexed*, was to attempt to inculcate this wider perspective on suffering among his readers. Two modern commentators and interpreters of his effort discuss it as such. First, Joel Kraemer, whose monumental biography of Maimonides looks to explain his thought as well as his life:

> If we consider the entire universe, we realize that it is not for the sake of a single individual or even for the entire human species. We must judge the world from a universal perspective, not from a limited human viewpoint. We must be aware that no being is alone, that we are all parts of a whole, all humanity and the totality of the universe. Then we feel serene, aware that the only evil is moral evil, and this depends upon us.[170]

Here we have a different angle on the dichotomy of human vs. natural evil. Maimonides, according to Kraemer, suggests that it is natural evil which isn't really evil. The only suffering then, is that caused by each other, and that we have the tools to address. This can be an empowering suggestion, but perhaps not a comforting one to someone suffering from disease and disaster. Again, dispassionately, Micah Goodman suggests a similar interpretation of suffering in Maimonides's thought:

> The individual tends to project his personal distress onto the whole of existence. If a rainstorm ruins one's long-planned outdoor event, he might, in disappointment and pique, look at the world as a terrible place. It is hard for him to step back from his dismay or sadness and ask whether, from the point of view of the farmer who is desperate for rain, the world is also terrible at that moment. People paint the whole of reality in the hues of their own experience. The unstated premise underlying the claim that the world is bad is a certain self-centeredness, that is, the world is supposed to satisfy personal needs and that when it does not do so it is failing in its purpose. Liberating oneself from this egocentric point of view saves one from turning one's own pain into a theological problem.[171]

In this interpretation of Maimonides's thought, he very much resembles the Greek philosophers who he so keenly read, particularly the Stoics, who emphasise the perspectival nature of evil. Take for example only one of hundreds of similar teachings among the late Stoics who have survived mostly through Latin literature:

> Nature's aim for everything includes its cessation just as much as its beginning and its duration – like someone throwing up a ball. How can it be good for the ball on the way up and bad on the way down, or even when it hits the ground? How can it be good for a bubble when it forms and bad when it bursts? A candle is a similar example.[172]

So What Do We Do?

We can combine together the two approaches we have seen – for they reach the same conclusion but begin at opposite ends: Maimonides teaches us that natural evil is really just a matter of perspective, and the rejection of omnipotence allows us to understand God's limitations in addressing our miseries. What is left is an incredibly potent role for human action.

A huge amount is attributed to human action – both the cause of suffering and its resolution. Regarding the cause, even a modern Maimonidean such as Ḥakham José Faur can reassure us that the flaws of the world are our fault: "the imperfections in the world are not the effect of a subaltern god, as per Gnostic theology, but the consequence of human failure to realise the 'image of God' within."[173]

This notion, that we have failed to manifest ourselves as adequate vehicles for the divine, is powerful and compelling. It allows us to understand the sufferings we inflict on one another while also offering a way to begin to resolve them. Mostly, it leaves us with a sense that our response to suffering should be action. God is our partner in suffering just as in Creation – the work of perfecting the world is a covenantal and contractual responsibility, one we eschew at our own peril. Rabbi Heschel, addressing a conference of Quaker leaders in Germany in 1938 articulated this beautifully:

> There is a divine dream which the prophets and rabbis have cherished and which fills our prayers, and permeates the acts of true piety. It is the dream of a world, rid of evil by the grace of God as well as by the efforts of man, by his dedication to the task of establishing the kingship of God in the world. God is waiting for us to redeem the world. We should not

> spend our life hunting for trivial satisfactions while God is waiting constantly and keenly for our effort and devotion.[174]

God is 'waiting constantly and keenly for our effort and devotion'. God needs us – or as Heschel famously put it when titling one of his books, God is in search of man. This shift in thinking, from attributing all our misfortune to God's punishment, to realising that suffering is a call to action, to work in partnership with the divine spark of Life, is essential for today's world. Modernity has made this call more obvious than ever before. If Rabbi Heschel, on the eve of the Second World War, in *Germany*, could assure his listeners of this, then we can bear to hear it today.

In 1952, the Swiss psychoanalyst Carl Jung published a small book which served as his only notable exegesis of a biblical story, *Answer to Job*. The book is ultimately a vindication of Christianity, in which Jung sees Job's story as a precursor to the New Testament narrative. This is upsettingly predictable. There are some interesting ideas, like the rather explicit suggestion that God had to sacrifice his own son (Jesus) in repentance for what God did to Job (who was completely innocent) – but ultimately, Jung's lack of knowledge and familiarity with the Hebrew text is on display in his analysis.

It is striking that a parable of suffering which is ambiguous, at best, in its meaning, should become such a by-word for our modern world. From Jung's attempt to analyse Job's morality to the *midrashic* take of *Good Omens*, Job has had many and extensive afterlives as a character. Yet, almost all of these engagements with Job's story get it wrong – or at least, don't understand it from the Jewish point of view in which the story is obviously written. Typically, this is because they are asking the wrong questions – and when one asks the right question, the answer can be surprising.

The Actual Answer to Job

The question that we should be asking of the Book of Job, according to Ḥakham Solomon David Sassoon, is this: who wrote it? Job, like many books in the *Ketuvim* (Writings) section of the Hebrew Bible, is anonymous and lacks much exposition. The story of Job takes place in an uncertain era and in an indefinite location. It could be anywhere, anytime – and perhaps that's the point. Just because no author signs off on Job doesn't mean we can't attempt to identify the voice behind the story, though, and Ḥakham Sassoon made an incredibly powerful argument for an unlikely source: Jeremiah.

In his *Siḥah al Iyyov* (Lecture on Job), Ḥakham Sassoon attempts to prove that the true author of Job is the prophet Jeremiah. He does so through literary comparison, similar use of language and ideas, and ultimately through comparing the moral message of both books. He is quite convincing, and in attributing Job to Jeremiah, the book takes on a whole new meaning. The 'answer to Job' which Jung and so many were seeking is, it would seem, already very much present, if only we see the link to the great Spokesman (Prophet) of Jeremiah. Job is, literally, a jeremiad.

It is worth reproducing Ḥakham Sassoon's lecture here in full, but we don't have space enough to do this. We will, however, translate (likely for the first time), a passage from it to demonstrate the point. The question of suffering and the answer that we might offer to Job as well as any other sufferer is not what we would expect. In the most Jewish way imaginable, Job's question (why has this happened to me and how can this represent the much-acclaimed divine justice?) is answered with another question – one that can shape our behaviour and our understanding of our own sufferings:

> **God says to Job: "Would you impugn my justice? Will you condemn Me to vindicate**

yourself?" [40.8] God has revealed here to Job that the root of Job's error is that he wants to see himself as free from any guilt. This is his intention when he argues against God, asking why God has given profit to the wicked rather than meted out justice to them. But, Job does all this, perhaps without even really knowing it, for a different purpose: '**Will you impugn my justice, condemning me to justify yourself?**' Job wants to see God as responsible and himself as completely blameless, as though he had no stake at all in the events of his life!

But God will not agree with him. God says to him: 'I'm not your servant to cleanse the world of wickedness so that you can live in peace and tranquility – that's not my job! I have placed people like you in the world in order that they will fight for justice and righteousness. If you have a strong feeling for justice, morality, and rectitude, then *you* need to do something about it. Don't sit there hugging yourself and crying out: 'Why has this happened to me?!' You have inverted the structure of creation – this is not the order which I set out in my world.

So God says to him: **"Do you have an arm like God's? Can your voice thunder like the divine?"** [40.9] That is, if you feel so strongly that you are able to speak against me about all the bad things and you know how to lift your voice against God.... then use that same energy to counter the wicked instead of arguing with God.

> **"Deck yourself with grandeur and eminence, clothe yourself in glory and majesty"** [40.10] Embrace the righteous anger you have wielded against me and use it against the wicked!
>
> **"Scatter wide your ranging anger, see every proud person and bring them low"** [40.11] Cherish your anger, use it against the arrogant and bring them down – why are you just sitting around?!
>
> **"See every arrogant person and humble them, bring them down where they stand. Bury them throughout the earth, hide their faces in obscurity. Then, even I will praise you, for the triumph you have won."** [40.12-14] I love justice and righteousness, but I love it more when human beings do right and justly and don't leave it all for me – so why haven't you done it?![175]

The question that Ḥakham Sassoon leaves hanging: *why haven't you done it?!*, completely inverts our expectations of Job. Rather than see Job, as Jung did, as totally blameless, Ḥakham Sassoon demonstrates how Job is being reprimanded for not taking some responsibility. The speech from the whirlwind is a rebuke of the expectation that it is God's responsibility to save mortals from suffering. In Ḥakham Sassoon's narration of this encounter, the lesson is obvious – Job's story is there to teach us to respond to suffering with action, to remind us of the incredible power we possess, and to confirm that, for better or worse, the world was not designed to be free of suffering.

In the midst of misery, this may be little comfort. Yet, when we can gain some perspective on our sufferings, perhaps we can encounter God, as Job does, and walk away motivated to redress the misfortunes of the world. We are not meant to relish suffering (God forbid), nor see it as productive punishment, expiation for sins, or a way of advancing our spiritual lives. We are meant to fight it where and when and however we can.

Our sufferings need not be dear to us, but neither should they challenge our conception of God. If we are willing to do away with omnipotence (which never should have been part of Judaism anyway) and willing to see our perspective within the framework of all Life – then we are left with the task, the sacred responsibility, to be God's agents and partners in creation, in crafting the perpetual present and imbuing it with a sense of goodness, justice, and righteousness.

In a famous exchange in the Talmud, we can see an apt response to suffering on display. Rabbi Ḥiyya is ill, and his friend and colleague visits him. Once they establish that his illness is not something he values and he doesn't see in it any reward, the answer is simple: action – collective, collaborative, creative action.

> Rabbi Ḥiyya bar Abba fell ill
> – and Rabbi Yoḥanan went in to visit him.
> He said to him:
> – Are your sufferings dear to you?
> He replied: Neither they nor their reward.
> He said to him: Give me your hand.
> He gave him his hand and he raised him.[176]

Chapter Eleven

Choose Your Own Death-venture // *Afterlife(s)*

When I die,
God will unravel my embroidery
thread by thread,
and seaward, cast my colours
to treasuries among abyssal depths.
Maybe God will transform them into a flower –
or perhaps a butterfly instead,
dark as the softest nights,
dim as the nights of life.

Zelda, When I Die

"Death", Neal Schusterman wrote in his novel *Scythe,* "makes the whole world kin." All who live, have lived, and will ever live are doomed to die. The pretense that, just maybe, there is some other way out dangles over our minds as a dangerous lure. In Judaism, death is correctly understood as universal, natural, and most critically, equalising. All distinctions are levelled by the soil of the grave. We give no attention to status, class or reputation when we treat the dead with dignity. Yet, while we all must die, we also share equally in the ambiguity of what comes next.

To ask, 'what happens after we die?' is to resign oneself to a dissatisfying silence in place of an answer. The Torah is honest – it claims no Fields of Elysium nor pearly gates to await us. The grave is a place of silence, where the dead remain and are unable to reach the light-filled land of life.

As Judaism grew and evolved, Jewish contact with Zoroastrian religion produced an idea of bodily resurrection (*teḥiyyat hamétim*), a concept which Jewish thinkers struggled to explain then, as well as now. Simultaneously, the Torah's bleak vision of the underworld was transformed into a bifurcated promise of two more descriptively endowed realms: *gan éden* (Garden of Eden) and *gé hinnom* (Valley of Children's' Screams)[177]. Lastly, the accretion of all these concepts of afterlives concluded with the addition of *gilgulé neshamot* (transmigration of souls). Gilgul (cycling) added a fourth voice to the quartet of afterlife beliefs, becoming positively mainstream by the mediaeval period.

These four ideas of 'life after death' (an underworld, the return of the dead, a 'good place' and 'bad place', and reincarnation) all coexist in Jewish thought today. A Jew who would like to know what to expect on the other side of the veil has options from which to choose. None of them are dogma, strictly speaking, although some have been favoured more or less among different communities, times, and places. We will explore a few of the sources behind all four, giving special attention to that which offers the most robust worldview to modern minds, *gilgul*. Before we do that, in keeping with the titular goal of this book, we must first explore what Judaism *does not* think happens after death.

Sorry, Not Sorry

There are no pearly gates, no harmonious reunions in fields of lavender and poppy, no winged angels with harps and halos, no infinite supply of your favourite ice cream flavour, no awards ceremony, no dewy-eyed courtesans waiting for you, and no exclusive poker game with sainted souls. Equally, there is no fiery punishment, nor icy wastes, nor torture-obsessed demonic enforcers. No pits of lava, or feces, or tar or anything – no pits of stuff. There are no Sisyphean or Promethean punishments of repeated body horror or menial chores. There is no Heaven and there is no Hell.

This is an important first step in understanding what Judaism does articulate about the afterlife. Once we are willing to do away with Hell (and who wouldn't?) as well as Heaven (harder to part with), we can breathe easier and evaluate the options before us clear-eyed. The whole Christian drama of salvation from Hell, the dominion of the Devil, and the absurd amount of high Renaissance torture porn that decorates the walls of churches – all of it – is wonderfully foreign to the Jewish imagination. Even within those texts that endorse a notion of 'a good place' and a 'bad place' the punishments in the bad place are temporary, purifying, and fairly minor, all things considered.

Critically, there is not some 'other place' where the dead presently are. All four of the views surveyed below accept that the interpenetration of the living and the dead is a given. This is well-illustrated by the term the Sages chose to refer to the afterlife: *olam ha-ba*. Often translated as 'The World to Come', this simplifies the grammar and sacrifices syntax. "The World that Is Coming" is the correct translation of *olam ha-ba* and that distinction is tense, meaningful and magnetic. The other world is not something that will occur later, it is coming, now, presently, in our lives and in our times. Life after life is constantly on its way, shortly to arrive to disrupt our lives with the experience of death.

If, as we have discussed previously, life is itself Divine, then how do we understand death? Death too is always on its way. Death is the World that Is Coming for it remains only ever just out of sight. The sneaking sense that death is just around the corner, that a momentary lapse in the routine of reality would permit it to penetrate our lives – that is what we mean by *olam ha-ba*.

The reason it is always so close, perpetually in pursuit, is because Life (which is God) is a matter of keeping Death at bay. Death is nothing more than the eventual and inevitable victory of entropy. The forces of chaos controlled through collaborative creation reach us sooner or later – and leave us with that pressing and unanswerable question: "...and then what happens?"

Holy Hades: She'ol

Robert Macfarlane, in his book *Underland*, narrates the Saami people's conception of the afterlife as a bizarro world – a realm in which everything is a "perfect inversion of the human realm, with the ground always the mirror-line, such that 'the feet of the dead, who must walk upside down, touch those of the living, who stand upright'"[178] Like many mythologies, the Saami's underworld is an alternate reality, a realm of the dead to match the world of the living – and like most, it is physically located under the ground. Both of these criteria are present in the Torah's underworld, She'ol, too.

She'ol is linked grammatically to the word for 'asking' or 'inquiring'. Presumably this is because the expectation was that one would ask things of the spirits of the dead, a necromantic form of sorcery evidenced by the Hebrew Bible in the famous example of the Pit Mistress of Ayin Dor.[179] This story is worth reading closely if we wish to understand what exactly She'ol might be.

Chapter 25 of 1 Samuel begins with the prophet's death. After nearly three chapters of tangents, the story returns to its theme in 28:3: "Shmu'él had died and been eulogised by all of Israel and he was buried in his home city of Ramah. Sha'ul had forbidden necromancy from the land." Two things stand out here: the strange juxtaposition of these two facts (like Chekhov's gun, telling us both that someone has died and that, by the way, necromancy was banned, is fabulous foreshadowing, and the fact that Saul's name (Sha'ul) is identical to that of the underworld (She'ol).[180] Despite his own edict, Saul is driven to seek out a Pit Mistress after his attempt to get God to answer his questions fails.

Having tried dream divination, stone-throwing (*urim)*, and asking the Spokespeople (*nevi'im*, or prophets) without success, Saul is pleased to discover that there is a Pit Mistress for hire nearby. He dresses in a disguise, ditches most of his royal bodyguard, and seeks this expert in ghost extraction in the dark of the night. He is clear about his wishes: "Use your pit magic, please, and summon for me a specific person?" She, evidently a law-abiding pit mistress, demurely deflects: "Surely you know what Saul has done, cutting off necromancy from the land. So what, are you trying to entrap me and get me killed?!" Saul swears an oath (a serious business in Ancient Israel) assuring her that no harm will fall upon her.

Evidently the oath is enough to bypass her reservations, as she immediately replies: "Who do you want me to call up?" After Saul explains that he wants the recently-deceased and highly-revered Prophet/Judge/Kingmaker Samuel, she recognises her inquirer, freaks out, and accuses him: "Why have you deceived me?!" Somehow again the king reassures her (through persuasion or coercion, very unclear which), and she sees: "divine beings coming up from the earth".[181] Saul cannot see what she can, and he has to ask her to describe her vision. Like a spiritualist medium at a séance she feeds him what he wants to hear: "I see an old man wrapped in a robe!".

Saul couldn't see his old friend emerge from below, but he can hear him, and he gets an earful. When Samuel realises that Saul has broken his *own* law to force him up from below he validates his previous prophecy, condemning Saul and confirming that his kingship is forfeit. After the whole ordeal, Saul is exhausted and miserable. The Pit Mistress looks after him, feeding him before she'll allow him to return home. The story ends there, but it demonstrates something important about the idea of She'ol: to the Hebrew Bible, it is taken for granted that the world of the dead is 1) under the ground, 2) accessible through magic and divination, and 3) similar to ours in meaningful ways.[182]

This story is worth looking at closely not only because it is so often misunderstood, but moreover, because it demonstrates how deep the idea of an underworld sat in the Hebrew Bible. Frustratingly, we have almost no direct descriptions of She'ol. It was so universal, so obvious, that the authors of biblical texts never bother to narrate its nature for the future reader. We are left to deduce from the references scattered through the Tanakh, including the story above, what She'ol was like. In many ways it resembles the ancient Greek notion of Hades, or the Sumerian Ereshkigal. She'ol was, as best we can tell, not unique – an underworld like other underworlds.

Genesis abounds with hints to She'ol's omnipresence in the life, and death, of its characters. To take but one example, when Ya'akov (Jacob) describes his grief at being told that Yosef (Joseph) is dead, the text narrates: "All his sons and all his daughters rose up to comfort him; but he refused to be comforted; and he said: 'I will go down to She'ol, to my son, while still mourning.'" [37.35] This melodramatic tone from one of our patriarchs is not exceptional, nor is the evocation of She'ol as place near at hand, just below the ground. In case there was any doubt, She'ol opens up (literally), when we read the story of Koraḥ and his abortive rebellion.

There, after Moses has seen off Koraḥ's challenge, an unusual punishment is decreed: Koraḥ and those who followed him will be devoured by She'ol, skipping the typically requisite medial step of actually dying:

> [...] and the earth opened its mouth and swallowed them up with their households, all Koraḥ's people and all their possessions. went down alive into She'ol, with all that belonged to them; the earth closed over them and they vanished from the midst of the congregation.

> All Israel around them fled at their shrieks, for they said, 'The earth might swallow us!' [Num. 16:32-34]

The scene is difficult to imagine, but yet again the story affirms the fact of Sh'eol, and how near at hand it is. All that's needed for the land of the dead to burst into the life of the living is a fissure in the earth, a crack by which death gets in and snatches up Koraḥ. Uncommon as this level of drama is, it reveals how fluent the Hebrew Bible was with an idea of an underworld. By deduction we can conclude that She'ol was believed to be a cavernous underland, where those who died dwelled in some recognisable form, unable to return to the surface world.

We know nothing of what might have occurred to those shades below in She'ol – only that they could not return, engendering a tragic hopelessness. Yeshayahu says of She'ol that, "[it] cannot praise You, death cannot celebrate You; those that go down into the pit cannot hope for Your truth." [38.18] Job similarly emphasises the bleak fate of that subterranean realm: "As a cloud fades away, so one that goes down to She'ol shall not come up." [7.9] The stuff of clouds, once dispersed, can never be put back together. The process cannot be reversed. So too, the journey to Sh'eol is one directional, and the entropy that causes the event of death continues even after, dispersing the person into increasingly vaporous wisps in the dark depths below the earth.

Back Again – Resurrection

Maintaining a belief in a She'ol-like underworld is difficult. No one wishes to think that their loved ones are trapped in a dark and dismal realm, unable to do anything but watch themselves disintegrate. Moreover, no one wishes to imagine the same fate for themselves. So, it is no surprise that other ideas, ones that offered more hopeful visions of life after death, easily took hold in the fertile but untilled soil of Jewish thinking on the afterlife. For many modern Jews, the belief in the resurrection of the dead is a given. This is due, in part, to Maimonides attempting to place it within his thirteen principles of Judaism (a deeply flawed and ultimately failed project). It is also because resurrection became the dominant belief in Christianity, and thus back-filled Jewish thinking in Europe, where an idea that once was nonsensical became normative.

Many Jewish sages have tried admirably to make resurrection make sense – but it is a doomed enterprise. Special credit goes to Ḥakham Ḥayyim David haLevi, who, in his *teshuvot* collection known as *Aseh Lekha Rav*, addresses the questioner who asks, how, in light of modern knowledge and contemporary science, we could possibly accept the notion of all the dead rising in their own bodies at some future time. Ḥakham HaLevi is masterful – he summons research from Elizabeth Kubler-Ross, scientific studies of near death experiences, and some slightly shady science from Descartes regarding the pineal gland to suggest a way forward. In his *teshuvah* he describes that resurrection will work through a tiny spinal bone called *luz* (almond), either identified as one of the cervical vertebrae or the coccyx[183] bone at the base of the spine, which he claims remains after decomposition, and, containing DNA in its marrow, can be used as a holographic source to recreate a new body.

For Ḥakham HaLevi, this bit of bone, together with the soul, will allow the body to be reformed. Frustratingly, this still doesn't answer many of the other key questions one might ask of resurrection: at what age is one resurrected? What if the body has been completely destroyed (coccyx included)? How can the more than fifteen billion people who have ever lived return all at once? Where does one return? Again, to his credit, he really does try and explain resurrection in a modern, logical method – but such a task is fated to fail. He writes about this model of projection:

> The idea of the resurrection of the dead is not so far from understanding by the human intellect. For example, what is this like? It is like a person who made idols and icons out of a mold that they had. If it so happens that one of the idols fell and broke, is it not easy for this person to fashion a new idol with the same form and image exactly as the first? They can do so using the same mold as before, from it they can make one just like the first. So too is the issue of a body that has died. The soul remains in the world of souls, and when the time comes to resurrect the dead, using that same soul as a mold, a new body can easily and simply be fashioned in the exact same image and form – because the same soul will enter it anew and give it form and image again as it had before.[184]

Compared to the idea of She'ol we saw earlier, this dynamic recreation of the body offers a more persuasive promise. Unlike She'ol it also has considerably more sources to rely on – although none from the Torah itself. Suggestions of an afterlife resulting from bodily resurrection only begin to appear in the prophets who lived during the Babylonian Exile (6th century BCE), a time during which Jewish thinkers came into close contact with the faith of Zoroastrianism, including its belief in resurrection. Two examples of prophetic sources which have often provided the prooftext for resurrection:

> Then God said unto me: 'Son of man, these bones are the whole house of Israel; behold, they say: Our bones are dried up, and our hope is lost; we are clean cut off. Therefore prophesy, and say unto them: Thus says the Lord, God:

> Behold, I will open your graves, and cause you to come up out of your graves, O My people; and I will bring you into the land of Israel. [Ez. 37:11-12]

> And many of them that sleep in the dust of the earth shall awake, some to everlasting life, and some to reproaches and to everlasting abhorrence. [Daniel 12:2]

Ezekiel and Daniel both were *au fait* with Babylon and its religious tendencies. The emergence of a concept of resurrection is only reasonable when that was the first idea of an afterlife they were exposed to other than She'ol, and the description of She'ol was so uninviting. We want to believe that there is some positive outcome awaiting us on the other side of death.

The Sages were well aware that resurrection has no biblical basis, and expended great intellectual effort to explain away this absence. In Sifré, an early Midrash, Rabbi Simai says: "There is no section in the Torah that does not deal with the resurrection, but we lack the strength to expound it."[185] Perhaps he protests a bit too much, as the overcompensating claim that the entire Torah deals with resurrection is difficult to justify.

Instead of trying to prove the point, many rabbinic texts simply imagine the logistics of resurrection. The Midrash teaches that God will make underground paths so that the bodies of the dead can roll along them to get to the land of Israel (Tanḥuma). The Talmud objects to the rolling when taught by Rabbi Ile'a, with a rebuttal by Rabbi Abba Salla Rava who claims: "rolling is an ordeal that entails suffering for the righteous!" Abayé then offers a compromise: tunnels are prepared for them in the ground instead.[186] If the Sages lived in an era of pneumatic tube systems, maybe they would see in their rapid transit an even better analogy.

Regardless of the particulars, the idea of *billions* of partially or fully decomposed (reconstituted from the *luz*?) bodies slamming through the earth's mantle in a madcap dash to get to the land of Israel has more the makings of a lighthearted zombie film than it does a serious theology about the afterlife.

While resurrection is very appealing in principle, it is hard to conceive of in practice. Despite the affirmations from many quarters that it is an unassailable component of Jewish belief, it is fairly late to Jewish thought, shows a great deal of foreign influence, and fails to address the self-obvious questions about its application that would occur to almost any listener. As unsatisfying as She'ol as an option for our post-death existence, resurrection ultimately ceded intellectual ground to another idea: that of otherworldly realms of pleasure and punishment, the good place and the bad place, *gan éden* and *gé hinnom*.

The Good Place & The Bad Place

The vision of resurrection and the grim depiction of She'ol are both complemented and compounded with the third major afterlife concept to be taken up by Judaism: *gan éden* and *gé hinnom*. Using these two places (the Garden of Eden and the Valley of Hinnom) as metonyms for supernatural realms of reward and punishment is the oldest component of the idea – the details of these places and their inhabitants were only filled in later.

For the Sages, *gé hinnom* was of very little interest. After-death punishment figured as a very small component of their worldview, and even when they indulged in speculating about it, the descriptions were underwhelming. There are so few clear sources on the nature of *gé hinnom* that by the time of Rabbi David Kimḥi (1160-1235), he is able to narrate in his commentary on Genesis a summary of the opinions available:

> Rabbi Shimon ben Lakish as well as his colleague Rabbi Yannai said that there is no such thing as the common conception of *gé hinnom* as a place of punishment lasting a long time. [...] Other sages said that there most certainly is such a thing as *gé hinnom*, [...] and Rabbi Yehudah bar Ilai claims there is neither a specific day, nor a specific place such as *gé hinnom*, but fire will come forth from the very bodies of the wicked and will consume them with its heat.[187]

Even in such a brief survey it is evident that *gé hinnom* is far from doctrine. It may be for a day, or for a year (a common belief today, when people say the Kaddish for parents who have died for a year on the basis that twelve months is the maximum stay in *gé hinnom*), or it may not be for any time at all. It may be a real place, or it may describe an experience, as Rabbi Yehudah suggests, of some sort of spontaneous combustion. Putting aside the particulars, we can largely disregard the bad place as a sort of boogeyman – no one is quite clear on what or where it is, and few Sages seem to be bothered enough by this fuzziness to attempt to articulate it better.

Instead, there is a robust literature which explores what the *good place* might be like. Often the Sages use the terms *gan éden* (Garden of Eden) and *olam ha-ba* (The World That Is Coming) interchangeably, implying an equality of experience. Most seem to have a positive place in the future world.

In fact, the Sages go to great effort to be *inclusive* with dozens of statements throughout rabbinic literature that begin: 'anyone who does ____ is guaranteed a place in the World That Is Coming'. That blank is filled by many things, including 'anyone who walks four cubits in the land of Israel'[188], 'anyone who recites Psalm

145 three times a day'[189], and 'anyone who has a dream in which they recite Kaddish'.[190] Perhaps the latter was a more common experience in Talmud times, but the point is clear. The goal of the Sages is to try and include as many as possible in the promise of life after death. They do not wish to condemn, but to commend.

This preference for the good place is present in even the earliest strata of sources. Probably the first clear exposition of the afterlife is from Bét Shammai, who the Tosefta tells us taught that:

> There are three groups: one is destined for eternal life, another consigned to eternal ignominy and eternal abhorrence, while those whose deeds are balanced will go down to *gé hinnom*, but when they scream they will ascend from there and be healed.[191]

This desire to redeem even the middling multitude is admirable, and the Talmud follows up on this teaching in its own discussion of the *bénoni*, the mediocre majority, people who are neither good nor bad, but 'whose deeds are balanced':

> Rabba said to Rav Naḥman: What happens to the souls of the mediocre people, who are neither righteous nor wicked? Rav Naḥman said to him: It is good that you asked me this question, for even if I were dead I would not have been able to tell you that! Shmu'él said as follows: These *and* those, the souls of the wicked *and* of the mediocre people, are handed over to Dumah, the angel in charge of spirits. But these, the souls of the mediocre people, have rest, and these, the souls of the wicked, do not have rest.

So while the souls of the mediocre are treated with suspicion, they avoid the punishment decreed on the purely wicked (a category which seems increasingly diminished). More than one might expect seem to be destined for the good place, for a spot in the world yet to arrive, for a seat at the tables of the righteous in the Garden of Eden. The wide circle of the righteous includes Jews and non-Jews, as the discussion of the afterlife tends to take a universal angle. Maimonides even codifies this when, in his Laws of Teshuvah he says: "the righteous among other nations have a place in the World That Is Coming."[192]

We saw in Chapter 8 that the view of the *sheva mitsvot bené no'aḥ* (7 Noahide *mitsvot*) allows for an appreciation of universal morality. This too allows for an afterlife which is not exclusive – it is a meritocracy open to all, even the mediocre, providing they attain a base level of morality and strive to do good in the world. This view is even captured by a charming vignette about two unlikely friends, Rabbi Yehudah haNasi (the compiler of the Mishnah) and his friend and confidant, Marcus Aurelius.[193]

> Once Marcus Aurelius asked Rabbi Yehudah haNasi: Will I be able to enter The World That Is Coming?' 'Yes!' said the Rabbi. 'But,' said Aurelius, 'is it not written, "There will be no remnant to the house of Esau?"' 'That,' Rabbi Yehudah replied. 'applies only to those whose evil deeds are like those of Esau.'[194]

The World That Is Coming is therefore free, open, and accessible to all – even Roman emperors! Yet, the Sages are still remarkably vague about what exactly one should expect from this idyllic afterlife. The Talmud suggests that there are three things which are 'samples' of The World That Is Coming in our own lives: Shabbat, a sunny day, and having sex.[195] Rather than imagine a scene with cloud-borne angels, pearly gates, and tinkling harp music, the Sages attempt to analogise the *good place* through the pleasures of life. Despite such a charming synopsis, other Sages sought to remind their students that any analogies we might seek are inherently insufficient. Rav, evidently, was wont to say:

> The World That Is Coming is not like this world. In The World That Is Coming there is no eating, no drinking, no procreation, no business negotiations, no jealousy, no hatred, and no competition. Rather, the righteous sit with their crowns upon their heads, enjoying the splendour of the Divine Presence.[196]

While it doesn't have quite the same ring as the trifecta of Shabbat, sun and sex – Rav's attempt to imagine *olam ha-ba* is also reliant on analogy, in this case that of a royal court. However the Sages conceived of life after death, these ideas of *gan éden* and *gé hinnom* didn't so much replace She'ol or the expectation of resurrection, but supplemented it. Adding to the layers of complementary (and occasionally contradictory) teachings regarding the afterlife, the final component is the idea of transmigration of souls (*gilgulé neshamot*), which, yet again, is compounded with the existing ideas to shape how we think about life after death.

Spun Right Round

The language of *gilgul* invokes the action of spinning. A *galgal* is a wheel – and the circular recycling of souls which *gilgul* envisions is akin to a wheel as well. Critically, *gilgul*, the Jewish concept of reincarnation, is notably different from that in Vedic (Hindu, Buddhist, etc) traditions, where *samsara*, the wheel of reincarnation, is seen as something to escape. In Jewish sources, *gilgul* is not a punishment *per se*, but a chance at refinement. We are given, these sources teach us, another shot to improve ourselves and the sparks that make up our souls. The wheel we envision is not one spinning in place, but moving ever ahead. With each revolution, with each lifetime, we aim to gain ground, to be better than before.

There are no references whatsoever to *gilgul* in the Torah, the Hebrew Bible, or rabbinic literature. It is, by all accounts, a late addition. The views of the afterlife we have surveyed (She'ol, Resurrection, Heaven/Hell) concatenate chronologically, building up over time like a layer cake. *Gilgul* is the frosting – added last, but also adding the most flavour. What is a cake without frosting, anyway? One way to understand this historical development is through functional theology. People adopt and adapt beliefs that *work* for them. If a belief doesn't help them, doesn't add to their life, then it is abandoned, substituted, or replaced. The doctrines of She'ol, of resurrection, and of *gan éden* and *gé hinnom* were each, in their own ways, incomplete and unsatisfying.

When reincarnation is added into the mix, all of the others are able to be interpreted through it – and since *gilgul* has entered mainstream Jewish thought in the mediaeval period, no further attempt has been made to add a new conception of the afterlife. This means that *gilgul* works – it makes sense. It is useful and natural, and it inherently appeals to a sense of justice. In fact, one of the first mainstream sources to mention the idea is Naḥmanides's commentary on Job, where he hints at the idea that Job may be suffering in part because of his actions in a previous lifetime.[197] We know that this wasn't a completely new idea though, as there is one source that discusses *gilgul* which precedes Ramban by several centuries.

Sa'adia Ga'on (882-942) was a leading thinker in the Abbasid Caliphate and one of the first authors to use Arabic. He was a philosopher as well as a scholar of Halakhah and he served as the clearinghouse and pivot point for the intellectual span of the Jewish world in the ninth century. He was no proponent of *gilgul*, in fact he condemns it, but his condemnation demonstrates the idea's antiquity. For Sa'adia to be so stridently opposed to *gilgul* it must have been prevalent long before him:

> I have found certain people, who call themselves Jews, professing the doctrine of … 'transmigration of souls.' Many of them would even go so far as to assert that the spirit of a human being might enter into the body of a beast or that of a beast into the body of a human being, and other such nonsense and stupidities![198]

While Sa'adia clearly had little time for *gilgul*, once Naḥmanides normalised talking about it in his commentary on Job, the concept took off in the nascent communities of scholars in Provençe and Castille who we now identify with the Kabbalah. When the Zohar was compiled in these communities in the thirteenth century, it included some of the first explanations of how *gilgul* might work, using the imagery of horticulture: "as long as a person is unsuccessful in their purpose in this world, the Holy Blessed One uproots them and replants them over and over again."[199] We return in order to accomplish what was left undone. Here, no limit on transmigrations is suggested, and no condemnation of their necessity – it is a part of the natural world – a metaphorical transplantation.

The Zohar is well aware that this may sound drastic, but it assures us that reincarnation is constantly happening, just slightly in the background:

> Truly, all souls, must undergo transmigration; but humanity does not perceive the ways of the Holy One, how the revolving scale is set up and people are judged every day at all time, and

> how they are brought up before the Tribunal, before they enter into this world and after they leave it. They do not even perceive the many transmigrations and the many mysterious works which the Holy One accomplishes with many naked souls, and how many naked spirits roam about, in the other world, without being able to enter within the veil of the King's Palace.[200]

Classic Zohar – loads of beautiful complex images, but without much practical detail. In some way, we have to appreciate that at least the Zohar is honest. We *don't* know how it works. Ever a mystery, acceptance of the idea of reincarnation isn't conditional on terms and conditions – it is simply a feature of nature, and like so many aspects of the natural world, we are largely unaware of its daily rhythms.

Later sources in Kabbalah attempt to give more detail as to how *gilgul* functions. None are wildly successful (any endeavour which attempts to say with certainty what life after death looks like is doomed to failure), but they are worth considering. The first great systematisation of *gilgul* comes at the hands of Rabbi Ḥayyim Vital, who incorporated *gilgul* centrally into his teaching. He describes in his autobiographical *Sefer haḤezyonot* how he came to understand his past lives and how his teacher, Rabbi Yitsḥak Luria, could identify anyone's previous soul-incarnations based simply on meeting them. In trying to clarify the process of *gilgul*, Vital helpfully lays out three primary reasons why it occurs:

> Regarding reincarnation of souls, why do souls reincarnate? There are various reasons why souls reincarnate: a) they have transgressed on a particular commandment of the Torah; b) To correct a commandment that was neglected

> and is lacking by them; and c) For the sake of others, to guide them and help them to correct.[201]

Excluding the final reason (which resembles the Buddhist concept of a *bodhisattva*), Vital expands and affirms the Zohar's claim: we return because we must. *Gilgul* is not a punishment, but another chance, an opportunity to do better. In this, Vital is also echoed by a later attempt at turning Kabbalah into a philosophical system, this time by Rabbi Moses Ḥayyim Luzzatto (Ramḥal):

> There is a core principle which guides all the ways of the world – and this is that which the highest wisdom has arranged in order to increase [the chance of] success, as I have explained. For a single soul will come to this world many different times in many different bodies. Through this one is able to repair at one point that which was corrupted at another point – or to complete that which was left unfinished. And only at the end of all these transmigrations will the future judgement occur, and thus the soul will be judged on all that which transpired during all the incarnations in which it was transmigrated and all the circumstances of each.[202]

We can see here the attempt to synthesise *gilgul* into the other approaches to the afterlife. Perhaps the soul reincarnates before eventually going to dwell in *gan éden* or to experience a form of resurrection at some future date. Making all four of these ideas work in tandem is not straightforward, nor necessary. The diversity of belief around the afterlife is precisely what provides Judaism such richness. What does Judaism teach about what happens after we die? Well, how long do you have? These four options are all presented to the curious inquirer, and none are mutually exclusive or completely comprehensive. Instead, we are empowered to pick and mix, to combine and create for ourselves a belief which is functional, which works, for us.

A model of this is Rabbi Elia Benamozegh, whose little tractate *Il Mio Credo* (My Faith) has been referenced before in this book, but is worth quoting once more, particularly his statement on the afterlife. In it, he attempts to combine together many of the ideas we've seen, but doing so in his own wonderfully idiosyncratic way:

> I believe that the justice of God is exercised everywhere and always, that everywhere is hell and everywhere heaven; on earth, in the stars, in what we see and in what we do not see. Hell where one suffers, heaven where one finds pleasure. Is it perhaps false then what the theologians say that, while here is where one lives, it is in the next life where one receives the reward? Indeed it is very true, because every phase of our existence, once it is completed, makes the creature descend or ascend by a step in the scale of Beings, and this elevation or abasement which forms the reward or the punishment are definitive, although not irreparable. I say not irreparable because the transmigration of souls, *Gilgul*, is a dogma in every respect worthy of the goodness and wisdom of God, who must prove and reprove so as not to irremediably condemn any of God's creatures. Gilgul is in agreement with the opinion of the best and greatest among ancient and modern thinkers; it is the supreme, almost unique, means to explain the apparent injustices that are seen on earth, and is, in short, almost necessarily required by science.[203]

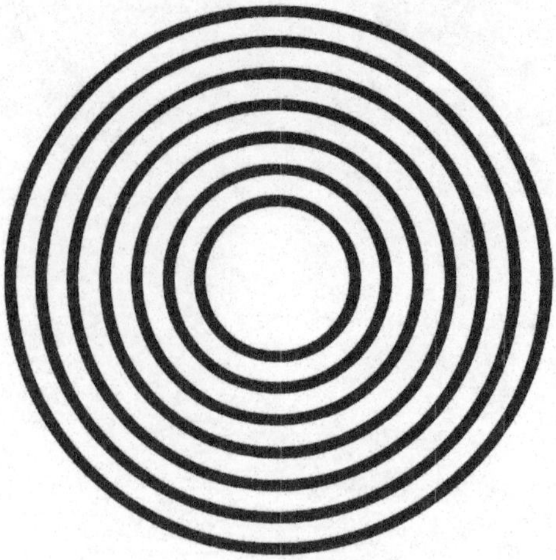

Chapter Twelve

Sacred Sevens // *Cycles*

Time is the substance I am made of.
Time is a river which sweeps me along, but I am the river;
it is a tiger which destroys me, but I am the tiger;
it is a fire which consumes me, but I am the fire.

Jorge Luis Borges, A New Refutation of Time

Frank Brown, an American biologist, did a rather strange experiment in 1954.[204] He took a bunch of Atlantic oysters from the seabed off of Connecticut and shipped them hundreds of miles inland to Northwestern University. There, he put them in brine in a sealed darkroom, shielded from any changes in temperature, water pressure, currents, or light.

Normally, oysters feed with the tides. They open up to eat plankton and algae when the tide comes in, and remain closed other times to protect themselves. He was curious - what would these molluscs do if they weren't able to feel the tide come in and with no environmental signals to indicate it? How would they cope? Would they continue to open, remembering when high tide was in New Haven, even when they were in Chicago?

Amazingly, they did, for two weeks. But then it got even stranger – gradually, their opening time moved later and later each day. After a few weeks a new stable cycle appeared, in which they opened at the same time every day, all in synchronised unison – but the new opening time was 3 hours behind the time that high tide was reached in New Haven. Brown was baffled, until he checked an astronomical almanac and realised that the new time correlated to the ***local*** state of the moon.

Of course, Evanston, Illinois is not near the sea. There are no tides. But the oysters were opening at exactly the time that there *would* be high tide, if there was sea in that spot. This was without any signals of light, heat, water, or temperature. How could they calculate the right time to open and remember it, communicate it, and organise themselves, even in their darkroom?

Brown's experiment became one of the most controversial in biology. He was ridiculed by his peers and largely sidelined from professional conferences. His ideas were dismissed as nonsense, yet, like many great scientists he was eventually proven right. Brown coined the word 'chronobiology' and hypothesized that there must be some mechanism in the oysters' biology that allows them to keep time, a sort of body-clock.

In the decades after Brown was laughed out of the room, this proved to be completely correct, with a whole field developing around what became known as circadian rhythms, chronobiology, and biological timekeeping. In 2017, researchers were awarded the Nobel Prize for discovering a gene which uses the Earth's magnetic field to keep time. Brown died before seeing his views vindicated, but our study of how we keep, perceive, and measure time owes a lot to him.

For many of us, time seems obvious. Like a story – there was a beginning, this is the present, and the future stretches out in front of us. Yet, this is more of a learned, collective hallucination. Italian physicist Carlo Rovelli's recent book, *The Order of Time*, suggests that we interpret events in a logical, sequential, progressive cause-and-effect fashion, only because we're not good at seeing detail. We have seen in our own explorations that creation is a common victim of this hallucinatory impulse – it is easiest to imagine creation as an event, rather than a jumbled anarchic process which is still underway.

The structures we use to process time may be a contrivance, but they are critical to our lives. They also are culturally quite variable.

Judaism has its own unique way of understanding time. Our take on time centres on how we understand past and future, how we divide up days, weeks, months, and years, and how we conceive of the creation, and extinction of the world – the end and beginning of all things.

Facing Backwards

Judaism is famously history-obsessed. Most of our holidays follow the comic (but accurate) tripartite trope of: 1) they tried to kill us, 2) we won, 3) let's eat. Yet, our fascination with history is not only because of how *much* of it there is, or its many ups and downs, each worthy of any historian's eager attention. Our obsession with the past is, in part, a product of the very way we think about time.

In English, when we talk about 'past' and 'future' or 'before' and 'after' we have a certain orientation. The past is behind us, it is what came 'before'. Before you go to the office, you eat breakfast. After you leave work, you will eat dinner. The words themselves reflect this – for instance 'after' originally meant something which was far away in the distance. When we think in English, we are facing the future. The future is in front of us. We say it all the time: 'He has his whole future in front of him,' or 'We've got to face the future' etc. Yet, in Hebrew, it is the opposite.

In Hebrew, *lifnim*, which means 'before' literally means 'facing' or 'in front of' as it is drawn from the word for 'face', *panim*. To talk about the past, we talk about it being in front of our face. And the future? The word for 'after' is *aḥar* and when we talk about something being 'behind' us it is literally, 'after us', *aḥaronah*. So we see that in Hebrew the orientation is the opposite. The past is in front of our faces, while the future is coming up from behind us. Thus you wouldn't say 'She has her whole future in front of her', you'd say 'She has her whole past in front of her' and 'We've got to turn our backs to the future'.

The past is in front of us, and the future behind. As we move forward, we move closer to our history. Meanwhile, the unforeseen future lurks behind our backs, always trying to catch up.

Carlo Rovelli wasn't the first to suggest that cause-and-effect time is an illusion, or that all that takes place are events unconnected to causality. Our Sages had a famous maxim, *én mukdam o muḥar batorah* – there is no 'before' or 'after' in the Torah. Events often happen out of order. The past happens ahead of the future. The Sages were willing and happy to see the Torah as a collection of events, the order of which could be understood in different ways, subjectively, flexibly.

This orientation towards time links up with our understanding of creation (Chapter 3) as well as afterlives (Chapter 11). Events imitate and interpenetrate time. Our history isn't something we left behind, it is right in front of us. The characters of the Torah repeat in our lives – literally through *gilgul*, and figuratively in the universality of their stories. With such an understanding of chronology, we can appreciate the incorrectness of another great myth told about Judaism in the Christian West: the association between Judaism and the invention of linear time.

Circles, Lines, and Spirals

Often you hear the view that Judaism ***invented*** linear time. Western scholars love to trot out this canard that it is Judaism, and the Hebrew Bible, which invents linear time. The trite contrast drawn between 'pagan' culture (which sees time as cyclical) and ancient Israel (who structure time as a line) is, at best, a dramatic oversimplification of a much more complex collection of concepts in Jewish thought.

This was the insight of the scholar Thomas Cahill, whose book *The Gifts of the Jews* suggests that the single biggest contribution of Judaism to civilisation is the idea that time is a linear thing – with a beginning and an end, and the possibility of change as it develops. This allows for capitalism, for technology, for science, for progress, etc. Our whole assumption of the world – that it is moving along a straight line, is, to Cahill, the result of the radical view of Biblical monotheism. Cahill, like most Christians, is reading the Torah through the eyes of the New Testament, and so finds ample evidence for this fabrication.

A key plank in the argument that Judaism is the author of linear time is an assumption that it is Judaism which introduces creation as an event which took place at a certain specific time. As we have seen, that isn't the case at all. The same scholars rely on a misreading of prophecy (see Chapter 7) to claim that Judaism also innovated the 'last day' and developed a clear eschatology. This also, is, at best, an exaggeration. Most of the prophets spoke to and about their own time and place. The few that looked towards the future, or spoke of the 'Day of the Lord' were speaking about what they saw as the near-term outcome of present events.

In stories we tell about the future, the inevitably apocalyptic ones feel inestimably Christian. There is no real Jewish apocalypse story – it just doesn't work. This was brilliantly noted by media critic Rachel Klein in a piece for the online magazine *HeyAlma*, where she attempted to articulate why plots which involved spiralling conceptions of time and time loops (films like *Groundhog Day* or shows like *Russian Doll)* feel inexplicably more Jewish than those in which the world ends in fire and brimstone:

> It is this cyclical motion, like an ever-winding spiral staircase, that is central to Jewish learning and life. Yes, time marches forward, but also, often, we find ourselves back where we started in some way, hopefully with new insights to change the outcome this time

> around. Yes, Jews keep our tragedies in front of mind, but rather than focusing on destruction and its aftermath, we adopt a model for day-to-day living that is more about iterative progress towards a goal.[205]

The one to one association between Judaism and linear time just doesn't hold up. However, Judaism's conception of time also is not completely circular. Like we saw with *gilgul*, the distinction between a wheel spinning in place (Vedic *samsara*) versus a wheel moving forward (Jewish *gilgul*) is echoed here: there is an important difference between a circle and a spiral – what Klein calls 'iterative progress towards a goal.'

A circular view of time argues that everything happens on a fixed track. Like the hands of a clock, time circuits around and returns to where it began, repeating the whole process over and over. A spiral is subtly but importantly different – rather than repeat, it revises. The same shape is in place but the dimensions differ, widening with each lap. We read the entirety of the Torah every year, but each time we are different. The shape persists but its form is flexible.

Part of this conception of time means that we are, by definition, anti-apocalyptic. Even when we discuss the Messianic Era, we do so in keeping with the rhythms and routine of life as it is now. The arrival of the rightful king of Israel to reclaim his throne and restore sovereignty (for this is what and who the Messiah is)[206] is not something which our Sages imagine interrupting the laws of nature or society. Maimonides puts it as clearly as possible in his *Laws of Kings and Their Wars*:

> One should not presume that the Messiah must work miracles and wonders, bring about new phenomena in the world, resurrect the dead, or

> perform other similar deeds. This is definitely not true. Proof can be brought from the fact that Rabbi Akiva, one of the greater Sages of the Mishnah, was one of the supporters of Bar Kokhba and would describe him as the Messiah. He and all the Sages of his generation considered him to be the Messiah until he was killed. Once he was killed, they realised that he was not the Messiah. The Sages did not ask him for any signs or wonders. The main thrust of the matter is: This Torah, its statutes and its laws, are everlasting. We may not add to them or detract from them.
>
> If a king will arise from the House of David who diligently contemplates the Torah and observes its *mitsvot* as prescribed by the Written Law and the Oral Law and as David his ancestor did, he will compel all of Israel to walk in (the way of the Torah) and rectify the breaches in its observance, and fight the wars of God, we may, with assurance, consider him the Messiah. If he succeeds in the above, builds the Temple in Jerusalem, and gathers the dispersed of Israel, he is definitely the Messiah. He will then improve the entire world, motivating all the nations to serve God together.[207]

This description of the Messianic Era is far from the apocalyptic nightmare scenarios which circulate so commonly in the thought of Christianity and Islam. For Judaism, with its helical conception of time, ever-spiralling out and in and back towards itself, there is no 'end of days', no 'rapture', no apocalypse. There is only the hope that, with good leaders and divine assistance, the world can be a better place than it is now, always improving through the collaborative partnership of creation, in which we honour our duty to prepare the perpetual present.

Sacred Sevens

Most cultures have affinities for certain numbers. Even individuals sometimes have a belief that some integers are 'good' and some 'bad'. While we don't cast moral aspersions on any particular number, we do sanctify one specifically: seven. Jews *love* a seven. There are so many significant sevens in Jewish thought it is hard to list them all. Here's just a few:

- The first verse of the Torah has seven words
- The creation story takes place in seven parts
- Shabbat is sanctified as the seventh day
- God visits sevenfold vengeance on Kayin
- There are seven *mitsvot* given to all humanity through Noaḥ
- Pharaoh's dream focusses on seven good years and seven bad ones
- The system of *shemittah* divides time into seven-year units
- Seven of those seven year units concludes with the *yovel*
- The blood of the sacrifices was dashed seven times on the altar
- Seven ancestors whom we count (three men, four women)
- There are seven days of Sukkot and seven days of Pesaḥ
- We count seven weeks (of seven days) during the Omér
- The seventh month of the year, Tishré, begins with Rosh haShanah
- The priests had a seven day period of purification for ordination
- The same seven-day period purified homes from *tsara'at*
- The Menorah has seven branches
- Zekharya has a vision of a seven-eyed stone in Chapter 3
- Yehoshua uses seven circuits around Yeriḥo to destroy its walls
- The Sages ordained that a wedding required seven blessings
- At a wedding the couple will often circumambulate seven times
- After the wedding, they receive guests for seven days
- When someone dies there are seven categories of mourners
- Those mourners are obligated to observe a seven day grief period

- Hebrew has seven letters which have two forms
- There are seven openings in the face
- In Kabbalah, it is the lower seven sefirot that govern reality

We could go on! Assuming a degree of confirmation bias, even if we exclude some for that we find that seven is the most significant number in Jewish thought. In that regard, we're not alone. Alex Bellos, a science journalist, conducted an online survey of peoples' favourite numbers back in 2014, received over 40,000 responses and came out of it with a clear and unequivocal winner: the number seven. Nearly ten percent of all respondents said seven was their favourite number! Bellos suggests a variety of reasons for why this might be in his book, but the simple answer is that seven is just special.[208]

The structure of sevens permeates Jewish thinking about time, from the week all the way up to the universal scale. There has long been a tradition to extrapolate from the biblical agricultural system of *shemittah* (in which one is meant to work the land for six years and then give it a '*shabbat*' year in the seventh in which it lies fallow) all the way up to the cosmos. The Talmud simply takes for granted that this seven-obsessed superstructure repeats, like a fractal, at all scales. It teaches: "Six thousand years shall the world exist, and one [thousand, the seventh], it shall be desolate."[209]

This would suggest that even the universe follows the sacred sevens, a concept that was eagerly picked up by Jewish mystical sources keen to try and figure out the age of the universe. One mediaeval work of Kabbalah, *Sefer haTemunah*, understands the talmudic statement above to refer to *one shemittah cycle only* – meaning that there would be seven cycles of these seven thousands years laid out as follows:

1	2	3	4	5	6	7
1000	8000	15000	22000	29000	36000	43000
2000	9000	16000	23000	30000	37000	44000
3000	10000	17000	24000	31000	38000	45000
4000	11000	18000	25000	32000	39000	46000
5000	12000	19000	26000	33000	40000	47000
6000	13000	20000	27000	34000	41000	48000
7000	14000	21000	28000	35000	42000	49000

In this system then, the universe would appear to exist for 49,000 years with the 50th one thousand-year period being the cosmic *yovel* - in which the universe returns to its primordial foundations. In the Torah the *yovel* (Jubilee) is a chance for all debts to be cancelled, all slaves to be free, and all land to return to its original ancestral leasehold. The cosmic *yovel* would similarly be a restart, perhaps all matter returning to a cosmic singularity in preparation for yet another cycle of boom and crunch, expansion and contraction.

Sefer haTemunah eventually became relegated to the margins of Jewish mysticism by the dominant school of Rabbi Yitsḥak Luria. However, before *Sefer haTemunah* was rejected entirely, another mystic took its theory of cosmic *shemittot*, and did some fabulously interesting maths with it. Rabbi Yitsḥak of Akko was a 14th century kabbalist and student of the Ramban (Naḥmanides). To take the theory of *Sefer haTemunah* and develop it into a more complete cosmological system, Yitsḥak of Akko connected the calculation[210] above with a key verse from Psalm 90: "a thousand years in your sight are but as yesterday."

Based on the interpretation of that verse, Yitsḥak of Akko understood one 'divine day' as one thousand times the length of a 'human year.' If that's the case, then a divine year would be 365,250 human years. Yitsḥak of Akko infers from the rabbinic idea that previous worlds were created and destroyed before ours that we are living in the 7th cycle of the universe, meaning that our universe was created 42,000 years ago. Connecting that age with Yitsḥak of Akko's 'divine years', the 42,000 divine years that have passed since the beginning of the world would be 15,340,500,000 human years, or 15.34 billion years ago.

The calculation is a bit silly, and there's little benefit to trying to prove that an itinerant rabbi living in the 14th century knew the true age of the universe. That said, lucky guess or clever maths, what this tradition of cosmological and chronological speculation demonstrates is how creatively Jewish sources approach time. To think in 'god-years' instead of human years, to imagine that the agricultural cycles of the earth are reflected in the stars, to look ahead of us and see the past – these are uniquely and wonderfully Jewish ways of encouraging us to think outside the dimensional box and make space for understanding time as part of our theology.

Reclaiming the Calendar

We began this book with a challenge. To be Jewish and yet to live in intellectual exile, to be Jewish but think like a Christian, is an affliction affecting modern Jewish life to a degree never seen before. Jews have always been swayed by the ideas, cultures, and beliefs of other peoples – sometimes through creative collaboration but more often through violent coercion – but, our modern world has erased many of the essential tethers that preserve an independence in Jewish thought. More than ever before, Jews have assimilated – not just in practice, behaviour, and culture – but in how we *think*. A key part of decolonising the intellectual landscape of contemporary Jewish life is about finding ways to reclaim and reestablish those tether points. One of them, and a key one, is the use of the Hebrew calendar.

To live within the Hebrew calendar is to inhabit a parallel

universe. The day begins at sunset (not midnight), the week begins on Saturday night (not Monday), the month begins when the moon is in full shadow (not at standard 30 or 31 day intervals), the year begins in the seventh month (not the first) and it's Tishré, not January. Everything about the way in which we flow through the fabric of time is different within the Jewish calendar. Our festivals bind us to the calendar and climate of the land of Israel, our months pull us into the tidal flow of the luminous moon, our weeks rebound again and again towards Shabbat, the jewel in the crown of our chronology.

Learning to live within the Hebrew calendar is not easy, but it is doable. With practice, we can inhabit two times at once. Like the oysters in Frank Brown's inland laboratory, with practice and persistence we can tether ourselves to the susurrations of the sea even when we cannot see outside. We can place ourselves again into the flow of Jewish time – looking at the past, working towards a future, spiralling ever onwards, outwards, upwards. *Time is the substance we are made of.*

Chapter Thirteen

The Shadow Symbol // *Conclusion*

We have come to sanctify the dark
Before the sun renews its light
In our hands, may light and flame
bejewel the tapestry of the night!

Seeds of fire and of light
Radiant within the night
Come up, darkness! Rise up, night!
Come up, to greet the light!

We will plant our fire's seed
Held enwrapped in darkness's weave
Seeds of fire and of light
Radiant within the night[211]

Symbols have a sway over us we rarely appreciate. The imagistic power of flags, logos and political iconography is omnipresent but constantly underestimated. We are unconsciously shaped by the symbolic language of our cultures and countries on a daily basis – a process which for most of us is rarely made to face any real analysis. After surveying various key topics in Jewish thought, it only seems appropriate to conclude by considering that power as a model and a methodology.

Ask yourself – what is the *symbol* of Judaism? The vast majority will respond with unhesitating immediacy that it is the Star of David. The six-pointed star (hexagram, really) is ubiquitous in modern Jewish life, from the flag of the State of Israel to synagogue décor and identity-bearing jewellery. Perhaps a small minority may hesitate and suggest one of the 'second-tier' symbols: the Menorah, the Shofar, the Lulav, the city of Jerusalem itself, a Ḥamsa or a pomegranate, the two tablets of the Law engraved by Moses, the letters of the word *ḥai* (living), a *mezuzah* or Torah scroll, or for a truly obscure choice, the mysterious four-branched letter *shin* that adorns the *tefillin* worn on the head.

This diversity itself is telling. Judaism is not a religion. There is no dogma and no hierarchy and only two mandated beliefs: 1) God's identity, and 2) God's singularity. Yet there are *dozens* of symbols that have stood in for the Jewish people over its millenia-long existence. Moreover, the one that the vast majority of people think of, the Star of David (more accurately, 'Shield' of David from the Hebrew *magén David*) is the thinnest, both historically and symbolically.[212]

Asking questions such as these is an example of the exercise this book is meant to inculcate, prompting us to realise that Judaism is not (or is only rarely) what we think it is. Unbeknownst to most, the Star of David is a complete newcomer to Jewish symbolism. It was only used as a marker of Jewish identity from the 17th century – no more than 500 years ago, a period of time which, relative to the breadth of the Jewish calendar, is like the blink of an eye. It was chosen by the Jewish community of Prague, who were permitted to fly their own flag over the ghetto (Josefov) after they aided the king during the Thirty Years War. For some reason, they chose a yellow hexagram on a red background.

That caught on, as it were – and by the 19th century, it was common for the Star of David to be seen in Jewish décor. A backstory was invented (that it was the symbol King David drew on his shields) for which there is no evidence[213] and the symbol was gradually adopted by the Zionist movement as a marker of Jewish identity and sovereignty, relying on the facile connection to the Davidic monarchy.

The flag which became that of the State of Israel upon its independence was almost very different, with Theodore Herzl originally proposing a white background that had seven golden stars[214]. While the Star of David has become accepted and normalised as a standard of Jewishness worldwide today, this happened largely by accident, with little design and even less interest in symbolic resonance.[215]

We need not ditch the Star of David, but the realisation of its superficial historical and symbolic dimension should prompt us to explore the question anew: what represents Judaism? A key contender is obviously the Menorah, the seven-branched candelabra that stood prominently in the ancient Temple, which, in ancient art and engravings became a metonym for the Temple, Jerusalem, and Israel. Another is the Shofar, connected to the story of the Akédah (Genesis 22) and to its numerous uses in the Hebrew Bible, from ritual instrumentation in the sacrifices of Leviticus to military application in the Israelite conquest of Canaan.

Others have their own merits – and there are so many they are difficult to enumerate. However, perhaps the most obvious symbol we could draw on is the one least likely to rank as notable. This underrated Jewish symbol which can aid us in thinking differently about Jewish texts is one of the very first: fire.

A Devouring Fire

The first appearance that God makes to Moses is surprising – it is not big and dramatic, there is no thunder and lightning, no smoke and quaking ground – all of that is saved for Sinai. Here, when God's voice is heard first in Moses's heart, it emerges from a rather unassuming scene: a desert shrub aflame, not burning up, nor going out, unconsumed.

This is remarkable – and the persistence of the symbol is deeper than we realise. Not only does the burning bush recur in the *mitzvah* to keep a flame constantly lit in the Temple [Ex. 27] but it also informs the story of Ḥanukkah and the practice in synagogues, based on all of the above, to keep a *nér tamid*, a perpetual flame. A synagogue should have no depictions of God. It should have no depictions of people either, but many have succumbed to the Christian-influenced fad of stained glass windows. At the least, it should not attempt to portray God – after all, that is one of the most essential and explicit *mitsvot*. God is depicted not by imagery, but by chemistry – a flame that never goes out.

Morissey may have sung about the soul in The Smiths' song *There Is a Light That Never Goes Out* but he probably didn't realise he was also evoking the Hebrew Bible, where in Mishlé (Proverbs) we read that *nishmat adam nér elohim* - the human soul is the divine lamp. The soul, which as we learned (Chapter 9) is a literal piece of God, is a light that never goes out. God, who is everything and nothing (Chapter 2) is a light that never goes out. The symbolism of the *nér tamid*, the Ḥanukkah story, the imagery of light and heat and flame – all of it points back toward that original encounter in Exodus 3. Yet, the fire imagery that represents God best is not a normal flame – like the *spark of darkness* of the Zohar, it is a flame bound by paradox.

In the story of the burning bush, the fire is described as 'unconsuming', the bush *énénu ukhal* (was not devoured). Yet, later, one of God's rare self-identifications utilises what appears to be the opposite language: "for your God is a devouring fire" (Deut. 4.24). This is hardly the first time such language has appeared. After all, the very first ritualised engagement between God and Abraham sees God appear like 'a smoking oven' and 'a flaming torch', devouring the pieces of an animal sacrifice (Gen. 15). A careful linguistic evaluation of the word, *ésh*, translated so often as fire, demonstrates that it is frequently used in an abstract sense, not unlike the metaphysical term 'being'. Fire is existence itself. God is life itself. It devours and is undevoured. It burns and consumes, creates and sustains. Fire can, when adequately controlled, preserve our very lives. When uncontrolled, it can take them from us. God gives and God takes, but the connection between faith and fire persists.

The sources that evoke this image are practically endless. God appears in a pillar of fire leading the Israelites out of Egypt (Ex. 13), God 'comes down upon Sinai in fire' in Exodus 19, God answers Elijah 'by fire' in I Kings 19, but when Elijah wants to hear God's voice, it is not in the fire at all. Jeremiah (23) compares God's word to fire – burning and burnishing. God spoke from the fire at Sinai as the mountain burned with fire (Deut. 4). Yet, Moses was not burned. In fact, in a famous *midrash*, Résh Lakish imagines that as Moses took down the Torah he was using fire itself as a medium:

> The Torah that was given to Moses, its parchment was white fire, it was written with black fire, sealed with fire, and bound with fire. As he was writing, he wiped the quill in his hair, and it was from there that he received the radiance of his face.[216]

The very light shining from Moses's face as he descended the mountain was black fire he accidentally brushed into his hair. This beautiful juxtaposition of the mundane (scratching one's face absentmindedly while holding a quill) and the magical (writing with black fire upon white fire) is fantastic – and fascinatingly, it exposes the very paradox of the image of fire. It is the black fire which Moses smears on his hair which then 'radiates rays from his face'. It is so bright and brilliant he has to cover his face with a veil. We have, in a sense, returned to where we started – a ray of divine gloom, a lamp of black light, a spark of total darkness.

The closest we can come to imagining God is to use the metaphor of fire. Yet, over and over again God, we are told, dwells in darkness and gloom. It is within the cloud that God is to be found – both in the Tabernacle (*mishkan*) and the Temple (*bét hamikdash*). Even Moses, when he goes up to Sinai, enters into the cloud. Revelation itself happens in the uncertain light of a gloomy mountaintop, and yet is described as a vibrant flaming fire. God is a devouring flame, yet the burning bush is not consumed. One suggestion on this comes from perhaps the earliest Jewish philosopher, Philo:

> Moses entered into the darkness where God was, that is into the unseen, invisible, incorporeal and archetypical essence of existing things. Thus he beheld what is hidden from the sight of the mortal nature, and in himself and his life displayed for all to see, he has set before us, like some well-wrought picture, a piece of work beautiful and godlike, a model for those who are willing to copy it. Happy are those who imprint that image in their souls.[217]

So how *do* we copy the model of Moses, and 'imprint that image' in our souls? As I hope this book has demonstrated, questioning our assumptions and embracing the paradoxes inevitably present in a spiritual quest is essential. We cannot begin to comprehend what Moses understood without first understanding how black fire could shine forth light, how a Being of flame could only be found in a cloud, and how a bush could burn and burn and never be devoured.

How to See the Burning Bush

The burning bush is an easy symbol to move past quickly, but for our purposes we need to understand what exactly happened when Moses encounters this bizarre phenomenon. The steps of Moses's awareness, acceptance, and accountability are ones which are instructive to us about how we too can encounter the numinous divinity in the world around us. Looking carefully at the first few verses of Exodus 3 verse-by-verse with an eye towards understanding how we can see the gradual revelation of the bush to Moses, we can identify four distinct steps, and begin to construct a rubric for shaping our own spiritual life.

I. Setting:

Now Moses, tending the flock of his father-in-law Jethro, the priest of Midian, drove the flock into the wilderness, and came to Ḥorev, the mountain of God.

Moses is in the desert, the wilderness. Empty spaces are critical. Surrounded by people and things, buzzing phones and noisy traffic, we can't quite hear the symphony of divine music around us. The voice is not audible – it is drowned out by all the noise. We have no hope of even reaching the eternal flame unless we can create space and time to listen. Isolation is the first stage – creating space to sit, to listen, to explore, to get lost is essential. The subtle light we seek can only shine in the utmost darkness.

II. Focus:

A messenger of God appeared to him in a blazing fire out of a bush. He gazed, and there was a bush all aflame, yet the bush was not consumed.

The passive tense here is interesting. It *appeared* to him. The divine is all around us but doesn't always appear. If we look carefully, we can see it just beneath the surface, but we have to be paying attention. More than that, this habit of seeing divinity in the world requires *sustained* attention, mindful, conscious focus. 'He gazed' – he looked at it *for a while*! Moses didn't just glance at the bush! Otherwise, how could he tell it wasn't burning up? Concentration and contemplation are the second stage.

III. Curiosity:

Moses said, "I must turn aside to look at this marvelous sight; why doesn't the bush burn up?"

Critical to the encounter is Moses' curiosity. How many people walked past the bush before him and didn't look long enough to realise how exceptional it was?! How many people noticed that, but didn't care enough to be curious about it? Having a posture of curiosity – of wonder and awe – these emotions which we can cultivate are critical if we are to find the encounter with the Divine in our lives. Curating our own sense of curiosity takes work, a courageous willingness to interrogate ourselves and others, and a feverish dedication to questions, not answers.

IV. Responsiveness:

When God saw that he had turned aside to look, God called to him out of the bush: "Moses! Moses!" He answered, "Here I am."

The culmination of this gradual revelation is dialogue. Moses *gazed* first, but then once he noticed, God saw. Like the analogy of a river

> or a radio – we have to tune ourselves in first before we can drink its waters or hear its broadcast. Moses changes himself through awareness and thought, creating the possibility of hearing the divine voice. Most importantly though, when that voice does speak – Moses answers. His curiosity is courageous enough to compel him to stand his ground and listen.

So how do we find God? First we get lost, then we pay attention, then we ask questions, and finally, we are offered the chance to answer the echoed query of the divine omnipresence, ordinarily hidden by routine and custom. When you hear your name called, you must answer: *hinéni.* Here I am. This four-part process is symbolised by the burning bush, and by its related iconographic language in the *nér tamid* and the imagery of flame and light, shining radiant darkness.

The process requires paradox – black fire shining forth and a spark of darkness illuminating the divine. It also requires unlearning much of what we *think* we know about Judaism. To see the bush aflame and to look long enough to realise it was extraordinary was a monumental task. We cannot take it for granted. If we were in Moses's sandals that day – would we have noticed such a paradoxical inversion – a fire that burns but doesn't devour?

This is the process that this book has attempted to teach and to model. To realise that Judaism isn't what we think means we first have to create enough distance, then look closely, ask questions, and find in ourselves the courage to respond, to not run away but to exclaim, '*here I am.*' To decolonise Jewish thought and reclaim our ideas, texts, and symbols – we have to be willing to see the question *as* the quest. The question is *at least* half the answer and the spark we seek to light our way may be, to our surprise, a spark of total darkness.

Additional Reading

Alter, Robert. *The Five Books of Moses: A Translation With Commentary*. W. W. Norton & Company, 2008.

Assmann, Jan.
——— *Moses the Egyptian*. Harvard University Press, 2009.
——— *The Invention of Religion: Faith and Covenant in the Book of Exodus*. Princeton University Press, 2020.

Barrows, Anita. *Rilke's Book of Hours: Love Poems to God*. Penguin, 2005.

Bellos, Alex. *Alex's Adventures in Numberland.* A&C Black, 2011.

Berman, Nathaniel. "Seekers of the Face: Secrets of the Idra Rabba (the Great Assembly) of the Zohar by Melila Hellner-Eshed." *AJS Review the Journal of the Association for Jewish Studies* 47, no. 1 (April 1, 2023): 185–88. https://doi.org/10.1353/ajs.2023.0011.

Bodhi, Bhikkhu. *The Noble Eightfold Path: The Way to the End of Suffering*. Buddhist Publication Society, 2010.

Borges, Jorge Luis. *Labyrinths: Selected Stories & Other Writings.*

New Directions Publishing, 1964.

Buber, Martin. *I and Thou.* eBookIt.com, 1970.

Cline, Eric H. *1177 B.C.: The Year Civilization Collapsed: Revised and Updated.* Princeton University Press, 2021.

Dennis, Geoffrey W. *The Encyclopedia of Jewish Myth, Magic & Mysticism.* Llewellyn Worldwide, 2016.

Diamond, James A. :"Maimonides: The Life and World of One of Civilization's Greatest Minds." *The American Historical Review* 114, no. 2 (April 1, 2009): 514. https://doi.org/10.1086/ahr.114.2.514.

Drob, Sanford L.

——— *Kabbalah and Postmodernism: A Dialogue.* Peter Lang, 2009.

——— *Kabbalistic Visions: C. G. Jung and Jewish Mysticism.* Taylor & Francis, 2023.

——— *Reading the Red Book: An Interpretive Guide to C. G. Jung's Liber Novus.* Taylor & Francis, 2023.

——— *Symbols of the Kabbalah: Philosophical and Psychological Perspectives.* Jason Aronson, Incorporated, 1999.

Faur, José.

——— *Homo Mysticus: A Guide to Maimonides's Guide for the*

Perplexed. Syracuse University Press, 1999.

——— *The Horizontal Society: Understanding the Covenant and Alphabetic Judaism*. Emunot: Jewish Philosophy and, 2010.

Fine, Lawrence. *Physician of the Soul, Healer of the Cosmos: Isaac Luria and his Kabbalistic Fellowship*. Stanford University Press, 2003.

Goodman, Micah. *Maimonides and the Book That Changed Judaism: Secrets of the Guide for the Perplexed*. U of Nebraska Press, 2015.

Gosden, Chris. *The History of Magic: From Alchemy to Witchcraft, from the Ice Age to the Present*. Penguin UK, 2020.

Graves, Robert, and Raphael Patai. *Hebrew Myths: The Book of Genesis*. Rosetta Books, 2014.

Gray, John.

——— *Black Mass: Apocalyptic Religion and the Death of Utopia*. Penguin UK, 2011.

——— *Seven Types of Atheism*. Penguin UK, 2018.

Green, Arthur. *A Guide to the Zohar*. Stanford University Press, 2004.

Hammer, Jill. *Return to the Place: The Magic, Meditation, and*

Mystery of Sefer Yetzirah, 2020.

Hammer, Jill, and Taya Shere. *The Hebrew Priestess: Ancient and New Visions of Jewish Women's Spiritual Leadership*, 2015.

Hellner-Eshed, Melila.
——— *A River Flows From Eden: The Language of Mystical Experience in the Zohar*. Stanford University Press, 2009.
——— *Seekers of the Face: Secrets of the Idra Rabba (The Great Assembly) of the Zohar*. Stanford University Press, 2021.

Holland, Tom. *Dominion: The Making of the Western Mind*. Hachette UK, 2019.

Horn, Dara. *People Love Dead Jews: Reports From a Haunted Present*. W. W. Norton & Company, 2021.

Jung, Carl G. *The Red Book: A Reader's Edition*. W. W. Norton & Company, 2012.

Kaplan, Aryeh.
——— *Meditation and Kabbalah*. Weiser Books, 1985.
——— *The Bahir: Illumination*. Weiser Books, 2001.
——— *ספר יצירה*. Weiser Books, 1997.

Magid, Shaul. *From Metaphysics to Midrash: Myth, History, and the Interpretation of Scripture in Lurianic Kabbala*. Indiana

University Press, 2008.

Marchant, Jo. *The Human Cosmos: Civilization and the Stars*. Penguin, 2021.

Markley, Stephen. *The Deluge*. Simon and Schuster, 2023.

Matt, Daniel C.

——— *God And the Big Bang, (2nd Edition): Discovering Harmony Between Science and Spirituality*. Turner Publishing Company, 2016.

——— *The Essential Kabbalah: The Heart of Jewish Mysticism*. Harper Collins, 2010.

——— *Zohar, the Book of Enlightenment*. Paulist Press, 1983.

Nirenberg, David. *Anti-Judaism*. Bloomsbury Publishing, 2013.

Patai, Raphael. *The Hebrew Goddess*. Wayne State University Press, 1990.

Schäfer, Peter.

——— *The Origins of Jewish Mysticism*. Princeton University Press, 2011.

——— *Two Gods in Heaven: Jewish Concepts of God in Antiquity*. Princeton University Press, 2020.

Scholem, Gershom. *On The Mystical Shape of the Godhead: Basic*

Concepts in the Kabbalah. Schocken, 2011.

Shapiro, Marc B. *Changing the Immutable: How Orthodox Judaism Rewrites Its History*, 2015.

Stavrakopoulou, Francesca. *God: An Anatomy*. Picador, 2020.

Steinsaltz, Adin. *The Thirteen Petalled Rose*, 1980. http://ci.nii.ac.jp/ncid/BA21674571.

The Zohar: Pritzker Edition, Volume One. Stanford University Press, 2004.

Unterman, Alan.
——— *Dictionary of Jewish Lore and Legend*. Thames & Hudson, 2012.
——— *The Kabbalistic Tradition: An Anthology of Jewish Mysticism*. Penguin UK, 2008.

Vicuña, Cecilia, and Ernesto Livon-Grosman. *The Oxford Book of Latin American Poetry: A Bilingual Anthology*, 2009.

Zohar, Zvi. *Rabbinic Creativity in the Modern Middle East*. Bloomsbury Publishing, 2013.

Endnotes

1 This translation is from the edition by Anita Barrows and Joanna Macy (Riverhead Books, 2005). I also owe my thanks to my friend Larissa Zeigerer who helped me to understand and refine the translation of this poem

2 *Pritzker Zohar*, Footnotes to Parashat Beréshit, I:15a

3 Mystical Theology 1.1 - these and other cognates are cited by Matt in his masterful footnote, cited above, on the subject, *Pritzker Zohar* Vol 1, I.15a

4 *Life of Moses* 2:163

5 A special shout-out to those students who have also become teachers through helping me edit early versions of this book and its ideas. Particular gratitude is reserved for Lee Starkey, Leonie Aigin, and Jacob Knight who did the difficult work of hunting down typographical errors and inconsistencies.

6 John Gray, *Black Mass*, p.28

7 Ibid p.73

8 Ibid p.2

9 ibid p.5

10 John Gray, *The Silence of Animals*, L 1084

11 For example, Maimonides begins The Guide for the Perplexed with an explanation of this term to mean that humans possess intellectual perception and moral decision-making abilities, reflecting God's intelligence and wisdom and not, God-forbid, any idea of bodily resemblance. This question of how to understand 'the image of God' as part of human identity will also be covered later in this book.

12 There are many for whom the label of 'spiritual but not religious' may be meaningful – and indeed, we should praise those who are transparent about being seekers. However, equally often, the concept of 'spirituality' is used as a way to exempt oneself from traditional religion, often accidentally replacing normative religious beliefs with alternative

ones that are equally problematic

13 José Faur, *Homo Mysticus*, p. 5

14 Mishnah Berakhot 1.2

15 Bereshit Rabbah 3.7

16 Tom Holland, *Dominion*, L 299

17 The Hebrew phrase used is never *aseret hamitzvot* (the 10 Commandments) but always and ever *aseret hadiberot* (the 10 Utterances). The point made is that while these are ten of the much larger cadre of commandments, what makes these ten unique is that they were spoken aloud by God and heard directly by the Israelites camped at the food of Mt. Sinai

18 This explanation, that they heard the first two, is used in many sources to explain the contradictions of the Torah's accounts of Sinai. The sugya in which the idea is first suggested is discussed more in Chapter 8 and is found in Talmud Bavli Makkot 23b-24a. There, Rav Hamnuna Sava points out that the word Torah equals 611 (using the system of gematria, 400+200+6+5 = תורה) and explains that this is because Torah is what Moses taught us but two of the mitsvot were heard directly from God. This simple teaching offers many wonderful insights, including a rebuttal to those who take the idea of torah min hashamayim too literally, as many do today. Judaism has always been happy to acknowledge that a majority of the Torah comes from God via Moses – after all, the second set of tablets are described as being written by Moses. Rashi in his commentary on this passage explains: "Torah (611 *mitsvot*) was taught by Moses and two were heard from God directly."

19 Micha Goodman, *Maimonides and the Book that Changed Judaism*, p. 33. Maimonides's own explanation of this comes from his Guide for the Perplexed (translation here from Goodman ibid): "This is their dictum: they heard I and thou shalt not from the mouth of the Mighty One. They mean that these words reached them just as they reached Moses our Master and that it was not Moses who communicated them to them. For these two principles, I mean the existence of the deity and being one are knowable by human speculation alone. Now with regard to anything that can be known by demonstration, the status of the prophet and anyone else who knows it are equal; there is no superiority of one over the other.

Thus these two principles are not known through prophecy alone."

20 This is purely anecdotal, and based on over a decade of working as a community rabbi. Initially, I was quite surprised that I needed to explain to my congregants that we don't believe in the devil, in Hell, or in the soul-destroying effects of pre-marital sex.

21 This common version of the quote is incorrect, and appears to be a paraphrase – the original passage in *Ich und Du* has been translated many ways. Here is an alternative with slightly more context, from the 1923 translation by Ronald Gregor Smith: "Life cannot be divided between a real relation with God and an unreal relation of I and It with the world—you cannot both truly pray to God and profit by the world. He who knows the world as something by which he is to profit knows God also in the same way. His prayer is a procedure of exoneration heard by the ear of the void. He—not the 'atheist,' who addresses the Nameless out of the night and yearning of his garret-window—is the godless man" [114] Buber himself seems to have endorsed this translation, as he commented on how best to render the German word *kammerfenster*. Buber explained in March 1937 that he was thinking of a *Dachkammer* (roughly equivalent to an attic or unfinished loft) and proposed the English words, "of his garret-window," adding (in German): "it is a poor student who lives in a garret; at night he opens the window and looks out into the infinite dark." This is recorded in the 1970 updated translation also published by T&T Clark in English and translated by Walter Kaufmann.

22 Maimonides uses the Arabic term *khayyal* in his Guide which is often translated as 'imagination' but, at least according to Ḥakham Faur, would be better rendered as 'illusion'. Faur has a fascinating discussion of Freud and Maimonides in Part 1 of his Homo Mysticus in which he suggests that Maimonides and Freud would actually agree on the fact that religion is an illusion – both though would also agree that whatever illusion religion is, Judaism is separate from it.

23 The *Guide*, referenced frequently throughout this book, remains enigmatic even a millennium after its publication. Many have attempted to dilute the radical message Maimonides promotes but the Guide remains a shocking text to many traditional voices. Leo Strauss famously suggested that the entire work should be read as an esoteric text, and that the beliefs Rambam holds are even more radical than they first seem.

24 Faur, *Homo Mysticus*, p. 21

25 Gray, *Black Mass*, p. 190

26 *Athens and Jerusalem*

27 Ibid p. 18

28 Not enough attention is given in Jewish history to placing our origin within the historical context of the Bronze Age Collapse. While no one quite can answer why all of the established societies of the ancient near east collapsed in the years between 1200-1000 BCE, there's little doubt that the practical result of such upheaval was a great deal of change and creativity in the culture of the region. One of the many outcomes of this period of chaos and catastrophe was the young polity of Israel and the text of the Torah. For a survey of the many, often uncertain, factors that contributed to this historical pivot point, Eric Cline's book *1177 B.C.: The Year Civilization Collapsed* is worth a read.

29 No one has better explored the 'Atenism Theory' better than Jan Assman, whose books *From Akhenaten to Moses: Ancient Egypt and Religious Change*, *Moses the Egyptian: The Memory of Egypt in Western Monotheism*, *The Invention of Religion: Faith and Covenant in the Book of Exodus*, and *Of God and Gods: Egypt, Israel, and the Rise of Monotheism* all explore the potential connection between the cult of Aten instituted under Akhenaten and the emergence of Israelite religion.

30 Aryeh Kaplan, in his commentary on Sefer Yetsirah, describes it similarly: "This teaches that one cannot focus for any length of time on any of the Sefirot. The mind can concentrate and see them as a 'flash of lightning' but only for an instant. Then one must return. One oscillates between 'running' and 'returning,' peeking for an instant, and then immediately returning to one's normal mental state." (L 1300)

31 *Everything and Nothing*, translation by Kenneth Krabbenhoft,

The Oxford Book of Latin American Poetry: A Bilingual Anthology, 2009

32 Jung is by no means the first to make this concept central – indeed, versions of it go all the way back to Heraclitus and others. Sanford Drob, a leading scholar of Jung (and of Jung's intellectual relationship with Jewish mysticism), summarises some of the many instances of the concept of coincidentia oppositorum in Jung's personal writing in *The Red Book*:

"The Red Book is replete with Jung's not as yet fully formed on the coincidence of opposites, and we see him struggling to make sense of the personal experiences that apparently led him to this notion. In the processes he considers a variety of oppositions: meaning and nonsense, fullness and emptiness, love and hate (343), action and thought (293), madness and reason (317), pleasure and thinking (247), above and below (315), etc. Jung tells us, for example, "immense fullness and immense emptiness are one and the same" (273), thinking and feeling "are each other's poison and healing" (248), and "If no outer adventure happens to you, then no inner adventure happens either" (263). (Blog post, 24 November 2009: https://theredbookofcgjung.blogspot.com/search?q=coincidence+opposites)

33 Even mundane examples of this in halakhic thinking can be found, such as that in Eruvin 13b about Sumakhus, who found 48 reasons to rule something impure and 48 reasons to rule it pure. The source of *eilu ve-eilu* follows that example and lays out a general principle regarding the historical tension between the school of Hillel and that of Shammai. The whole *sugya* in Eruvin is worth studying to see how the idea of creative tensions is applied in rabbinic thinking.

34 There is actually a rather obscure Jewish mystical text called Shi'ur Komah which expends hundreds of pages discussing the anatomy of God's body. All the measurements are in absurd scales, typically accounted in parasangs, the imperial unit of distance from the Achaemenid Empire – perhaps the equivalents of today's light years to us.

35 This is from the Pataḥ Eliyyahu, a passage from Tikkuné haZohar 17a. The fuller context of this short quote offers even more evidence for the additive approach to theology: "Greatest in the Worlds, You are one, but not in counting. You are the highest and most hidden of all, there is no mind that can conceive of You." In the same

passage we also get a glimpse of the negative pole of monotheism – a jarring inclusion leading us towards a paradoxical acceptance of both everything/nothing: "You have no name, for You fill and complete all names. When you leave from them, all names remain like bodies without a soul. You are wise, but not with wisdom. You understand but not with understanding. You have no place, but your power is known to humanity, in how you conduct the world through law and mercy, for there is goodness and justice in accordance with our deeds."

36 There is a complex and important argument that many of the ideas of Kabbalah which regain normalised acceptance in the mediaeval period, are continuous with the pagan and polytheistic principles of the ancient world. Raphael Patai famously argued in his book The Hebrew Goddess that the figure of the Shekhinah in Kabbalah is in fact a reincarnation of the war and love goddess of ancient Canaan. In a sense, this is true - and the quaternary relationship between the four primary deities identified in Canaanite sources (Él, Atirat, Ba'al, Anat) does have an echo in the partsufim system of R' Luria, where God is expressed through the four primary personalities of Abba, Imma, Ze'ir Anpin and Nukva.

37 This phrase has its own interesting history, with two variants common in siddurim: ḥai olamim (Ever-Living One) and ḥei olamim (World-Life). Maimonides, predictably, discusses this and comes down on the side of the latter, suggesting that God in the world is analogous to the heart in the body: "The world and all its parts endure because of something unseen—namely, God. It is only for this reason that man is called a microcosm: We, too, have something in us that governs all the rest. That is why, in our tongue, God is called the Life of the world; as it says, He swore by the Life of the world (Daniel 12:7)." (I.72, Goodman translation)

38 To Maimonides, this was the great heresy of Christianity, that it confined God to a human body. Joel Kraemer writes: "Maimonides was convinced that belief in God's corporeality is worse than idolatry, for the object of worship is not God at all. A God in human form, with human emotions, was not the Lord, God of the universe, but a fabrication of the human imagination." Kraemer, *Maimonides*, L 3334

39 Benjamin, Mara. "There Is No Away". https://www.mdpi.

com/2077-1444/13/4/290

40 See, for instance, Micah Goodman's masterful *Guide to the Guide* where he writes: "The idea that God is beyond language is profoundly important; it means that God is utterly different from the world. The doctrine of negative attributes is founded on God's absolute otherness." p. 10

41 That is, a zero (nothing) can be transformed into an infinity symbol (everything) with nothing more than a slight modification, a gripping of both sides and a bit of torque

42 https://www.thetorah.com/article/before-the-beginning-between-ancient-and-modern-cosmology

43 This is the position conventionally taught by most modern sources of Kabbalah and Ḥasidut – see for example, Rabbi Adin Steinsaltz's masterful work of popular theology, *The Thirteen Petalled Rose*, where he says: "To bridge the abyss, the Infinite keeps creating the world; His creation is not the act of forming something out of nothing, but the act of revelation. Creation is an emanation from the divine light; its secret is not the coming into existence of something new but the transmutation of the divine reality into something defined and limited – into a world." p. 20

44 The Gemara asks: Was fire created at the conclusion of Shabbat? Wasn't it taught in a *baraita*: Ten miraculous phenomena were created in heaven on Shabbat eve during twilight, and were revealed in the world only later? They were: Miriam's well, and the manna that fell in the desert, and the rainbow, writing [*ketav*], and the writing instrument [*mikhtav*], and the tablets of the Ten Commandments, and the grave of Moses, and the cave in which Moses and Elijah stood, the opening of the mouth of Balaam's donkey, and the opening of the earth's mouth to swallow the wicked in the incident involving Korah. [Talmud Bavli Pesaḥim 54a]

45 "At the start of God's creating..." – six items preceded the creation of the world; some of them were [actually] created, and some of them God contemplated creating, [though God did not actually do so]. The Torah and the Throne of Glory were created. Torah, from where is it derived? As it is stated: "The Lord made me at the beginning of God's

way" (Proverbs 8:22). The Throne of Glory, from where is it derived? "Your throne stands firm from earliest time, [You are from eternity]" (Psalms 93:2). The patriarchs, Israel, the Temple, and the name of the messianic king – God contemplated creating them [before the world, but did not]. The patriarchs, from where is it derived? "Like grapes in the wilderness [I found Israel, like a first fruit on the fig tree, at its beginning [bereshitah] I saw your fathers]" (Hosea 9:10). Israel, from where is it derived? "Remember Your congregation, that You acquired from old times" (Psalms 74:2). The Temple, from where is it derived? "Throne of glory, exalted from the beginning, [is the place of our Temple]" (Jeremiah 17:12). The name of the messianic king, from where is it derived? "May his name endure forever. His name is praised before the sun" (Psalms 72:17). Rabbi Ahava ben Rabbi Ze'eira said: Repentance as well, as it is stated: "Before the birth of mountains" (Psalms 90:2), and at that same time, "You bring man down until he is crushed, [and then You say: Return, sons of man]" (Psalms 90:3). [Bereshit Rabba 1.4]

46 "God saw everything that God had made, and, behold, it was very good" Rabbi Abbahu said: From here we learn that the Holy Blessed One continuously created worlds and destroyed them, until God created the current ones, and said: This one pleases me, those did not please Me. [Bereshit Rabba 9.2]

47 "This is the legacy of the heavens and the earth on the day that they were created" (Genesis 2:4). What did it reject? God had been creating heavens and earth and examining them. They were not pleasing to God, and so God would restore them to emptiness and disorder. When God saw these [current] heavens and earth, they were pleasing to God, and so God said: "This is the legacy of the heavens and the earth," but what came before was not a legacy. [Shemot Rabbah 30.3]

48 These are the nine hundred and seventy-four generations that were before the creation of the world and were swept away in the blink of an eye because they were wicked. [Midrash Tehillim 90.13]

49 Whence were the heavens created? From the light of the garment with which God was enrobed. God took (of this light) and stretched it like a garment and (the heavens) began to extend continually until God caused them to hear, "It is sufficient." Therefore God is called Almighty (El Shaddai), who said to the world: "It is sufficient," and it

stood (firm). Whence do we know that the heavens were created from the light of God's garment? Because it is said, "Who covers yourself with light as with a garment; who stretches out the heavens like a curtain" (Ps. 104:2). Whence was the earth created? God took of the snow (or ice) which was beneath God's Throne of Glory and threw it upon the waters, and the waters became congealed so that the dust of the earth was formed, as it is said, "God said to the snow, now be earth" (Job 37:6). [Pirké deRabbi Eliezer 3:7-8]

50 "One of the definitions of the name 'Human' or 'Adam' is likness (*domeh*) to the Divine. For, like God, humanity creates the worlds in the image of itself. The physical human form, in the assemblage of its several parts, also constitutes a system that is a sort of model of the inner network of all the worlds. The structure of the human is a paradigm of the structure of the worlds; it is the key to the order of the mitzvot; and it is also the configuration that symbolizes the system of relationships among the worlds. All of the organs of humans correspond to higher essences in other worlds. The general structure of the human body is homologous with with the order of the ten Sefirot, every part of the body of a person being congruous with a particular Sefirrah."

51 Beréshit Rabbah 11.6

52 Zohar 2:161a-b (Pritzker)

53 This is a frequently-cited but misquoted version of 2 Samuel 23:3. The origin of this interpretation, which seems to directly contradict the plain meaning of the verse, is likely the Zohar (or its own sources). See Zohar III:15a (Pritzker) where the verse is purposefully inverted and affirmed: "The blessed Holy One rules humanity (2 Samuel 23:3); who rules the blessed Holy One? As it were, the righteous (ibid.), for the blessed Holy One decrees and they abolish."

54 Levi Yitsḥak of Berditchev, Kedushat Levi commentary on Vayakhel

55 Ramḥal, Derekh haShem 1.2

56 R' Yehudah Lév Ashlag, Talmud Eser haSefirot, 1:19 (Histaklut Penimit 4:2), see also Zohar I.5a

57 Hakham Ben-Tsiyyon Uziel, Hegyoné Uziel, Sha'ar 2:5

58 Horizontal Society, p. 12

59 This point is easily missed by those who aren't used to the difficulties of reading the Torah. Without vowels and punctuation, the Torah in its natural state is like a quantum conception of the electron. Until it is observed, the electron could be anywhere. Once it is measured, its position is fixed – but only so long as it is under the experimenter's eye. Similarly, the Torah can mean many things. We fix it by applying a tradition of vocalisation, punctuation, and cantillation – but the text remains ever able to free itself of our imposition and assert other meanings.

60 Ibid. p. 34

61 Ibid. p. 32

62 This irony is mindbending. The Torah is not a record of speech (it cannot be, because consonants alone cannot represent speech). By being a text *qua* text and not a text which acts as an aide memoire for a speech (as epic poetry such as Homer would have been), it falls into a completely different category. Faur cautions us against the tendency to see the Torah as yet another document of an ancient society by putting tremendous emphasis on the practical nature of writing the Torah. Excluding specificity means allowing for diversity.

63 Ibid. p. 83

64 Ibid. p 86

65 Ibid. p. 84

66 See Deut. 17:14-20

67 Faur, *The Horizontal Society*, p. 106

68 Ibid. p. xviii

69 Unsurprisingly, a similar point is raised by John Gray in Black Mass, although he fails to carry it to the logical conclusion as Faur does: "Antisemitism is co-eval with the appearance of Christianity as a distinct religion: Jews were persecuted from the time of Rome's conversion from paganism and throughout the Christian Middle Ages, while medieval antisemitism was reproduced in the Reformation by Luther. However, while antisemitism has ancient Christian roots, the project of exterminating Jews is modern." (*Black Mass* ibid, p. 64) The

reason that extermination is a modern manifestation is only because it is modernity which offered the tools of industrialised slaughter – the underlying motivation not just to suppress Jews but to destroy them is certainly consistently present throughout Christian history

70 Faur, *The Horizontal Society*, p. 96

71 Ibid. p. 92

72 Ibid. p. xviii

73 Ibid. p. 92

74 Ibid.

75 While Faur is strident on this point, there's no doubt that cultural bias, racism, religious discrimination, xenophobia and many other comorbidities help explain the disease of antisemitism. Faur is suggesting only that the cause, the real root of the nearly-universal hatred of Jews is due to our uncompromising rejection of hierarchy in favour of horizontalism. That doesn't make it the exclusive cause of antisemitism, only the primary one.

76 Faur, *The Horizontal Society*, p. 93

77 Ibid. p. 49

78 Ibid. p. 51

79 There is a single, often-cited midrash that God threatened to murder the Israelites if they refused the Torah, implying the covenant was entered into under duress. This is a hyperliteral reading of the phrase *taḥtit hahar* in Exodus 19.17, describing the encounter at Sinai. The plain reading of the verse implies that the words *taḥtit hahar* mean 'at the foot of the mountain' or 'at the base of the mountain' but can be read hyperliterally as 'underneath the mountain'. Most know the idea through Rashi's commentary on this verse, which refers to a longer and more interesting sugya in Talmud Bavli Shabbat 88a, which has parallels in Avodah Zarah 2b, Mekhilta Baḥodesh 3, etc.), where Rabbi Avdimi bar Ḥama says: 'The Holy Blessed One lifted the mountain over them like an [inverted] barrel (giggit) and said, If you accept the Torah, all will be well: but if not, this will be your burial place'." This bizarre suggestion by Rabbi Dimi is furiously rejected by others in the Talmud, with Rabbi Alma bar Ya'akov suggesting that if we were to

accept such an idea, it would undermine the entire foundation of the Torah, in addition to contradicting the text in every other instance, which emphasises the Israelites' consent and agreement. Unfortunately, this misquoted midrash has become one of those rabbinic texts to be frequently used and abused without context in our contemporary world of meme-able Torah.

80 Louis Jacobs, *We Have Reason to Believe*, p. 67

81 The question of whether the Torah records real speech is a complex one, which cannot be fully addressed here. Rabbi Jacobs in *We Have Reason to Believe* gives a few examples of rabbinic traditions which affirm that it is not a direct record of a verbal act, but rather, evidence of an encounter. Rabbi Jacobs concludes the seventh chapter of his book with a thought-provoking analogy which he derives from Emil Brunner. In his words: "Brunner asks us to think of a gramophone record. The voice we hear on the record is the voice we want to hear, it is the actual voice of the artist who delights us, but we hear it through the inevitable distortions of the record. We hear the authentic voice of God speaking to us through the pages of the Bible-we know that it is the voice of God because of the uniqueness of its message and the response it awakens in our higher nature-and its truth is in no way affected in that we can only hear that voice through the medium of human beings who, hearing it for the first time, endeavoured to record it for us." p. 81

82 The United Synagogue, the organisation which launched a vicious public attack on Rabbi Jacobs, can be seen as a facsimile of the Church of England, copied and pasted artificially onto Jewish communities. For a long time the United Synagogue insisted that their clergy be called 'Reverend' and wear the Anglican vestments (including what is affectionately known as 'the dog collar'). For such an assimilationist structure to criticise Rabbi Jacobs for upholding the traditional Jewish view of the Torah is absurd.

83 Faur, *The Horizontal Society*, p. 53-4

84 Ibid. p. 51

85 Talmud Bavli, Bava Metzi'a 58b-59a, trans. Adin Steinsaltz, adapted

86 Faur, *The Horizontal Society*, p. 72

87 Ibid. p. 75-6

88 Here the Jewish people, not the modern State of Israel

89 Faur loves to use this phrase as a foil – the 'European humanism' he decries is, in his work, often counterposed to the Israelite approach

90 Faur, *The Horizontal Society*, p. 79

91 Ibid. p. 82

92 The assumption is that the word *perushim* is what became preserved in the Koine Greek term 'Pharisee'.

93 This title is now so familiar to us, but it really is quite mundane. Meaning 'greater,' rav might be translated as 'master' or 'teacher' but is really just an honorific. With the addition of the first person possessive suffix it becomes Rabbi, a title still used today.

94 While our tradition refers to Ben Zakkai's interlocutor as Vespasian, its more likely that the Roman in question was actually Vespasian's son, Titus. On 1 July 69, Vespasian was proclaimed Emperor while on campaign in Judea, the last in a chaotic year known as 'The Year of the Four Emperors'. Vespasian left Judea before the end of 69 and charged his son Titus with leading the campaign to crush the Jewish rebels.

95 There are many points of disagreement between these two schools of thought, and it is symptomatic of the entire approach to the Mishnah. To take but one example from Mishnah Shabbat 1:7: "Bét Shammai says: one can only sell something to a gentile, or load their donkey, or give them a burden to carry on Friday as long as there's enough time for the gentile to arrive at their destination before Shabbat. Bét Hillel permits selling, loading, or giving things to gentiles even if there isn't enough time." It may seem like an inconsequential difference, and to some degree it is – but the point remains that the Mishnah affirms, records and even celebrates the multivocal method of making law.

96 The term 'Codes' refers in particular to two specific works of rabbinic literature: Maimonides's Mishneh Torah and Rabbi Yosef Karo's Shulḥan Arukh. Each of these streamlines the diversity of the

Mishnah, Talmud and rabbinic responsa – transforming the law into a single voice. While this makes Halakhah more accessible (which is good), it also makes it opaque, and hollows out much of the creativity that characterises texts like the Mishnah and Talmud.

97 Rabbi Jacobs did not see himself as founding a new 'movement' – quite the opposite. He only wanted to combat what he saw as increasingly-extreme interpretations of Jewish texts in the Orthodox world, bringing it back towards the historic centre. As he said himself in a retrospective look at the 'Jacobs Affair': "To see halacha (Jewish law) in dynamic rather than static terms is in no way a rejection of halacha. On the contrary, historical research has shown, this is the halachic approach; in its later development no less than in its formation [...] We were not rebels. The real rebels were the United Synagogue and kindred "establishment" organisations who had moved away from the tolerant, liberal (with a lower-case "l"), tradition of Anglo-Jewry in favour of a harsh, rigid, uncompromising – not to say obscurantist – approach, foreign to the mood of the community." This piece was published in *The Jewish Chronicle* on 19 December 1986.

98 Imagine many who proudly claim the label of 'orthodox' today saying, as HaLevy did in 1989 that 'there is nothing so flexible as the flexibility of Halakhah'! (*Yearbook of Israel's Chief Rabbinate* (Shana beShana, 1989), pp.185–6.

99 Hopefully a few quotes will help to illustrate the point. All of these represent the widely-accepted views of mainstream, traditional, conservative voices – all of whom were aiming to preserve the vibrant and dynamic Jewish tradition inaugurated by the ancient Rabbis and saved from destruction by Yoḥanan ben Zakkai:

> *For Judaism, unity is not only of God; it is also of the world and of the entire human race. The image of divinity on earth is not the Jew; it is the human being.*
>
> *Eliyyahu Benamozegh, Israël et L'humanité 1914*
>
> *Permission was given to our Sages in each generation to innovate new Halakhah according to the changes in time*

and place – it is only thanks to this that the Torah has been maintained and we are able to walk on the path of Torah and mitsvot.

Rabbi Ḥayyim David haLevy, Aséh Lekha Rav, 7:236-7, 1989

Even an actual prohibition can be abolished once the reason for it no longer exists or is applicable.

Rabbi Yosef Messas, Otsar haMikhtavim 1884

The Torah has sustained us throughout the ages and will sustain us in the future, as long as we are ready to see in it a vital force which can be applied to changing life in changing conditions.

Rabbi Solomon Gaon, Planning for the Future, 1951

In each generation - living conditions, changes in values and technical and scientific discoveries - create new questions and new problems that require solutions. We cannot look away from these issues and say 'Anything new is prohibited by the Torah.' Nor can we simply declare these matters permissible, either! Nor may we let them remain vague and unclear, each person acting however they wish. No, it is our duty to search the Halakhah, to derive responses to current issues from what they [our ancestors] already explained.

Rabbi Ben-Tsion Uziel, Mishpeté Uziel, 1955

100 The notable exception, reinforcing the point of the first chapter, are the two elements of mandatory Jewish belief – God's identity and singularity

101 Maimonides, Mishneh Torah, Hilkhot Dé'ot 1:3-4, trans.

mine

102 Interestingly, 'atonement' means being alone, and only started being used in for the idea of a spiritual reconciliation from the 1680s

103 Adin Steinsaltz, *The Thirteen Petalled Rose*, p. 56

104 Maimonides, Mishneh Torah, Hilkhot Teshuvah 5.5: "Human knowledge cannot comprehend this concept in its entirety for just as it is beyond the potential of people to comprehend and conceive the essential nature of the Creator, as [Exodus 33:20] states: "No person can perceive Me and live," so, too, it is beyond people's potential to comprehend and conceive the Creator's knowledge. This was the intent of the prophet's [Isaiah 55:8] statements: "For My thoughts are not your thoughts, nor your ways, My ways." Accordingly, we do not have the potential to conceive how The Holy One, blessed be God, knows all the creations and their deeds. However, this is known without any doubt: That people's actions are in their [own] hands and The Holy One, blessed be God, does not lead them [in a particular direction] or decree that they do anything." This matter is known, not only as a tradition of faith, but also, through clear proofs from the words of wisdom. Consequently, the prophets taught that a person is judged for their deeds whether good or bad. This is a fundamental principle on which depends all the words of prophecy.

105 Zohar II:33b

106 See the fantastic meta-analysis study of Thomas Curran and Andrew P. Hill for the APA: https://www.apa.org/pubs/journals/releases/bul-bul0000138.pdf

107 The source of this aphorism seems to be elusive, but it is quoted frequently in *maḥzorim*

108 From Erets Ḥefets

109 *What Really Happened in the Garden of Eden?*, p. 239-241

110 *What Really Happened in the Garden of Eden?* p. 261

111 Deuteronomy 30.11-15

112 Interestingly, the concept didn't begin in the world of fandom, but in theology! The first instance appears to be a 1973 work of theology by E. Frank Tupper

113 Oxford English Dictionary, "retcon (n.)," December 2023, https://doi.org/10.1093/OED/5177398449

114 In Judaism, the 'Prophets' are the Nev'im, a collection of individuals who each authored books in their names which eventually became canonised into the Hebrew Bible. In fact, the acronym used to refer to the Hebrew Bible in Hebrew (TaNaKh) includes the Nevi'im as one third. They are featured in the practice of reading Haftarot in synagogue and are quoted frequently in the liturgy. There are often considered to be three 'major' prophets (Isaiah, Jeremiah and Ezekiel) and many minor prophets as well as prophetic works which overlap with historical writing (Samuel, Kings, Joshua, etc)

115 A 'prophet' is properly referred to as a Navi (masculine) or Nevi'ah (feminine). Unlike many other roles of spiritual leadership in the Hebrew bible, women feature in the list of prophets, even if a considerable minority. The Talmud says (Megillah 14a) that there are seven female prophetesses: Sarah, Miriam, Deborah, Hannah, Abigail, Huldah, and Esther.

116 A reference to Talmud Bavli Ḥagigah 14b and the famous story of 'The Four Who Entered the Orchard' there, and the complex literature of the Heikhalot in which rabbis worked to actively stimulate an experience of Nevu'ah in order to engage in a sort of astral travel. For more on this fascinating genre of mysticism, see below in our survey of Kabbalah Nevu'it or the work of scholars such as Peter Schäefer and Rachel Elior.

117 Maimonides, Mishneh Torah, Hilkhot Yesodé haTorah 7.1. The use of this particular prooftext from 1 Samuel is telling, as the context gives a real window into the phenomenon of Nevi'im (Spokespeople) in the time of Saul and Samuel.

118 This claim, which is cited frequently but found predominantly in Talmud Bavli Sanhedrin 11a: "After the last of the prophets, Ḥaggai, Zekharya, and Malakhi, died, the Divine Spirit of prophetic revelation departed from the Jewish people" The Talmud itself, however, then goes on to discuss all the others who may have had access to the divine Voice. The insistence that Malakhi was the final prophet may have been in part a polemic – both against Christian claims regarding John the Baptist and Jesus and against the emerging Muslim idea that Muhammad was

the final prophet, *khatam an-nabiyin.*

119 See, for example, *Guide* II.32: "

120 *Maimonides and the Book that Changed Judaism*, p. 25

121 For a brief summary in English, see Dov Schwartz's article "The Hebrew Auditory Logic and the Revival of Prophecy" in Tradition 26.3 (1992)

122 Maimonides, Mishneh Torah, Hilkhot Yesodé haTorah 7.2

123 Ibid. 7.3

124 This fourth part has been censored in almost every publication of Sha'aré Kedushah, with the notable exception of the 2003 printing done by Rabbi Amnon Gross.

125 Sha'aré Kedushah 1.2

126 Ramban al haTorah, Leviticus 19.2

127 Sha'aré Kedushah 3.3

128 Interestingly, this word is very hard to translate and is used to mean 'abstraction' as well as the act of undressing another person. So is it 'stripping' things back to their essence? Or is it expanding and abstracting them to new complexities? The paradoxical nature of the word is likely one of its selling points as a concept for Rabbi Vital.

129 Sha'aré Kedushah 3.5

130 Voluntary and desirable spirit possession does play a role in Kabbalah, with the phenomenon of ibbur (in which a fragment from the soul of a righteous ancestor is invited to cohabit with the possessed) being prominent in many Renaissance-era Kabbalistic texts.

131 Ibid. 3.7

132 Numbers 11.24-29, adapted from the Everett Fox translation

133 Talmud Bavli Makkot 23b-24a

134 Ibid. In Hebrew, all letters can represent both a phonemic consonant and/or a numeral. This allows for any number to be converted into words/phrases that equal it and for any word to be understood as a number. The word 'Torah' adds up to 611 (Tav/400 + Vav/6 + Résh/200 + Héh/5 = Torah/611)

135 Azharot poems, Sefer Halakhot Gedolot, and the Sefer haMitsvot of Maimonides are only a few examples.

136 Ibn Ezra's Yesod Mora is illuminating here. Ibn Ezra, like most critics of the 613 mitsvot idea, believes it to be a significant underestimate: "And in the pursuit of truth, there is no end to the number of mitsvot, as the poet said, 'I have seen an end to all perfection; Your *mitsvah* is exceedingly broad.' (Ps. 119:96) And if we were to count the principles, the general rules, and the enduring laws, the *mitsvot* would exceed six hundred and thirteen." (Chapter 2)

137 Two common examples of this idea are the Kuzari, by Rabbi Yehudah haLevi, which is explicitly polemic, and the Tanya, by Schneur Zalman of Liadi (the first Chabad rebbe). The Tanya in particular is guilty of promoting a sort of metaphysical racism as it suggests that non-Jews either don't have souls or have impoverished ones. This strange particularism was the basis for one of the many critiques levelled against Ḥasidism.

138 In threatening Pharaoh during the Exodus story, God routinely affirms this idea, such as Ex. 4.22: "So you should say to Pharaoh: God says, 'Israel is my first born son.'"

139 Arguably, the one that poses the biggest challenge is idolatry – although what we mean when we say 'idolatry', particularly in the modern world is not easy to define.

140 *Il Mio Credo*, 14

141 HaArévut/Matan Torah 19

142 See Isaiah 42.6, 49.6, 60.3

143 A recent Pew report suggests that the worldwide Jewish population will only regain its pre-Holocaust levels in 2060 at the soonest. "The Changing Global Religious Landscape…". pewforum.org. April 5, 2017.

144 From the essay "On Prayer" in *Judaism, Human Values and the Human State* (1995)

145 Likuté Torah, Shelaḥ 40a

146 *Guide for the Perplexed*, III:26

147 Talmud Bavli, Shabbat 118b

148 Likkuté Moharan, 5.2

149 Devarim Rabbah, Nitsavim 8.5

150 Lawrence Fine, "Tikkun: A Lurianic Motif in Contemporary Jewish Thought" in *From Ancient Israel to Modern Judaism: Intellect in Quest of Understanding–Essays in Honor of Marvin Fox*, Vol. 4, ed. Jacob Neusner et al

151 Isaiah 1:14-17

152 Midrash Tanḥuma, Shemini 15b (Buber)

153 HaArévut/Matan Torah 12

154 Mishneh Torah, Hilkhot Temurah 4.13

155 Orḥot Tsaddikim, Hakdamah: **כשאין בידך מידות טובות - אין בידך תורה ומצוות, כי כל התורה תלויה בתיקון המידות**

156 Vilna Ga'on, Even Shelémah, 1: **כל עבודת ה' תלוי בתיקון המדות, שהם כמו לבוש להמצוות וכללי התורה, וכל החטאים מושרשים במדות.**

157 In the Christian tradition these books largely became labelled as 'Apocrypha' and included in some bibles in a supplementary fashion, but in Jewish tradition, there isn't even a word for these extrabiblical books that didn't make the cut

158 https://ndpr.nd.edu/reviews/spinoza-s-heresy-immortality-and-the-jewish-mind/

159 For a modern articulation of this concept, see Jay Michaelson's *Everything is God: The Radical Path of Nondualism*

160 Moses Cordovero, Elimah Rabbati, 24d-25a, translated by Daniel Matt in *The Essential Kabbalah*, p. 24

161 TES, 1.1.Histaklut Penimit 1, p. 14

162 Quoted by Rabbi Art Green in his book, *Ehyeh: A Kabbalah for Tomorrow*

163 TES, 1.1.Histaklut Penimit 3-4, p. 15

164 Rabbi Elia Benamozegh, *Il Mio Credo*, p. 17

165 See, for example, Bhikkhu Bodhi's Noble Truths, Noble Path: "Personal continuity exists without a self that persists through the process" p. 92. Notably, Bodhi, like most Western exponents of Buddhism, is Jewish.

166 For years I have used this lovely little book and the stories therein as a way to introduce and frame Yizkor during synagogue services. Eagleman, who is a neuroscientist, offers thoughtful and comic constructions of possible afterlives, an exercise which prompts the reader/listener to really think carefully about what they do believe regarding what awaits on the other side of death, and how that then shapes the way in which we live here and now.

167 Abraham Joshua Heschel, "Teaching Jewish Theology in the Solomon Schecter Day School," The Synagogue School 28 (Fall, 1969): 12. Rabbi Heschel's daughter, the scholar Susannah Heschel has affirmed this many times. "I do not find divine transcendence and omnipotence the most salient features of most classical Jewish theology. On the contrary, rabbinic and medieval texts more often present God as engaging in empathic resonance to human suffering than as an omnipotent ruler of the universe" (Susannah Heschel, contribution to Commentary magazine's symposium "What Do American Jews Believe?" in Commentary 102 [August, 1996]: 49).

168 *Moral Grandeur and Spiritual Audacity*

169 Abraham Joshua Heschel, 1967, "What We Might Do Together"

170 Joel Kraemer, *Maimonides*, L 7204

171 Micah Goodman, *Maimonides*, p. 45

172 Marcus Aurelius, *Meditations*, Book VIII:20

173 José Faur, *The Horizontal Society*, p. 24

174 Heschel, A speech in Frankfurt-am-Maim in 1938, published as 'The Meaning of this Hour'. This speech is really worth reading and rereading in its entirety – it is one of the most beautiful examples of oratory on record in Jewish sources

175 Ḥakham Solomon David Sasson, Natan Ḥokhmah LiShelomoh, p. 144-145

176 Talmud Bavli, Berakhot 5b

177 This is a guess, at best. It appears that the name Hinnom was originally a proper name (The Valley of Hinnom's Son), but thanks to the associations of the physical location (a valley just outside Jerusalem) with child sacrifice in the Hebrew Bible, the word took on a metonymic meaning implying 'wailing'.

178 Robert Macfarlane, *Underland*

179 This has been purposefully not rendered as the Witch of Endor as she is neither a 'witch' in the conventional European sense, nor is Endor the same, but rather Én-Dor in a semikhut phrase, implying the same to be Ayin Dor, which means either: 1) Ancestors' Eye, or 2) Ancestor Fountain. Both convey much more accurately a sense of the place's purpose and the ways in which this ba'alat ov (Pit Mistress) uses it. The word 'ov', based on parallels in other cognate languages and literature, was a well or pit from which it was believed the spirits of the dead could be drawn up out of She'ol

180 The difference, of course, is in their vocalisation – but as most Hebrew texts are written without vowels, it would be incredibly easy to confuse Sha'ul and She'ol.

181 This is a fascinating use of the word *elohim*, which, when appended to a singular verb we read as God (capital G), but when used in other contexts can mean judges, noblemen, powers, etc. Here, it seems to mean 'those which lived, which very much reinforces the idea in this book that God = Life *(elohim = ḥayyim)*. When she activates her pit magic she sees *elohim olim min ha-arets*, literally, "gods coming up from the earth". These spirits are called elohim because all lvings things are elohim.

182 Samuel's clothes in She'ol are recognisable and he is aware of his memories from life – carrying on a conversation with Saul no different than might be recorded if they were both still on this side of the dividing line between life and death

183 Fascinatingly, this idea is also prominent in the Hadith. The Hadith collection of Abu Hurayrah records: "The whole (body) of the son of Adam will be consumed by the earth except for the tailbone, from which he was created and from which he will be created anew."

The question of who influenced who is, as usual, impossible to discern – but it is worth noting that there are Jewish sources that discuss the recreation of the body from the *luz* bone that are contemporaneous with Islam. See for example, Kohelet Rabbah 12:5 (6th-8th centuries): "'The almond tree will blossom' – Rabbi Levi said: This is the nut-sized bone at the top of the spinal column. Hadrian, may his bones be crushed and his name expunged, asked Rabbi Yehoshua ben Ḥananya; he said to him: 'From where does a person blossom in the future?' He said to him: 'From the nut-sized bone at the top of the spinal column.' [Hadrian] said to him: 'Show me.' What did [Rabbi Yehoshua] do? He brought him the nut-sized bone at the top of the spinal column. He placed it in water, but it did not dissolve; in fire, but it did not burn; in a mill, but it was not ground. He placed it on an anvil and struck it with a hammer. The anvil split, the hammer split, but it was to no avail."

184 Ḥakham Ḥayyim David haLevi, Aseh Lekha Rav 2:5

185 Sifré Devarim 306.25, dated to 2nd-3rd century CE

186 Talmud Bavli Ketubot 111a

187 Radak on Genesis 6.3

188 Talmud Bavli Ketubot 111a

189 Talmud Bavli Berakhot 4b

190 Talmud Bavli Berakhot 57a

191 Tosefta Sanhedrin 13.3

192 Maimonides, MIshneh Torah Hilkhot Teshuvah 3.4

193 The identification of this particular Roman emperor is controversial. The Talmud almost always just calls him 'Antoninus', which has led to a common assumption that it is Antoninus Pius. It could be Pius or Aurelius, or some other figure, but the shocking point remains that the leading Jewish figure of the time was close personal friends with Roman royalty. The likelihood that it is Marcus Aurelius is based on the dates (Yehudah was patriarch from 161-200 CE and Aurelius reigned from the 160s-180 when he died), as well as on their philosophy (many teachings of the Sages share a great deal in common with Stoic philosophy, of which Aurelius was a student and exponent). One small example of the rich literature detailing this unlikely friendship is from

Beréshit Rabba 67:

Antoninus sent the following message to Rabbi Yehudah: "The treasury is empty. Tell me what to do." Rabbi Yehudah led the messenger into his garden and in his presence he pulled out some large radishes and planted small ones in their stead. When the messenger asked him for a reply, R. Yehudah said that none was needed. The messenger returned to Antoninus and reported that Rabbi Yehudah gave no answer to the question. "Did he do anything in your presence?" Antoninus asked and the messenger related what he had seen. Antoninus understood the hint and he discharged some officials and appointed others in their place. In a short time the royal treasury was again filled with gold.

194 Talmud Bavli Avodah Zarah 10b

195 Talmud Bavli Berakhot 57b

196 Talmud Bavli Berakhot 17a

197 See Ramban's Pérush al Iyyov published in the Mossad haRav Kook edition of Kitvé Ramban

198 R' Sa'adiah Gaon, *Book of Beliefs and Opinions*, vi. 8

199 Zohar I:186b

200 Zohar III:99b

201 R' Ḥayyim Vital, Sha'ar HaGilgulim, Hakdamah 8

202 R' Moses Hayyim Luzzato, Derekh HaShem, 2:10

203 R' Elia Benamozegh, *Il Mio Credo*, 17

204 This story is told beautifully by Jo Marchant in her incredible book *The Human Cosmos: Civilization and the Stars*

205 "A Case for Why Time Loops are Inherently Jewish", Rachel Klein, 13 June 2022 for HeyAlma

206 An entire chapter could be devoted to this subject, but we have to be satisfied with only the briefest explanation. In Judaism, the Messiah (*mashi'aḥ*) is nothing more or less than the rightful heir to the throne of Israel, the long-lost son of the Davidic monarchy. While Christianity has warped this concept into that of a supernatural saviour, Judaism awaits a purely political and fully human leader. The

conception of the Messiah in Judaism is authentically far closer to that of Aragorn from Lord of the Rings than the figure of Jesus as understood by Christian doctrine. Aragorn is the rightful heir to the human realm of Gondor, but has renounced his claim, living as a ranger in the wild. When he eventually returns to claim the throne, it ushers in an era of renewed sovereignty. It is Aragorn for which we hope, not Jesus.

207 Maimonides, Mishneh Torah, Hilkhot Melakhim uMilḥamotéhem 11.3-4

208 This survey was covered by numerous online outlets and discussed in Bellos's book *Alex Through the Looking-Glass: How Life Reflects Numbers and Numbers Reflect Life.*

209 Talmud Bavli Sanhedrin 97a

210 The full interpretation Rabbi Yitsḥak offers is fascinating to read. It can be found in his work Otsar Ḥayyim, Chapter 77

211 These words are a rewording of the popular Israeli folk song Banu Ḥoshekh leGarésh (We Come to Banish the Darkness). This (I think, improved) version was compiled from the several fascinating rewrites done by Rabbi David Seidenberg and Rabbi Jill Hammer and can be found on R' Seidenberg's website neohasid.org as well as the Open Siddur Project (oppensiddur.org)

212 If we were to use a star as a symbol, you would think it would have seven points, as seven is a significant number! Six is not – and this alone shows the thinness of the *magén david*

213 In fact, the six pointed equilateral star was originally associated with David's son Solomon and his mythical magic ring that could control demons. Hence it was known in Jewish, Christian, and Muslim communities in the ancient world as the 'Seal of Solomon'.

214 While it might be tempting to see this as a more authentic Jewish iconography (seven!), Herzl explained in Der Judenstaat (*The Jewish State*) that the stars would be about socialist legislation on working hours: "I would suggest a white flag, with seven golden stars. The white field symbolizes our pure new life; the stars are the seven golden hours of our working-day."

215 Interestingly, the same phenomenon seems to have befallen

Muslim communities, in which the primary symbol used to identify Islam, the star and crescent, actually comes from Muslim communities co-opting the symbol from the Sasanian Empire when they conquered it. The star and crescent figured prominently in the iconography of the Zoroastrian Sasanian Persian Empire, and spread from below into the symbolism of its colonial occupiers, the Muslim armies of the 7th and 8th century. It was only adopted as the flag of the Ottoman Empire in 1844, and this was largely due to the historical antecedent of Byzantine history in Ottoman-occupied territory. The first use of the symbol is in Anatolia, but by the pagan king Mithridates IV around 300 BCE of Pontus, himself of Persian origin.

216 Devarim Rabbah 3.13

217 Philo, *The Life of Moses*, I, 158

Printed in Dunstable, United Kingdom

74608106R00181